Being All Equal

Global Issues

General Editors: Bruce Kapferer, Professor of Anthropology, James Cook, University and Chair, UCL and John Gledhill, Professor of Anthropology, Manchester University

This series addresses vital social, political and cultural issues confronting human populations throughout the world. The ultimate aim is to enhance understanding - and, it is hoped, thereby dismantle - hegemonic structures which perpetuate prejudice, violence, racism, religious persecution, sexual discrimination and domination, poverty, and many other social ills.

ISSN: 1354-3644

Previously published book in the series:

Michael Herzfeld
The Social Production of Indifference: Exploring the Symbolic Roots of Western Bureaucracy

Being All Equal

Identity, Difference and Australian Cultural Practice

Judith Kapferer

BERG

Oxford • Washington, D.C.

First published in 1996 by
Berg
Editorial offices:
150 Cowley Road, Oxford, OX4 1JJ, UK
22883 Quicksilver Drive, Dulles, VA 20166, USA

Berg is an imprint of Oxford International Publishers Ltd.

Library of Congress Cataloging-in-Publication Data

A catalogue record for this book is available from the Library of Congress.

British Library Cataloguing-in-Publication Data

A catalogue record for this book is available from the British Library.

ISBN 1 85973 101 5 (Cloth)
1 85973 106 6 (Paper)

Typeset by JS Typesetting, Wellingborough, Northants.
Printed in the United Kingdom by WBC Book Manufacturers, Bridgend, Mid Glamorgan.

Contents

Preface

When I was very young, there was a children's radio serial called *The Search for the Golden Boomerang*. I have utterly no memory of the plot, theme or characters, only of the regular portentous announcement in the style of the times. Now I have written a book about the ceaseless human quest for community, and it seems to me that the Golden Boomerang is a fitting metaphor for that search in Australia: community is precious, it is supremely worth striving for, and it forever returns to inspire our dreams of being in the world.

My own vision of that lifeworld is, I think, very Australian – simultaneously individualist, and egalitarian. But as a sociologist, I endeavour to see that world through the eyes of others with whom I share it, others sometimes quite like me, sometimes quite unlike. I have traced out here various aspects of Australian cultural practice which, no doubt, many will find to be an idiosyncratic selection of activities, events, people and places – the social relations built on different (of gender, of class, of race and ethnicity) and their manifestations in the living out of everyday lives. What I have tried to show is that these mundane happenings, formed in arts, histories, politics, economics, philosophies, are a universal human work undertaken in a particular human situation which is late twentieth century Australia, but still resonating through other times and other places.

I have been very conscious, in the long process of research and writing, of my own deep need for community, for companionship, support and attachment. And I have everywhere discovered that need in others. Australians, it has been said, have a talent for bureaucracy, with all its cautious, officious, going-by-the-book implications. But with very few exceptions I have met with little but courtesy, interest and goodwill from those, usually nameless, from whom I have sought assistance and advice, and I thank them for that. As well, and too many to name, I want to thank countless friendly guides, curators, librarians, garage mechanics, bus drivers, newsagents, motel operators, town clerks, local historians and tourism advocates in South Australia, Victoria, New South Wales and Queensland, whose local and specialist knowledges have kept me fascinated, in good spirits and on the roads around the country. As have my Monaro neighbours, the Elluls and the Hartigans.

For financial assistance, I particularly wish to thank Dr. Michael Lawson and Dr. Robert Withers for their good offices in securing for me, and Louise Marks and Beverley Palmer for administering, over many years, small grants from the Flinders University Research Budget. Belinda Niederer's 'infrastructural support' – dealing with my technological incompetence – has been invaluable.

I owe an enormous debt of gratitude to the Netherlands Institute for Advanced Study in the Humanities and Social Sciences, a scholar's paradise where I spent a glorious year as Fellow in 1991–2. The disparate group of historians, anthropologists, classicists, economists, linguists sociologists and philosophers with whom I spend that year provided a stimulus and an inspiration which has yet to fade. Their lunchtime conversations, their weekly seminars, the cheerful assistance of technicians and librarians and the unobtrusive and learned directorship of Dr. Dirk van der Kaa, combined to produce that sense of community which is so rare in large universities today as to be little more than a faint memory. The heart of community, in St. Augustine's words, lies in conversations and jokes together, reading together and the mutual rendering of small attentions. NIAS provided all this for me.

There are others with whom I share conversations and jokes, reading and affectionate attentions, my friends Judy Gill, Christina Haskin, Sue Howard, Felicity Hughes, Denis Grundy. As well, I have colleagues at Flinders who, from time to time share rueful jokes and commentaries on the state of the academy with me. All these continue to remind me, in the welter of academic bureaucracy and administrative warfare, that universities are still the best places to engage in research and scholarship.

It is a rare pleasure for me to have my family gathered together in the same place at the same time – on this page. Above all others I owe to them gratitude for their loving support over many years. To my mother, Alison Champain, for her unwavering hospitality, devoted moral support and diligent research assistance; to my son,

Roland Kapferer, determined guide, serious philosopher and good friend; to my daughter Michaela Kapferer, exuberant, incisive and eagle-eyed explorer of popular culture – to these I offer my heartfelt thank, with love. And to Bruce Kapferer, anarchist anthropologist, an indomitable idealist who embraces all of humanity with a ferocious passion, a generous teacher, an inspiring companion and heroic seeker after community – to him I dedicate this book, as too small a recompense for all that he has given me.

Judith Kapferer
Adelaide

Acknowledgements

Grateful thanks are due to the following who have given permission to use extracts from their works: Francis McQuilton, from *The Kelly Outbreak*,Melbourne: Melbourne University Press in Chapter 2; Mudrooroo Nyoongah, from *The Australian Higher Education Supplement*, 27/1/93: 14, and David Trigger from his review in *The Australian Higher Education Supplement*, 20/1/93: 19 in Chapter 2.

The following publishers have granted permission to reproduce extracts from works published by them: Curtis Brown, for extracts from Geoffrey Dutton's *The Australian Heroes* in Chapter 3; Harper Collins (Australia) for extracts from Russel Ward et al. *The Greats* in Chapter 3 and extracts from The Australian Stockman's Hall of Fame *Outback*, in Chapter 9.

The Commonwealth of Australia has given copyright permission to reproduce extracts from the following: Joint House Department (1989) *Australia's Parliament House: The Meeting Place of our Nation*, Canberra: AGPS in Chapter 9; Royal Commission into Aboriginal Deaths in Custody (1991) *Report, Overview and Recommendations*, Elliott Johnston QC, Canberra: AGPS in Chapter 10; Commission to Advise on Australia's Immigration Policies, (1988) *Immigration: A Commitment to Australia*, Dr. Stephen Fitzgerald, Canberra: AGPS in Chapter 11.

The following newspapers have given permission to reproduce copyright material from their publications in Chapter 12: *The Guardian Weekly* © (8/3/92), *The Observer* © (1/3/92), *The Sydney Morning Herald* (26/2/92; 29/2/92), and ©Times Newspapers Limited, 1992 (28/2/92).

CHAPTER ONE

A Profession of Being All Equal

> As for us, added the Old Man, we make a profession of being all equal, our glory consists in being all alike, and to be dignified with the same care, and in the same manner. . . . [Gabriel de Foigny, *A New Discovery of Terra Incognita Australis* 1676, in Berneri, 1950]

On 20 September 1822, eight convicts escaped from Macquarie Harbour on the wild west coast of van Diemen's Land (modern Tasmania). Their ghastly tale is related by the historian Robert Hughes [1987: 219–24], often in the words of Alexander Pearce, who survived to tell it when he was recaptured:

> Within a week [of the escape] the weather turned to gales and sleet. . . . Then they finished the last of their rations. Hungry, cold and failing, the band struggled for another two days. . . . But now the fugitives were straggling. . . . No man felt able to gather all the wood for a fire. *In the feeble hysteria of exhaustion, they began to squabble about who should do it; in the end, each convict scraped together enough twigs for himself, and eight little fires were lit.* Kennelly made what might or might not have been meant as a joke. 'I am so weak. . . . that I could eat a piece of a man.' [my emphasis]

> In the morning [Pearce's narrative continues], there were four of us for a feast. Bob Greenhill was the first who introduced it, and said he had seen the like done before, and that it eat much like a little pork. . . . 'I will warrant you,' said Greenhill, 'I will well do it first myself, and eat the first of it. *But you must all lend a hand so that you may all be equal in the crime.*' We then consulted who should fall. Greenhill said, 'Dalton; as he volunteered to be a flogger, we will kill him.' [my emphasis]

Dalton was despatched with an axe and co-operatively butchered and eaten. In the ensuing weeks, two of the escapees disappeared and were eventually found near death on the shore of Macquarie Harbour, 'still with pieces of human flesh in their pockets'. Bodenham was the next to be killed and eaten, and in the last week of October he was followed by Mather. Shortly afterwards, Travers, who had become ill and feverish, followed them, being unable to keep up with Greenhill and Pearce, and since 'his flesh would answer as well for Subsistence as the others'. Greenhill and Pearce struggled on for some days, each in fear of the other. Eventually, Greenhill fell asleep, and Pearce took the axe, and killed him, taking part of his arm and thigh for further sustenance; at the end of November, he was recaptured.

There is one society in the known world that was formed from an anti-social impulse, a society made from scratch, from deep lacerations in the social and political body of an arrogant metropolis, the British imperial state, a culture cobbled together from the rags and tatters of the underclass of Georgian England, washed up on harshly unwelcoming shores, brutalized and brutalizing. The cruelty of convict transportation, the viciousness of the penal colonies, the wreckage of human relations which formed the basis of Australian society, all simultaneously expressed and engendered the Hobbesian War of All Against All, that nightmare that so terrorized the rulers of late eighteenth-century Europe. The wonder is that this society, formed so inauspiciously from a small band of rejects and outcasts, with no social organization of their own, no community of feeling, no common interest, not only survived, but finally flourished. Unlike the Pilgrim Fathers of the United States, Australia's early involuntary settlers had no faith, learning or culture which bound them together; unlike the Jews of the Diaspora, they had no sense of oneness in exile, no tradition or hope. It is the ongoing construction of that social and cultural formation which is the focus of this book.

Hughes' story of convict cannibalism encapsulates two aspects of Australian historical and contemporary social practice which give some hint of the way a society could be formed from such unpromising beginnings. The uneasy conjunction of individualist solutions to a common problem (the lighting of 'eight little fires') with egalitarian demands for partnership in a common enterprise ('all equal in the crime') has been characteristic of Australian social relations for two centuries. The example may be bizarre, but it is not difficult to trace these two apparently conflicting impulses in the everyday lives of Australians. Ideologies of egalitarian individualism, the politics of difference and identity, are everywhere to be discerned in the people, places, activities and events I examine here. They include the gendered creation of heroes and villains (Chapter 3), the symbolic and practical uses of public space (Chapters 4 and 9) and private housing (Chapter 5), the management of families and of higher education (Chapter 6), popular festivals and exhibitions (Chapters 7 and 8), the definition and practice of Aboriginality (Chapter 10), multiculturalism and athleticism (Chapter 11), and the rhetorics of nationalism (Chapter 12).

What I offer in the pages that follow is an extremely partial (in both senses of the word) guide, personal and patchy, through partially known and understood, and differentially valued terrain, territories of the mind and heart as well as of a physically demarcated geopolitical ground. In doing so, I am conscious that I speak of only one of many Australias, of the people, places and customs with which I am most familiar. There are many others.

I argue that the agency which mediates between ideology and culture is mythology. It is mythology which structures and manipulates the relations between state[1] and people, drawing upon more or less widespread and collectively held understandings of being in the world to establish and maintain a certain spectrum of those understandings as characteristic of a social formation, an identity, a national self. This mediation is of course unequal in that it pits a powerful organized body against a diffuse mass already subject to the controls of state institutions and apparatuses. But the rhetoric of democracy, upon which the state is dependent for its very legitimation, is limited in the degree to which the agents of that state can impose beliefs and practices which are popularly felt to be in some way alien. The ideologies of the democratic capitalist state are drawn from the cultures of the people, moulded, mythologized, reworked and represented to them as artefacts of their own making and choosing – which indeed they are, but subtly altered to serve an interest beyond that of an aggregate of individuals, beyond a collectivity of free wills. My project is one which seeks to *de-mythologize* those aspects of culture which are borrowed in the creation of ideologies of the nation state and capitalist social formations, to rupture, if only momentarily, the mythological bonds which attach people to state, culture to ideology.

The themes and threads I gather together are those of people, nation, state and community, of the collectivity and the individual, the one and the many, the partial and the total. In their kaleidoscopic and sometimes conflictual juxtapositions they speak of oneness, the overcoming of social and cultural difference as the expression of what Schutz [1962] called 'we-feeling', what Deleuze [1991] in another context[2] speaks of as intersubjective idealism, and what Australians broadly understand as 'the nation'. For while individuality (often expressed and enacted as individual*ism*) is highly, perhaps supremely valued by Australians, the vision and experience of community (however subverted by the mythopoesis of nationalist passion and by the egocentricity of individualism itself) is a constant and cherished ideal.

In unpicking and re-weaving the multiple realities, meanings and identities which both hinder and facilitate the constitution of community, I have frequent recourse to the idea of *Geschlecht* as expounded by Jacques Derrida in his 1987 essay on Heidegger's Hand. The term itself is virtually untranslatable, but Derrida makes the point, quite explicitly, that, 'according to the contexts that come to determine this word, it can be translated by sex, race, species, genus, gender, stock, family, generation or genealogy, community' [1987: 162] and sometimes, according to the broader usage of French translators, 'humankind, human species, human race.' Central to the concept is the idea of shared characteristics, a commonalty of roots and origins discernible in the bearing of characteristic marks and imprints. And significantly, these need not be physical marks:

> *Geschlecht* is an ensemble, a gathering together. . .an organic community in a nonnatural but spiritual sense and those who belong to 'this circle, this alliance of spiritual freedom. . .would belong to "our *Geschlecht*"'. [1987: 163; Derrida is analysing and quoting Fichte's usage here]

The most telling of Derrida's translations of *Geschlecht* for my purposes is 'stock', and not only because it has a peculiar resonance in a culture which takes commercial stock-breeding and biogenetics extremely seriously, to the extent of referring in certain circles to estimable human forebears and the assumed magical heritability of morality and character as 'good stock'. Indeed, in 1914 the Sydney urban reformer R.F. Irvine maintained that it is

> only by successively improving the conditions of life that its good stock, if we are fortunate enough to get it, can realise itself and produce the results expected of it. Every breeder knows this. . .the problem of how to produce a superior civilisation is both biological and sociological. [cited in Hoskins, 1994: 4–5]

The non-material sense of the word 'stock' (*Geschlecht*) is loaded with meaning, with its manifold connotations of collective sharing, of communal intersubjectivity, of bonds understood to connect those who think and feel alike, who share a life-world and a common spiritual orientation to it. Schutz [1962] stresses the centrality of the stock of knowledge at hand, of what is taken for granted in the social relations of 'the paramount reality' of everyday life and the specialist stocks of knowledge required in particular situations – 'finite meaning provinces' – within it. It is these stocks of knowledge that I interrogate in the unravelling of the relations between people and state and the mediating role of mythology in the structuring of these relations.

My central question revolves around the patterned relations of individuals in society, the imagination, creation and practice of human sociality, which I take, for the moment, to be a broad definition of culture. Particularly and substantively I focus on an examination of discursive practices of difference and identity in a specific social formation which is Australia in the late twentieth century. And I do so because such a study has the potential to illuminate or rejig perspectives on aspects of everyday life which form an unquestioned cultural stock, an ancient store from which differently placed social actors draw in the prosecution of public and private ends.

The often bitterly felt gap between the imagination of social harmony and equality and the experience of daily conflict and oppression does not falsify the potency of the dream of egalitarianism in Australian cultural practice. Nor does it deny the common enjoyment of the pleasures of mass society. The widespread participation and interest in physical activity and the equally widespread denigration of cerebral activity and the horror of pretension, the simple joys of beach and barbecue, of entertaining family and friends, the domestic division of labour, are all much more closely attuned to the practices of Hoggart's (1958) English working class than they are to the American leisure class of Veblen's (1970) more caustic vision, though they are engaged in by bourgeoisie and proletariat alike. It is these shared understandings and practices, along with the state's provision of welfare benefits, high taxation and the regulation of industrial labour, that have produced the tenacious if increasingly besieged mythology of a workers' paradise and a 'working-class culture' in Australia.

The ideal of a classless society, celebrated as fact by earlier historians vilified, as fiction by revisionists, is always at the forefront of the Australian egalitarian imaginary as a goal more nearly achievable in Australia than anywhere else in the world. And yet the social division of labour is only one of the ways in which Australians are ranged, sometimes ferociously, against each other. Racial-ethnic and gender divisions, for example, run strong and deep, forever threatening the abiding mythologies of egalitarianism and individualism.

Australian egalitarianism pays scrupulous attention to individual and group differences and is founded in assumptions about equality *in nature* [B. Kapferer, 1988]. Those who are considered equals are those conceived of as identical in nature. This is a conception expressive of the Enlightenment view (and that of Gabriel de Foigny) of the noble savage as the pristine individual, unsullied by social structures and constructed social orders. By those defining the situation of equality, those sharing such a natural identity are thought of as equals, to be treated with the utmost fairness. Those not identical in nature – women, Aborigines, Asians, for example – are not conceived of as equals, and indeed are often thought to be 'naturally' inferior.[3] That some may be more fortunate or lucky than others is taken to be 'natural' and more deserving of financial reward or social esteem than those who have 'artificially' (through cunning, sharp practice, learning or the manipulation of networks) achieved economic or social success. *Socially constructed* and therefore artificial differences in wealth and status in no way excuse pretentiousness, snobbery or arrogance in social relations, and are to be ignored. This equivalence in social relations takes particular account of the individual as the essential 'human being' in whom society is always already present, the source of an ideal sociality based on *natural* equality. It also skews Australian egalitarianism in ways which are frequently the very antithesis of egalitarian ideals.

Much Australian social policy is directed towards overcoming the separation and fragmentation induced by divisions between individuals and groups, whether these differences be mythologized as natural *or* artificial. Legislation outlawing discrimination on the grounds of race, ethnicity, creed, physical disability or gender is regularly enacted in the attempt to persuade Australian citizens into a more all-embracing sense of community than that espoused by egalitarian individualism. But the very individualism and egalitarianism which produce the struggle for community and solidarity can also produce further fissions, so that the attempt to treat all groups and individuals with scrupulous fairness has the potential to generate new definitions of identity and difference, which in their turn negate the dream of community.

The battle to achieve consensual validation of the economic and political project of the state by the people under its governance cannot be won by coercion and legislation alone, though these may be important elements in its overall strategy. Paralleling the popular struggle to overcome separation and difference is the state's work of achieving popular unity of purpose for a nation in which division and conflict are engendered by the very organization of that state in its capitalist formation. In this work, the ideological state apparatuses enlist the aid of popular mythologies, beliefs, values, traditions, legends and prejudices – all the discursive practices of popular culture which can be turned to account in the interests of social harmony and common economic purpose.

As a brief example of the kinds of discursive practice I examine in this book, I offer some comments on the institution of naming The Australian Of The Year, a government-supported tradition established in 1960, the record of which is displayed in Parliament House, Canberra.

Case 1. Australian of the Year 1960–1995

1960	Sir MacFarlane Burnet	Medicine
1961	Joan Sutherland	Opera
1962	Alexander (Jock) Sturrock	Sailing
1963	Sir John Eccles	Medicine
1964	Dawn Fraser	Swimming
1965	Robert Helpmann	Ballet
1966	Jack Brabham	Motor racing
1967	The Seekers	Popular music
1968	Lionel Rose	Boxing
1969	Lord Casey	Governor General
1970	Cardinal Gilroy	Religion
1971	Evonne Goolagong	Tennis
1972	Shane Gould	Swimming
1973	Patrick White	Literature
1974	Sir Bernard Heinze	Orchestra
1975	Professor John Cornforth	Chemistry
1976	Sir Edward (Weary) Dunlop	Surgery
1977	Mrs Raigh Rowe	President, CWA
1978	Galarrwuy Yunupingu	Civic leader
1979	William Henry (Harry) Butler	Conservation
1980	Professor Manning Clark	History
1981	Sir John Crawford	Education (agriculture)
1982	Sir Edward Williams	Anti-Drugs campaigner
1983	Robert De Castella	Marathon
1984	Lois O'Donoghue	Civic leader
1985	Paul Hogan	Film and Television
1986	Dick Smith	Philanthropist
1987	John Farnham	Popular music
1988	Kay Cottee	Sailing
1989	Allan Border	Cricket
1990	Professor Fred Hollows	Medicine
1991	Archbishop Peter Hollingsworth	Community service
1992	Mandawuy Yunupingu	Building Aboriginal/ Non-Aboriginal Understanding
1993	Dating system changed	
1994	Ian Kiernan	Environmentalist
1995	Arthur Boyd	Artist

Summary Comments

1. The number of Aboriginal people represented (5 out of 35: Rose, Goolagong, G. Yunupingu, O'Donoghue, M. Yunupingu) is disproportionately high relative to numbers in the overall population. The value of Aboriginal people as mythologized standard-bearers of natural, physical Australianness is indicated here, as well as a recognition, belated and tinged with guilt, of their accession to full citizenship, their struggle for improved civil rights, and the Commonwealth Government's project of Reconciliation.
2. The number of women (7 out of 35: Sutherland, Fraser, Goolagong, Gould, Rowe, O'Donoghue, Cottee) is disproportionately low. While this says something about the lesser status of women in public life, it also confirms the value placed on natural attributes – a talent for singing, athletic excellence, or being feminine in a maternal, nurturant way – as grounds for admiration and acknowledgement in a culture of egalitarian individualism.
3. Natural physical prowess, and individualism, are stressed in the largest single category of achievement recognised as 'typically' Australian – that of sports. It might be noted that not a single sporting *team* is honoured.

By examining and analysing such aspects of public culture in Australia, I seek to unravel their significance for the establishment and maintenance of sociality and community in the midst of the conflictual and divisive activities of everyday life. In this endeavour I adopt Sahlins' approach of regarding culture as *praxis*:

> 'Praxis' I should like to confine mainly to the sense of productive action. . .including. . .both the objective and subjective aspects of the process: on the one hand, the historically given means and relations of production; on the other the experience men have of themselves and the objects of their existence in the course of productively transforming the world through a given instrumental mode. [1976: vii]

As Sahlins points out, this approach enables the explication of the discursive practices of a particular social and cultural formation, seeing 'the culture in the praxis, the symbolic order in the material activity' [1976: 3], but without ever granting determinant status to one or the other. Thus the people, places and events I address in this book are to be understood as the concerted productive action of diverse human beings, social action in which cultures are produced, refracted, reproduced, transmitted and transformed in the universal human process of being-in-the-world. The paramount reality of everyday life is to be discerned in the finite meaning provinces of specific social action, whether that action be as concrete as the building of a Parliament House or attendance and/or participation at an agricultural show or an athletic contest, or as abstract as the mythologizing (by journalists, historians, poets or painters) of folk heroes and villains, past events and future projects.

Notes

1. Throughout this volume I have tried to avoid the charge of reifying the State, but with, I am afraid, indifferent success. There is a structuralist legacy to be grappled with here. While it is clear that 'The State' has neither programmes nor projects of its own (and that the term is very often a gloss for 'a dominant class and its subalterns'), I do not wish to imply that it has no existence in political theory and political practice. That would be to suggest too great a faith in human, even individual agency to change what is and to deny the power of statist ideologies in Australian social thought.
2. Deleuze's reference is to what he sees as 'the two illusions' already traversed in philosophy's dream of dominating the other disciplines – objective idealism and subjective idealism. He claims that philosophy's dishonourable 'falling back upon the universals of communication' is an attempt to give the discipline 'an imaginary mastery of the workplace and the media (intersubjective idealism)' [1991: 475]. But the universals of communication are just what are essential to the creation of that intersubjective idealism which lies at the heart of the constitution of community, of what Derrida [1987] calls *Geschlecht*.
3. In his autobiography, Paul Hasluck mentions the attitude of a Chief Protector of Aborigines in Western Australia, who believed 'that anyone with an Aboriginal ancestor must be treated as an Aboriginal and regarded as being *different in nature*, in entitlements and way of life from all other Australians and all other human beings'. [1977: 211, my emphasis]

CHAPTER TWO

Ideology and Public Culture: The Work of Mythology

The legitimation of the control of the modern nation state over disparate groups within its national borders is a constant primary concern of the state. Ceaseless repressive and ideological work is required to achieve and maintain the hegemony of those shared meanings of nationality and citizenship which buttress and protect the legitimacy of the state, its forms of administration and structures of power. In this process, the cultivation of a nationalist mythology is of the utmost significance. But such a mythology, singular and unique, is always coming up against the equally well-developed and well-protected mythologies of other nations. It is this situation that keeps questions of national identity and national prestige in the forefront of public discussion – of sports, of the arts and entertainment, of patriotism and service to 'the nation'.

Australia is, in a well-worn phrase beloved of politicians, a multicultural society, a place called 'home' by a population 25 percent of which was not born in the country or have at least one parent who was not. It is the attachment of these erstwhile foreigners that the Australian state seeks to ensure, without, at the same time, alienating those whose residence and presumed loyalty is of longer duration. The mid-twentieth century abandonment of earlier and often *ad hoc* practices of containment and suppression, even genocide, in favour of official policies of integration and assimilation, directed at both Aboriginal people and immigrants of diverse provenance, eventually gave way to more clearly formulated policies of multiculturalism. This change in bureaucratic terminology and political practice reflects an increasing sophistication on the part of state instrumentalities over the last two centuries in their efforts to assure the loyalties of all citizens.

Throughout its short modern history, Australia, like many other nations of the New World, has actively encouraged immigration until very recently, thus quite rapidly overwhelming the indigenous population. The reasons for this encouragement are not far to seek: they are intertwined with the political, economic and commercial aspirations of European imperial expansion in the seventeenth, eighteenth and nineteenth centuries. With the twentieth-century granting or wresting of independence by or from colonial powers, the nations of the New World themselves adopted the economic motivations and many of the cultural habits which had been so central to their settlement and development under colonial rule.

The Australian imperative to 'populate or perish', current in the period immediately after 1945, was as much founded in economic ambition as it was spurred by political and racist fears of the 'yellow peril' to the north. Its longest lasting effects were the postwar baby boom and the wave of European immigrants seeking work, freedom and stability far from nightmare memories of war and degradation, with government-assisted passages for the British and other favoured nationalities. The softening of a tough masculinist image in the country's advertising was contemporaneous with a softening of the discourses of racial and ethnic harmony which were gathering strength in the Western world generally.

Since the global economic downturns of the 1970s and 1980s and the move from labour-intensive to capital-intensive high-technology industries, Australia, like other importers of human raw materials, has reversed its immigration policies, resisting the blandishments of all but the most stringently scrutinized refugees, the relatives of Australian citizens, those with money to invest or those with skills of which there is a shortage in Australia. As the perceived need for national unity and ideological consensus (fuelled, once again, by international economic competition) is hammered home by the ideological apparatuses of the state, the unity of the Australian people is stressed at every turn, often to the extent of implying a lack of patriotism in those who criticize, for example, Australian economic performance or the quality of Australian products. Exhortations to 'buy Australian' or to 'advance Australia' are the staple fare of local advertising, even though they tend to contradict other exhortations to imitate the industrial relations or managerial practices of foreign economic competitors, and even though labelling regulations are so vague as to obscure the fact that, for example, only the label on a can of fruit may actually have been 'made in Australia.'

The accentuation of national *unity*, of purpose, temperament, will, *Geschlecht*, is what nationalism is all about. *Diversity*, on the other hand, is what lies at the heart of multiculturalism: diversity of character, language, custom and tradition. The problem for the Australian state is one of achieving unity in diversity without appearing to elevate the value of any one cultural strain above any other; of retaining the 'good' (i.e. useful, creative and productive) elements of diverse cultural stocks while eliminating the 'bad' (i.e. divisive, suspicious, combative) for the benefit of *all* Australians. Certainly this would appear to be the overt purpose of the state's adoption of policies of multiculturalism over the last quarter of a century, with the development of 'ethnic' broadcasting, the promotion of what are called 'community languages' in the schools, and the encouragement of a reverence for what has come to be a very broadly defined 'cultural heritage' in the community at large.

Nationalism, as Bruce Kapferer points out, 'makes culture into an object and a thing of worship. . .the political is made religious' in the process of nationalism.

> This is effected through the sacralization of the culture of the nation, the two being inseparable in modern nationalism. The culture that is sacralized is highly distilled, spiritualized, and as the *essence* of the nation defines the conditions of its unity. [1988: 209, my emphasis]

One of these conditions is the belief that we are all equal before God. National unity cuts across and is expected to negate political differences and ethnic, religious, gender and class conflicts, subsuming old enmities and installing the common weal as the highest goal of every individual. Treason, disloyalty, tax evasion and unemployment ('dole-bludging') are anathematized in the same breath by agents of the state as failures of citizenship, which, though it has its rights and benefits, also exacts corresponding (some might say greater) duties and responsibilities. These crimes take on the added status of sins, of a sacrilege against the nation, rather than (merely) crimes against the state.

Case 2. Anthem and Flag

The sacralizing of any nation is well illustrated by its national anthem. Around the world, nation states invoke divine providence in glorifying and sanctifying their cause and firmly attaching their citizens to their national project (as defined by dominant groups or combinations of power elites of various kinds), whether that project be represented as war or peace, economic domination or survival, moral regeneration or global political supremacy.

For instance, the British national anthem, *God Save The Queen/ King*, seeks divine intervention in preserving the monarchy, the symbol of the nation, and in granting victory to that nation: 'Send her victorious, happy and glorious. . ..' While the exact nature of the monarch's victory is unclear in the first verse, the second (in, significantly, *Hymns Ancient and Modern*) suggests a warlike stance, similar to that of the French national anthem:

> O Lord our God arise
> Shatter our enemies
> And make them fall.
> Confound their politics
> Frustrate their knavish tricks
> On Thee our hopes we fix
> God save us all.

The French anthem stresses glory and blood, calling its citizens to arms against tyranny, while the anthem of the United States of America again employs the imagery of vigilance as the price of liberty, and of battle against those who would deny it. While these republics no longer call on a Supreme Being to support the righteous cause of the nation, the solemn weightiness of warlike images and the hymn-like quality of the melodies recalling the Church Militant make powerful messages of nationalism sanctified by religion. The sacred songs of war, in Australia as elsewhere, have the same effect, hallowing death and destruction in terms of 'the supreme sacrifice' made by the fallen who died to protect their land from invasion, or to save the ideals of their nation and way of life – democracy, racial superiority, imperialist dreams or the divine right to rule. Such songs, many of them hymns (*O God our help in ages past*; *Lest we forget*), are amenable to performance on the instruments of the Christian church, particularly the organ and the trumpet. Songs like Blake's *Jerusalem* or Elgar's *Pomp and Circumstance No. 1* spring readily to mind:

> Land of hope and glory, Mother of the Free,
> How shall we extol thee, who are born of thee?
> Wider still and wider, shall thy bounds be set,
> God who made thee mighty, make thee mightier yet.

By contrast, *Waltzing Matilda* is not a song destined to stir the blood or stiffen up the sinews to great heights of self-sacrifice and devotion to patriotic duty. The tune, played on fiddle, piano accordion or mouth organ, is rollicking, and the lyrics verge on the scurrilous. The jolly swagman is a crook, a vagabond who lives by petty thievery; he respects neither the ruling class of squatters, nor their law-enforcing agents, the troopers. He commits suicide rather than submit to arrest:

> Up jumped the swagman and sprang into the billabong
> 'You'll never take me alive,' said he.
> And his ghost may be heard as you pass by the billabong –
> 'Who'll come a'waltzing Matilda with me?'

No doubt the swagman's lack of moral fibre is one reason why, when Australia chose a new national anthem for itself in 1984 and relegated the colonialist *God Save the Queen* to the archives of an imperial past, he was passed over in favour of the altogether more exalted *Advance, Australia Fair.*[1] This despite *Waltzing Matilda* being identified with Australians on parade grounds, in taverns and beerhalls around the world, and despite the lyrics of *Advance, Australia Fair*'s requiring alteration: 'Australia's sons' became 'Australians all', for example, thus avoiding offence to Australia's daughters and invoking the entire population of whatever ethnic or racial background in its call to rejoice. The old second verse, with reference to 'gallant Cook' who 'raised old England's flag, the standard of the brave' on our shores – 'With all our hearts we love her still, Britannia rules the waves' – has been relegated to abashed oblivion, to be replaced by a multiculturalist vision, stressing open-handed sharing, not colonialist conquest.

As with many other national anthems, the Australian version takes freedom as its central value:

Australians all, let us rejoice,
For we are young and free.

Zambia is 'strong and free;' the United States of America is 'the land of the free.' But there is also a strong emphasis on materialist values and the work ethic, both of which are rare in other nations' praise poems: 'We've golden soil and wealth for toil' and 'We toil with hearts and hands.' There is also no mention of a divinity: we conclude that the advancement of Australia is predicated upon the toil of its people alone, and also, perhaps, that many of these people do not subscribe to a Christian faith. The anthem also makes much of the beauty and abundance of the land itself rather than the glories of its past and the assumed innate qualities of its people. In the same way, the flag of the Aboriginal people – black, red and yellow – focuses on natural phenomena: skin colour, the red desert earth and the sun.

There has indeed been sporadic controversy over the Australian flag, most particularly from Australians of non-British descent or those with republican inclinations, who find the Union Jack's inclusion in the banner offensive. While the major part of the flag, with the five stars of the Southern Cross representing the states and the seven-pointed Pointer representing the federated states and territories, would appear to be unobjectionable, depicting a political arrangement in unworldly and suitably ineffable images, new designs are offered from time to time. Almost all would remove the Union Jack from its position of dominance, most would change the colours of the flag – very often to green and gold, considered since 1984 to be 'national colours' as worn by Olympic teams and suchlike – and many would feature a spray of wattle or a kangaroo rampant. Such designs are generally criticized as lacking in dignity, while another, that of the flag raised over the Eureka Stockade during the miners' rebellion of 1854, has been tarnished in the eyes of many because of its adoption by both a militant trades union (the Builders' Labourers Federation, which flies it from gantries and cranes on building sites) and a shadowy right-wing organization known as National Action, advocates of white supremacy and racist violence.

The Australian flag is what Roland Barthes calls a 'full' signifier: sanctioned by tradition, instantly recognizable, triggering a plenitude of sentiments in the hearts of the citizens who toil beneath it. The flag is what the Australian state expects Australians to die for. That so many have done so in the past and will undoubtedly continue to do so is potent testimony to the work of the mythologizers (the mass media, the schools, the churches), whose task it is to soften the horrors of the needless suffering and death of young Australians in other peoples' wars and to allay the grief of those left behind to grow old, wearied by age and condemned by the years.

Defining Culture(s)

Within the academy and in wider intellectual circles, the concept of 'culture' is fiercely contested. The terrain upon which these battles are fought is itself a matter for contestation: whose definitions of 'culture' and cultural significance will prevail, and what are the implications of preferring one definition over another? In approaching these questions, I begin with what I take to be one of the broadest, least contentious and therefore initially most useful of these definitions as expressed by the American anthropologist Clifford Geertz: 'Believing, with Weber, that man is an animal imprisoned within webs of meaning he himself has spun, I take culture to be those webs' [1973: 5].

These 'webs' or patterns of meaning, spun in the everyday practices and commonplace interactions of social life, reflect and express the shared and generally taken-for-granted understandings, judgements and assumptions of a social group – a family, a community, an association, a nation – about a way of life, about who 'we' are, and how 'we' do things in contradistinction to other groups – 'they' – who do the same things in different ways.

The larger and more differentiated the social group, the more difficult the achievement of taken-for-grantedness, the generation and maintenance of a 'we'-relation. More difficult, but also more imperative in a world of contentious nation states whose governments and ruling elites are desperate (that is not too strong a word) to create and sustain those sentiments of patriotism and national pride whereby all or most of the diverse fractions of a populace can be persuaded to equate individual altruism and individual self-interest with what is incessantly promoted as the higher morality of the public or national interest, the common good.

As Herzfeld notes, the everyday negotiability of meaning, the contextually relative understandings of morality in everyday life, have no place in statist discourse, which requires the imposition of a system of *absolute* values as 'eternal verities', of which the most crucial is the very existence of the state itself. For it is the conflation of social identity with morality which permits the construction of cultural boundary markers between one community (of class, occupational group, ethnicity, gender, locality, nation or state) and another: moral disapproval pronounces a sentence of social exclusion and legitimizes it.

> It is perhaps a truism that the nature-culture distinction is not given in nature, but culturally created and constantly recreated. What happens when a statist ideology supervenes is not merely that nature becomes 'culturalized,' but that culture itself becomes more sharply defined, with a concomitant rigidification of the 'meanings' – now said to be discovered rather than invented – in nature: context gives way to eternal verity. [Herzfeld 1986: 89]

The task of defining the common good and the national interest and equating them with private and individual benefit falls principally and most explicitly on officially recognized and supported bodies within the nation state, controlled and directed through the great bureaucracies of government, the 'public' or 'civil' service. Whether or not that government is democratically elected makes no difference to the centrality of this task. Whether those bureaucracies are known as the Ministry of Culture or the Senate Standing Committee on Arts and Science, the Department of Education or the Congregation for the Propagation of the Faith, by no means denies, indeed it affirms, the supervention of statist ideology in the construction and imposition of a set of absolute moral values '*in the service of the State*.' Shifting cultural constructions of 'common decency' are transmuted into and codified as 'public morality.' By the same reifying alchemy, nation becomes synonymous with state, the people with society. An offence against 'public morality' (sometimes 'community values') incurs a 'debt to society,' to be paid by incarceration or by the enforced performance of 'community service' – the repair of vandalized public property, for example.

The process of transformation is a process of mythologization, of myth-making. It is a process of gathering up widely shared, often inchoate and ill-articulated but always situationally specific understandings of being in the world (all the elements of a culture) and refashioning them as timeless truths, encoded in law and sacralized in ritual, protected by the might of the very state which has organized their transformation.

In Australia, the apparatuses of the state which are most centrally concerned with public myth-making are the institutions of formal education controlled, funded (in varying degrees) and organized by the federal (national) Department of Employment, Education and Training, and what have come to be called, in another telling phrase, 'the cultural (or culture) industries' (cf. the 'cultural Ideological State Apparatus' of Althusser, 1971). The latter include all those who are engaged in the production and distribution of narrowly defined 'cultural' goods and services ('cultural', in that they are promoted as having little or no immediate use value in a material sense; rather, their effect is on the mind and spirit): works of art, musical productions, galleries, museums, public entertainment, public ceremonial and spectacle, the organs of mass communication (the press, radio, television) and information provision (libraries, data-banks, citizens' advice bureaus and bureaus of statistics).

The educational apparatuses of the state and the formal organizations of the culture industry are not the only contenders for the controlling voice in what counts as culture. Beyond them, and thus not always within their direct sphere of influence, is a plethora of more fluid groups, voluntary associations like the Country Women's Association, the Returned Services League, sporting groups, ethnic associations and charitable foundations. There are also political lobbies representing economic interests and utilizing culturally loaded slogans appealing to democratic freedom of choice or to the essential and equally mythicized relation of agriculture to the land: the National Farmers' Federation or the Australian Medical Association. Also, and perhaps most significantly, there are bodies (usually but not always religious in orientation) which claim to represent and define the values of 'the community', or the pressing need for change in those values: various churches, anti-abortion 'pro-life' organizations, the Women's Electoral Lobby, Aboriginal land rights movements, the Wilderness Society, etc.

While the apparatuses of state control may deem all such groups to be representative of merely 'sectional' interests, thus implying the existence of an overarching national interest, they nonetheless fall well within the sphere of the indirect influence of bureaucratic government control through economic and political necessity. Many, indeed, operate with the support of government ministries and departments, even when such bodies have oversight of conflicting interests, as, for example, the Department of Environmental Affairs, which constantly has to seek a balance between commercial and conservationist demands. Moreover, as the beneficiaries of government grants or tax concessions, or of media attention, all these legitimate groups do actually accede to the idea of their position as the tributaries of a mainstream, as sectional interests ultimately devoted to the national interest. In return, as more or less formally organized entities recognized and extolled as shining examples of the freedom of expression and toleration thought to be the *sine qua non* of democratic debate in a pluralist society, they serve to demonstrate the benevolence of the state *and its legitimacy*.

Not so more obscure groups and individuals – writers of letters to the editor, the National Socialist movement, street gangs, graffiti artists – who question the legitimacy of the currently dominant forms and processes of statist morality and statist discourse. Those who cannot be ignored or suppressed as harmless eccentrics can be marginalized through ridicule or criminalized as morally and socially deviant, in need of 'rehabilitation.'[2]

The designated spokespeople of all such pressure groups are regularly accused of failing to represent the unanimous views of their entire constituencies. Whether they be appointed or elected, professional association presidents, trades union representatives, university Vice Chancellors, government ministers, bureaucrats or public relations experts, such spokespeople are frequently required to articulate opposing views within their own organizations, almost invariably within strict time limits which do not permit a canvassing of all their members. In these situations, what is produced as 'the' position of the organization is frequently the position of a powerful minority (a board, a council, a committee) proffered and often accepted as the consensual position of the majority.[3]

Within any sociocultural formation, certain ideas and activities are conceived of as centrally important to the ongoing prosecution of daily life and principled engagement within it, and to its evaluation as good or bad, productive or unproductive, beautiful or ugly, significant or trivial. In reading (comprehending and interpreting) Australian cultural production, many of these ideas and activities appear, in different guises, to be so ubiquitous as to merit the term 'central'. This is not to posit some Parsonian central value system, in which the majority of social actors (with the exception of some imperfectly socialized 'deviants') subscribes to and upholds essentially similar judgements of social and moral rectitude. It is rather to suggest that there are common issues and problems which confront social actors and demand to be resolved by them – common, in that they are widely shared and that they keep reappearing over time. That judgements of worth may and do differ radically, that the solutions proposed by one group of actors may be and are radically opposed by others, serves only to demonstrate the ubiquity and obduracy of the *problems*, not agreement about the values and beliefs which are brought to bear on their solution.

Many of these central problems are expressed in terms of antitheses and antipathies: the proper relation between, for example, individual benefit and the common weal, or tradition and progress, or public and private morality. Others are subsumed under all-embracing terms like the nature of social justice, gender, class and ethnic relations, democracy, criminality, liberalism, racism and so on. Still others are assumed to be matters of personal taste or opinion, to which any individual is 'entitled'. Historically grounded and incessantly reworked, the wrangling and debate, the frequently vehement confrontations between differing and opposed understandings of all these issues, produces the characteristic fabric of a culture.

That some threads of this fabric are thicker and stronger than others indicates the power of specific social groups and institutions to gain the acquiescence of other, less powerful ones in their definitions and delineations of the situation at hand. Such acquiescence may be expedient or self-serving, enthusiastic or resigned, but its achievement is always considered crucial to the production of economic stability and political order in a society which characterizes itself as a liberal (or sometimes, under a Labor government, a social) democracy.

Defining the Mainstream: Dominance and Subordination

Geertz' definition of culture with which I began now appears to be so broad and bland as to have little purchase on the questions of power and domination which are central for an understanding and analysis of social order and social control in contemporary mass societies. Social beings cannot be usefully conceptualized as atomized individuals spinning their private webs of meaning without regard to the webs of others and the activities of larger and stronger predators. Like W.I. Thomas' famous dictum [1928], that if men define situations as real then they are real in their consequences, Geertz' definition is comforting to those who wish to get on with their own lives without interference. It is also most appealing to peoples who value individualism highly. But it does not begin to offer an explanation for the ways in which some people, or some collectivities of people, can impose, by force or moral suasion, their definitions of the situation on others.

Not that there is a shortage of explanatory theories in the social sciences and elsewhere. The Hobbesian problem of order, the search for answers to the question why human social groups and the individuals within them are not constantly at war with each other, has had a long fascination for social theorists, exercizing the imaginations of philosophers, politicians and priests for centuries. And indeed, Hobbes' questions are vital ones, never more so than in a world of contentious states jockeying for global domination, a world in which Hobbes' three causes of quarrel – competition, diffidence and glory – remain as great a threat as ever to the safety and survival of humankind.

> The only way to erect such a common power, as may be able to defend them from the invasion of foreigners, and the injuries of one another, and thereby to secure them in some sort, as that by their own industry, and by the fruits of the earth, they may nourish themselves and live contentedly; is to confer all their power and strength upon one man, or upon one assembly of men, that may reduce all their wills, by plurality of voices, unto one will: which is as much as to say, to appoint one man, or assembly of men, to bear their person; and every one to own, and acknowledge himself to be author of whatsoever he that beareth their person shall act, or cause to be acted, in those things that concern the common peace and safety; and thereby to submit their wills, every one to his will, and their judgements, to his judgement. [1962: 132]

While the desire for peace, security and social order in any age is so widespread as to be universal, the answers as to how such a state is to be achieved and maintained become ever more complicated. Hobbes' three causes of quarrel remain, played out through the application of diverse cultural logics in diverse social formations. But what is central to the solutions offered in contemporary mass society always turns on the power relations of that society. Who has the power to define the situation of peace, security and social order? And in those societies characterized as open, or liberal, or democratic, who is granted the right to that power and on what (cultural) grounds is that right granted?

Western social theory has, until very recently, revolved around two main schools of thought regarding these questions, the one emphasizing the achievement of social order through socialization into a common cultural system, the other stressing the achievement of order through the control exercised by one powerful (ruling) group over others less powerful. The first has consensus as its defining characteristic, the second, conflict. Each has been vehemently opposed to the other under the banners of 'the common culture' thesis and 'the dominant ideology' thesis respectively [see Abercrombie et al., 1980].

This is a revealing choice of terms. Where 'common culture' has a fine democratic ring to it, 'dominant ideology' smacks of totalitarianism and chicanery. 'Culture' speaks of what is 'natural' to human beings, of 'common sense'; 'ideology' raises spectres of conspiracy, false consciousness and misrecognition of the 'real' conditions and relations of existence. A dominant ideology implies that most human beings are easily led, subject to massive confidence tricks on the part of ruling elites – cultural dopes, as Garfinkel [1967] calls them. A common culture, on the other hand, implies that they are very well able to recognize their conditions of existence and to change them – that as creators of culture they are, rather, cultural sharpies [see Moerman, 1968].

The dualisms of modernism (mind/body; real/ideal) have, in recent decades, been challenged if not replaced by the fluidity and eclecticism of post-modern thought (see, for example, Lyotard, 1984). The positivist faith in observable and verifiable reality has been nudged, if not toppled, by the widespread interrogation of objectivism. As a result, in the arena of the humanities and social sciences, at least, defining the culture concept has achieved a new urgency and a new militancy. The comfortable certainties of the old division of labour in academic specialisms have all but disappeared. A blurring of boundaries has occurred between the Arnoldian camp, which conceives of culture as the best that has been thought and said, the 'high' culture, culture-with-a-capital-C camp, and the so-called anthropological camp, which utilizes a far broader conception of culture as a whole way of life, encompassing both the best and the worst, the material and the ideational. And that blurring has been brokered and orchestrated to a great extent by the new mythologists in the academy, gathered into cross- or multi-disciplinary enclaves with significantly amorphous labels, the most common of which is 'cultural studies'. The following tale of academic wrangling, begun as a book review and reported over several weeks in the Higher Education Supplement of *The Australian* poses a number of questions about post-modernism and post-colonial responses which, though they remain for the most part unanswered, highlight many of the cultural dilemmas facing Australians at the end of the twentieth century.

Case 3. Trigger versus Nyoongah[4]

A review of Bob Hodge and Vijay Mishra's 1993 book *Dark Side of the Dream: Australian Literature and the Post-Colonial Mind* [Sydney: Allen and Unwin] was headlined in *The Australian* [20/1/93: 19]:

> No place for vague radicalism in Cultural Studies.
> Cultural Studies are all the go in universities at the moment but are we talking radical critique or vacuous posturing?
> asks DAVID S. TRIGGER[5]

Trigger, an anthropologist from the University of Western Australia, begins his review with a critique of the 'hybrid discipline' of cultural studies and the propensity of its practitioners to display a self-righteous and politically motivated antagonism to 'conventional academic disciplines,' seen within cultural studies as discursive regimes which manipulate 'Australians' popular readings of their culture and identity'. Hodge and Mishra's book, he says, 'purports to be a study of Australian "character" via an examination of literature and other "texts". The general aim is to uncover the "dark side" or allegedly invisible aspect of Australian culture, namely our colonial history.' Trigger questions the possibility of 'reading' Australian culture from literary and other texts, without reference to the study of social action – 'that is, from what members of Australian society actually do and say in the course of their everyday lives'. Further, he accuses the authors of using methods which 'rest simply on presentation of allegedly privileged speculations by the researcher', thus pretending to depict a wider Australian consciousness.

According to Trigger, Hodge and Mishra allege that anthropologists and historians 'silence the authentic Aboriginal voice while making Aboriginal culture a fetishised object of endless fascination.' Yet their own analysis of texts produced by Aboriginal people is, he claims, largely unsupported by the texts themselves:

> One aspect of their reading of a painting by Peter Skipper (an Aboriginal man from the West Kimberley region) is an example. In the painting, joined-bar forms indicate stylized sandhills, according to the artist; they happen to be shown as located in the west and north, in the direction of the area of white settlements. Yet, in an extraordinary leap of imagination, Hodge and Mishra interpret these shapes as characterizing the spaces of civilization and white men's ways, seeming 'not unlike the bars of a cage, symbols of regimented existence'. In short, a painting the artist says represents sacred waterholes in a larger landscape and the presence of powerful religious forces is read as a text 'coming to terms with the position of Aborigines in white Australia, using traditional resources to express a twin sense of alienation and belonging'.

Trigger's central point is that 'the analysis from cultural studies effectively silences the voice of the artist and imposes the view that all cultural productions by Aboriginal people necessarily entail direct comment on the experience of colonialism.' This is, he adds, 'a crude romanticization, almost sycophantic in its intended construction of Aboriginal culture. . ..' He concludes by suggesting that 'Australian cultural studies will have to do much better than this if it is to survive'.

A week later, Mudrooroo Nyoongah from Murdoch University in Western Australia provided a reply to Trigger's review [*The Australian* 27/1/93: 14] under the headlines

Turning the tables on Anthropologists
Last week David Trigger criticized aspects of the cultural studies approach to Aborigines.
MUDROOROO NYOONGAH responds.

Nyoongah's main point is that disciplines like anthropology, as 'part of the apparatus of control which [has] ensured the continuance of the colonial system', will have to take seriously the critiques of feminists and others who charge anthropology with misreading the objects of its study through the ideological lens of 'western patriarchal thought' in texts which are 'open to [a] deconstruction which too often reveals their inadequate discourse and level of objectivity. . ..' Attacks on newer 'methodologies' such as those of cultural studies are, he suggests, an expression of 'the inertia of conservative societies refusing to change'.

Nyoongah points out that *The Dark Side of the Dream* is 'co-authored by a white man and a black man' and that 'the very nature of the enterprise is vastly different from a text of anthropology written from the position of subject and other, or if you will, with the dominance of the anthropologist clearly established from the beginning.' While he concedes that cultural studies texts like *The Dark Side of the Dream* may also be open to dispute, and that Trigger's discussion of the Skipper painting has some force,

> I doubt that it can be established as appropriation, although the reading may be disputed, but [the interpretation] does establish for Peter Skipper's art pieces a political dimension as claimed for Arnhem Land bark paintings by Galarrwuy Yunupingu: 'Our painting is a political act. Unfortunately non-Aboriginal people often remain ignorant of this fact, or deliberately choose to ignore that element in our work.'

'The charge of patronizing Aborigines must be queried', Nyoongah concludes. 'Aboriginal culture . . . is by its very nature – as indigenous to Australia – unique and different from the products of what is usually termed "mainstream" culture, which is European-derived.' Anthropology, he suggests, 'might maintain its life or regain its health by simply renaming itself cultural studies'.

Both Trigger and Nyoongah are presenting the kinds of arguments which might be predicted from their own academic orientations, even if these arguments might also be considered to be extreme statements by many of their colleagues. Trigger presents the case for scholarly authority in the analysis of otherness, Nyoongah the case for the primacy of lived experience in the analysis of a collective self. Trigger refers to the subjects (objects) of his researches in the third person, as 'they' or 'them'; Nyoongah speaks of 'we' and 'us'.

Modernist anthropology, particularly so-called 'cultural' anthropology, which has focussed principally on 'material culture'

– that is, an anthropology which has as its subject matter the concrete objects and artefacts of social formations other than what is taken to be 'our own' – has long been accused of the kind of cultural elitism to which Nyoongah refers. Such charges have often been justified, and in many famous cases incontrovertibly demonstrated. And this, more often than not, by anthropologists themselves.

Unlike literary scholars and critics, or sociologists, who in general work within cultural traditions and linguistic conventions to which they are native, anthropologists have tended to focus their researches in societies in which they are themselves alien. The changing designation of such societies – as, for example, primitive or tribal (both outdated, and ideologically unsound) or non-Western (inaccurate, and fraught with paternalist connotations) or pre-literate, pre-industrial, under-developed (patronizing and politically naive) – not only expresses the frustration of practising anthropologists in search of a neutral terminology, it also speaks of the fury of cultural members who wish to *define themselves* as active subject, not passive object.

The yardstick of 'our own' (literature, art, music, language, custom, history) as the standard by which otherness and difference are observed and evaluated has, except in recent years, been implicit and taken for granted. In anglophone cultures, the field of 'comparative literature', for example, defines works written in English (or American, or Australian) as mainstream. They are the benchmark with which other works, in translation, are compared. The literary concentration on value(s) – the good, the true, the authentic – and on a canon of great works, or classics, is a corollary of using 'our own' (whoever 'we' are) as touchstone.

Like conventional literary studies and other forms of 'high' culture criticism, though in a broader and more self-conscious sense, anthropology is, almost by definition, a comparative study. But like cultural criticism, the comparative stance of anthropology is redolent with the assumptions of an elite mainstream to which all other cultures must surely aspire. In both fields, questions of taste and preference arise, as well as hierarchies of value.

What is important about these questions is the way in which they point to the classification and framing of knowledge (see Bernstein, 1971) as a powerful tool in the hands of those whose major concern is to delineate the inclusivity or exclusivity of social groups, the definers of us and them. By what criteria are individuals to be granted inclusion amongst 'us'? As for the 'elitist purity' of traditional academic disciplines, so for the politically correct stance of the new regimes, women's studies, cultural studies and Aboriginal studies. The language and tone is different, but the tactics and ends are the same: control over inclusivity and exclusivity.

As Trigger's reply to Nyoongah [*The Australian*, 3/2/93: 22] suggests, 'politicking within the academy' has much (too much, in his view) to do with the kind of debate in which they are engaging. Authors like Hodge and Mishra, who subtitle their work 'Australian Literature and the Post-colonial Mind', should, in Trigger's view, stick to their literary critical last, leaving the analysis of Aboriginal culture to those whose education and training qualifies them to do so. Nyoongah, on the other hand, suggests that if researchers like Trigger insist on maintaining the colonialist arrogance of pure, single-discipline boundaries, then anthropology is dead.

Hodge and Mishra's reply to Trigger's review of their work also indicates the basic difference in their understandings of what constitutes a political stance, within or outside the academy:

> We accept that our book does argue a particular politics, and we do not apologize for that. For too long literary criticism has avoided the political, assuming that it could be neutral on matters of culture. [*The Australian*, 3/2/93: 22]

Trigger himself, they say, citing his book as an 'illustrious' example of an interdisciplinary study and his work for the Royal Commission on Black Deaths in Custody ('a valuable contribution to the study of media representations of Aborigines') as 'an impeccably politically correct intrusion into Cultural Studies which we applaud,' misrecognizes, by denying it, the unavoidability of political engagement 'in matters of culture.'

So what exactly are these 'matters of culture?' Scholars in interdisciplinary fields like cultural studies, and others who are proud to recognize and announce the essentially political nature of their work, have often been very careful to define culture in what they say is 'the broad anthropological sense' (see, for example, McQueen, 1988.) For them, pushpin is always going to be as 'good' as poetry. And anything (museums, libraries, galleries, but also children's games, television soap opera or media representations of Aborigines) may be read as a text which informs the reader of some carefully patterned way of seeing: 'Our painting is a political act.'

On the other hand, those who remain attached to the idea of disciplinary exclusivity take for granted that culture is the output of the *cultivation* and refinement of aesthetic sensibilities, the proper object of study for the liberal arts. Pushpin for them will never be as good as poetry. And this remains true, if in a special sense, even for those iconoclasts who move outside the classical canon in their studies (see, for example, Eagleton, 1990; Greenblatt, 1991): While some are more overtly 'political,' and others move beyond the great works and 'masterpieces' to the analysis of mass-produced pulp fiction, minority genres like the detective novel or science fiction and fantasy, their first interest remains a literary one. Their focus of interest may be celebrated as new or execrated as jejune; their critical techniques range across fields like psychoanalysis or sociology, which are understood by their supporters to be enlightening and emancipatory, and by their opponents as obfuscatory, speculative or inappropriate; the conservative old guard decries the loss of purity, while the Young Turks revel in their 'impurity' and 'hybridity.'

The essential dispute is still between schools of thought within the same arena. One group has a narrow and clearly defined understanding of what is an appropriate focus for the liberal arts (the humanities) and what constitutes (high) culture. The other aims to broaden this focus and to redefine (popular) culture. But what anthropologists have long considered to be culture – customary arrangements of kin and family relations, or village politics, economic exchange or religious practice, the social relations of everyday life in an alien society – all of these become transmuted into 'popular' culture when the same lens is turned upon 'our own' daily lives. One person's exotic is always, or almost always, another's mundane. And one person's important text may very well be another's ephemeral fancy.

It is here that assumptions of value, whether repressed or spelled out in literary criticism, muted in 'value-free' social science, or warmly addressed in critical anthropology or sociology, become themselves the subject of dispute. Furthermore, this dispute is by no means a storm in an academic teacup. It centres on the question of who has the controlling voice in defining the ideological dominance, the hegemony of one social group as the common culture of an entire social formation.

Mythologies of Public Culture

In one sense, the imposition of the ideal of a common culture *is* a storm in an academic teacup, at least to the extent that the majority of the populace has little interest one way or the other in the ambivalent outcomes of academic disputes, particularly when those disputes are conducted in learned journals or in the pages of broadsheet dailies with paltry circulation figures. And this is nowhere more so than in a determinedly and aggressively egalitarian society like Australia, where 'academic' is a pejorative term with connotations of marginal usefulness, and intellectual work is suspected as being an elaborate trick on the part of an arcane minority [see Kapferer and Kapferer, 1993]. A trick, moreover, which is transparently unsuccessful, if its point is to convince outsiders that the liberal arts sections of the academy, at least, are doing anything more than feathering their own nests by being paid, by taxpayers, to engage in the kinds of activities that others regard as leisure pursuits of individual interest.

What is more important, to both outsiders and insiders, is the mass publicizing of the world views of powerful ruling groups, whether they be designated by analysts as power elites, or the ruling class, or the establishment, or accepted, however sceptically, by consumers of that publicity as the government, the experts, the system, or 'them'. But it is the widespread public display of power and influence which underpins the idea of what has been called 'the public culture' in industrial society [Horne, 1986]. The public culture is comprised, in the first observable instance, of a patterned repertoire of public events, public people and public places which gather up a plurality of multivocal symbols with the effect of concentrating attention on aspects of, say, national pride or community solidarity. Again, the categorization of insiders and outsiders is a crucial outcome, and it is the public nature of these people, places and events which allows for the widest possible net to be spread, to include the greatest number of people within the insider category.

The public culture is enacted within a public arena. As such it is dependent, in contemporary industrial and post-industrial social formations, upon the work of the publicizing organs of the state: free education in 'public' schools, for example, but also free medical treatment in public hospitals. 'Free to air' television and radio stations, however, or government subsidized or controlled telecommunications and postal services, are more difficult to designate as public in this sense, since the latter have monopolies or near monopolies, and the former are generally not much patronized by 'the public', as audience rating figures demonstrate. To Australian ears, there is a world of difference between the understanding of 'public' radio, for example, and 'state' radio: public provision is grudgingly necessary, state provision is a totalitarian infringement of civil liberties. And while public schools have long been synonymous with state schools, public hospitals are more often referred to as 'government-funded' than as state institutions, again because of overtones of coercion and monopoly control. There is a semiotic consensus that, for the majority of Australians, private is good, to be equated with independence and autonomy, and public is bad, speaking of dependence and humiliation. But 'state', with its strong implications of oligarchy and totalitarian repression, is worse still.

The concept of 'public culture', particularly in liberal democracies, stresses the openness of these societies to 'constructive' criticism and to the possibilities of democratic social change. As a phrase implying the shared nature of ideals and beliefs and values about democracy, public culture loses its possible pejorative connotations, especially when compared with State culture. It also, and not coincidentally, underpins distinctions drawn in capitalist social formations between high culture and popular culture, distinctions which might be understood as expressions of elitist snobbery or cultivated sensibility on the one hand and populist boorishness or liberated eclecticism on the other.

In both cases, 'public' is opposed to 'private' in a way that produces some anguish in cultures which value individualism at least as highly as egalitarianism. Private and personal choices, particularly in matters of 'high' cultural consumption, are regularly promoted as nothing other than a cherished democratic freedom to disburse one's time and income in whatever way one pleases. Public choices are conceived of as being made on behalf of those who have neither the time nor the funds to choose (schools, medical services) for themselves, while recognizing that there is a limited supply of public money to finance a very wide choice. Indeed, this limited funding does not in general apply to the production or consumption of 'popular' culture, which is assumed, not without foundation, to be well catered for by private enterprise and also to be a matter of private choice.

So there can be no such thing as a 'private' culture in terms of what is individual, idiosyncratic, peculiar to a single person. But what are otherwise called subcultures serve to mark off, to 'privatize', some aspects of a wider culture, taking unto themselves as definitional certain practices and ways of being which are unusual, or oppositional, or defensive or specialist. Thus we hear of corporate or productive culture, for example, or 'the culture of poverty', or youth culture.

And these subcultures are named most readily by the mass media, by scholars and researchers, by those whose opinions are taken to be informed and influential in public affairs. Which is to say, for example, that the culture of poverty is not named by the poor, but by those who are officially charged with the oversight of their welfare. Corporate culture, in a somewhat different way, is a term popularized by those who speak with authority on behalf of powerful business conglomerates, extolling the common bonds which exist among those in the same enterprise.[6] Productive culture is a designation for particular kinds of work practices and industrial relations which are understood by those who use the term to be more up to date, more cost effective, more efficient, faster and more 'competitive' than work practices (like 'featherbedding' or penalty rates) which are scorned as outdated and inefficient, or adversarial industrial relations which are premised upon a conflict of interest between employers and employees.

That such 'cultures' are limited to specific subgroups in no way lessens their impact upon 'outsider' understandings of what poverty, business or productivity are 'really' all about. In fact, I would argue that they provide stark examples of the ways in which the power and authority to define the situation of poverty, for example, is all-important in the process of reducing the multiple meanings of poverty in a wider non-specialist world (starvation? disease? malnutrition? straitened circumstances? inability to service debt? inefficient use of limited resources?) to the ideology of a single specialist group. And within that group – of welfare workers, charitable foundations, individual volunteers, lobbyists – what are often euphemistically referred to as 'philosophical' disagreements about policy and practice are resolved by agreement to present a publicly united front which dismisses 'internal' disagreement as superficial. Furthermore, the public façade of a specialist body, with the power of expert and esoteric knowledge to legitimate its expertise in a public forum, is such that those without the esoteric knowledge, but with respect for the expertise, and with the support of opinion leaders and image makers, mythologizers, in the mass media and elsewhere, can come to accept and embrace a subcultural ideology as an element of a common culture, a current in the 'mainstream.'

That other subcultural groups (racial/ethnic minorities or radical feminists, for example) have yet to achieve such acceptance is indicative of the oppositional nature of their political practice, as well as of divisions among them which militate against the presentation of a unified line of argument. Abusing ideals of consensus and disturbing 'mainstream cultural values' – indeed, deriding 'the mainstream' as elitist or oppressive, fundamentally self-serving, self-satisfied and *undemocratic* – threatens to expose that mainstream for what it actually is: a dominant ideology.

The finite meaning provinces of specialist, private subcultures – their taken-for-grantedness and common sense – are rarely open to the scrutiny or critique of outsiders except in so far as they are thought to be fair and impartial, their critique demonstrably 'constructive' and well within the parameters already set by the subcultural gatekeepers and their publicists/guardians. It is through the work of the mythologizers, who mine the cultural seams of everyday life and refine the raw materials of everyday meaning-making, that finite meaning provinces come to masquerade as the paramount reality of everyday life. The webs of meaning spun by powerful social groups begin to encompass the meanings of the less powerful and come to be definitional not only of the public culture, but of culture itself.

For 'the public culture' is only a more polite, less contentious term for 'dominant ideology', a term lacking in the dialectical rigidities of Marxian analysis and the residual suspicion of conspiracy which grounds critiques of the dominant ideology thesis. The term 'culture' – especially culture with a small 'c' – has none of the meanings of mistakenness and wrong-headedness attributed to the term 'ideology' in party political parlance and radical critique, and as such it can be 'ideologized' with near impunity. For hegemony is not a confidence trickster's method of imposing a dominant ideology when public coercion and intimidation are no longer legitimate. It is achieved not through guile and mystification, by playing upon the false consciousness of cultural dopes, but through drawing upon and re-mythologizing the most deeply taken-for-granted elements of a cultural logic, a

Geschlecht, and its discursive practices. Hegemony expresses a master social narrative, taking to itself aspects of less powerful narratives as tributaries to a mainstream, but like other master narratives, it is as much open to question and resistance, analysis and deconstruction, as, for example, the literary canon, the disciplines of the academy or the architecture of the modern.

Notes

1. While most Australians know the words of *Waltzing Matilda* and especially its rollicking chorus, few, to the constant annoyance of politicians and other nation-builders, are well-versed in the words of *Advance Australia Fair*, certainly beyond the first verse:

    Australians all, let us rejoice,
    For we are young and free.
    We've golden soil and wealth for toil,
    Our home is girt by sea.
    Our land abounds in Nature's gifts
    Of beauty rich and rare -
    In History's page let every stage
    Advance Australia Fair.
    Chorus: In joyful strains then let us sing, Advance Australia Fair.

    Beneath our radiant Southern Cross
    We toil with hearts and hands,
    To make this Commonwealth of ours
    Renowned of all the lands.
    For those who've come across the sea,
    We've boundless plains to share.
    With courage let us all combine:
    Advance Australia Fair.
    Chorus.

2. This term resonates with the meanings attached to habitus in Bourdieu's usage, with connotations of taken-for-grantedness and unquestioning acceptance of a social practice which is *doxic*.
3. The 'manufacturing of consent' through the quotation of expert opinion is addressed in Chapter 6. The phrase, originally used by

Walter Lippmann, [1965], was revived in the early 1990s in a film of the work of the social critic Noam Chomsky.

4. I am endeavouring to use what I take to be surnames here, although people I have consulted on the issue are unsure about applying contemporary Western usages to a naming system that works in radically different ways for 'tribal' people or those who have adopted 'traditional' names. Cf. the use of Yunupingu in Chapter 1.
5. The full text of David Trigger's review, 'Australian Cultural Studies: Radical Critique or Vacuous Posturing?' is in *Anthropological Forum* VI, 4: 607–613 (1993), as is Hodge and Mishra's reply, 'Anthropology and/or/as "Cultural Studies?" A Response to Trigger' (pp.614–618.)
6. And utilized by those who perceive their own smaller commercial interests to be aligned with the corporate bases of contemporary capitalist enterprise.

CHAPTER THREE

The Discourses of History: Larrikins, Scarlet Women and the Apparatus of Capture

> The whole idea of trying to define an identity is a bit silly. The moment you step into Australia, your actions and thoughts are already shaped by all the years of history. That's enough of an identity. If you ask for any more, you start to have to deny other bits of people's identity which may be equally important to them. [C. Kukathas, lecturer in politics, cited *Sydney Morning Herald* 26/6/93: 44]
>
> Australia is one of those few countries which actually relishes its diversity. . . . Under the umbrella of an overall commitment to the nation and its uniting values and institutions, a society of great richness and variety as well as remarkable harmony has evolved. To reinforce this commitment to national unity, we must continue to develop the special Australian identity. We need strong national identity to give us more strength of purpose. We need it abroad to leave no one in any doubt about who we are and what we stand for. [N. Bolkus, Minister for Immigration, cited *Sydney Morning Herald* 26/6/93: 44]

The discovery, definition or creation of a 'national identity' has long formed the principal task of nationalist mythologizers, most particularly in times of political and economic uncertainty and perceived loss of faith in a secure collective future. As the Commonwealth of Australia, established as a federation of former British colonies in 1901, nears the centenary of its existence as a nation state, questions about 'who we are and what we stand for' become more and more insistent. At every turn, groups of people with particular understandings of race, ethnicity, political allegiance, personal autonomy, characteristic tastes and behaviours can be seen to be in more or less open competition to establish claims to being really, essentially, archetypally Australian. Aboriginal people vie with White landowners and transnational mining companies for control over vast tracts of potentially productive land; people of non-English-speaking background wrestle with taken-for-granted Anglo-centrism; generations clash over ideas about the proper behaviour of young men and, particularly, young women. Religious affiliations, family traditions, custom, morality and manners are thought (by commentators in the parliaments and the mass media) to have been jettisoned in favour of a dangerous individuated, atomized hedonism or, alternatively, a despairing collective lassitude. And neither of these escape routes from reality has the capacity to endow us with the greater strength of purpose so greatly desired by the Minister for Immigration. As the fractures and fault-lines of our *Geschlecht* become more obvious and more sinister, as We become a host of disconnected object-selves, strength of purpose appears to be unfocused, national unity a dream lacking in direction and conviction.

At the same time, tens of thousands of Australians conceive of themselves as 'ordinary' men and women, with little interest in or contribution to make to the great national purpose, whatever it may be. For many, 'identity' is a treasured individual characteristic, a composite wrought from melding together a unique genetic endowment and life history, a haphazard, aleatory lived experience, accidents and coincidences, sometimes shared with known or unknown others, sometimes solitary. No doubt this is what Chandra Kukathas refers to as the 'bits' of identity which are differentially important to different individuals. For such individuals, it is 'all the years of history' which shape (even determine) national identities. To be sure, history shapes individual identity also, but only partly, for the ideologies of individualism hold that each individual has the capacity to choose, to change, to overcome or succumb, and only specifically, for the same ideologies teach that all are different, and differently capable of grasping opportunities or turning events to personal advantage. Individuals have biographies; nation states have histories.

The sufficiency of history to shape a national identity is questionable. What is also necessary is an acceptance, by the majority, of that identity as shared and unifying, as embodied in 'uniting values and institutions' which give 'us' strength of purpose and demonstrate that unity and strength to outsiders. The belief in a shared historical purpose is something that requires to be learned, and learned formally in a multicultural, pluralist society, one divided and categorized along lines of class and gender, race and ethnicity. The effective achievement of national unity, national strength of purpose and respect for national institutions requires the mythmakers and marketing managers to capture the hearts and minds of the citizenry. Physical coercion will not produce the intense commitments sought by military commanders or athletic coaches or the creators of national scholastic standards. Emotional and intellectual involvement are at least as important, even more so in a social formation which prides itself on its commitment to the processes of democratic governance and social justice.

The surveillance and control of corporeal entities is achieved through the utilization by the agents of the state of all the repressive apparatuses and mechanisms which that state has at its command. But the moulding of wills, the manufacturing of consent and embracing of the ideals of others as one's own, can only be achieved through constant ideological suasion. Not beating into submission, but seduction, captivation and enchantment are the most successful devices in effecting the capture of passion and imagination [cf. Deleuze and Guattari, 1987]. And history is perhaps the most powerful net of all for ensnaring a nationalist imagination and ensuring loyalty and commitment to an ideal of national unity.

Heroes, Hagiography and the Question of Identity

Recent Australian history, like so many other New World and colonial histories of the post-Enlightenment period, is studded with the stories of 'great men'. In the case of Australia, colonial governors, discoverers and explorers, inventors and adapters provide the framework within which the history of a specific era is, or has been, written. The names of Phillip, Macquarie, Brisbane, Bourke, Hindmarsh (governors), Tasman, Cook, Fleurieu, Flinders, La Perouse (discoverers), Sturt, Hume, Eyre, Forrest (explorers), Rouse and MacArthur (inventors) resound through the history of the last two hundred years, providing the names of towns and suburbs, streets and highways, electoral districts, mountains, rivers, lakes and deserts. The names of the English ruling class are also prominent, of course: Sydney, Melbourne, Victoria, Adelaide.

Children learn these names (or at least those which are locally relevant) in primary school, names which form signposts in the narrative history of Australia since European colonization and settlement. Irish, Scots, Welsh and English placenames attest to the sense of exile which burdened many of the settlers (Ballina and the Castlereagh, Glen Innes and the Macleay, Llangothlin and the Gwydir, Tamworth and the Clarence) while jostling for map space with names like Namoi, Pokataroo, Warrumbungle, Yamba and Coonabarabran. Map space, but also, as a newer, more socially sensitive history teaches, actual land space as well, for it is no longer possible to conceive of the Liverpool Plains as the explorer Cunningham did in 1823, as 'a million wild acres' [see Rolls, 1981] ripe for settlement and agricultural development, belonging to no one but the Crown, whose representative, the Governor, had the sole power to bestow it.

Place names around the country also convey a stark impression of doomed projects and failed dreams: the search for an inland sea or for fertile pastures beyond the coastal plains is punctuated by Mount Disappointment, Mount Misery, Mount Desolation and Mount Hopeless. The desperation and suffering of the convicts at Port Arthur and Port Jackson are long continued in the daily experience of pioneers and smallholders battling drought, flood and fire in an age-old struggle for survival. The viciousness of relations between these same pioneers and the local indigenous people is horribly evoked in signposts, like one in the Riverina: Poisoned Water Holes Creek.

The historical imagination of Australians and the discourses that flow from it have, until recently, been bounded by an understanding of the land as harsh and unwelcoming, to be tamed only by the good offices of benevolent government and the honest toil of diligent yeomen labourers. It is a history of tribulation and striving, in which the generosity and fortitude of 'the common man' are to be found within both the ruling class and the lower orders. It is a history of individuals, brutal and self-seeking as well as compassionate and honourable.

It was not only natural disasters which beset those who populated the pages of the school history books, however. Courage, will and enterprise were also required to conquer situations of everyday poverty and degradation, which were thought to be the product of avarice and ignorance, sloth and ingratitude. While few of the rulers believed that these vices were anything but 'natural' to the working class, many believed in the redemptive powers of a new beginning in a new land, the social and personal gains to be had from independent, autonomous labour and wise governance. The assumption of linear progress which colours the tales of misfortune overcome also informs, and is informed by, a kind of utopianism which sees Australia as a land upon which the ideals of the Enlightenment and the hopes of the nineteenth century – radical, socialist, democratic, egalitarian – might be inscribed.

Through the margins and footnotes of the history books spread rhizome-like the stories of other men and women, far less respectable than Governor Lachlan Macquarie of New South Wales, and far less powerful than his predecessor, the brutal Governor Bligh. Many of them, ordinary labourers for the most part, are nameless, gathered together under the rubrics of 'convicts, diggers, shearers, stockmen' or 'Anzacs'. But they are almost invariably depicted and popularly recalled as men, with the possible exception of the much less well-known women of the west, memorialized in George Essex Evans' poem of that name. In loneliness and isolation, they cleared the land and tilled the soil, dug the gold and shore the sheep, unprotected from either natural disaster or human rapaciousness and malfeasance by distant governments, in Sydney, Adelaide, Brisbane or, in the final analysis, London. And it is their struggles against oppression and degradation which are valorized in legendary tales of rebellion, strikes, bushranging and warfare.

While a few individual women are remembered in songs and stories of the bush – Lawson's mythic drover's wife, for example, or Judith Wright's grandmother [see Wright, 1959] – more are remembered in an urban environment, as merchants like Mary Reibey [see Irvine, 1982], as what would now be called 'social workers' like Caroline Chisholm [see Heney, 1943] or as actresses or dancers like Lola Montez, who entertained working men and scandalized the local bourgeoisie. From the earliest days of settlement, the role of women was to support men: to maintain male authority over children or servants, to be servants and/or sexual partners to soldiers, freed convicts, new settlers and freeborn 'currency lads.' Ultimately, the authority of women was conceived of as moral, and their moral authority was called upon, as it still is today, to bolster the authority of the family, the church, the school and the state itself. Thus women were and often still are popularly conceived of, in Anne Summers' [1975] memorable portmanteau phrase, as either 'damned whores [or] God's police'.[1]

Histories of the Australian people (as opposed to histories of the Australian state) remain few and marginal to the interests of the people themselves, though recent years have witnessed a flowering of academic interest in local history, labour history, women's history and Aboriginal history [see, for example, Connell and Irving, 1980; Reynolds, 1982; Macintyre, 1985; Burgman and Lee, 1988; Bulbeck, 1991]. Many of these works, which endeavour to include hitherto largely neglected contributors to the making of Australian history in narratives of progress and mythologies of political power, are conceived within the same Enlightenment vision as the earlier stories of great men. Many still share the speculative and mythologizing tendencies of an older 'big-picture' historiography, romanticizing and embellishing the 'good,' justifying or defending the 'bad,' and maintaining their devotion to an arborescent model of human history. Many also are conceived in a spirit of redressing past injustice, explaining and legitimating the claims of groups or individuals to greater respect, or accusing the previous holders of power and authority – and their biographers or apologists – of oppression and self-aggrandizement.

Central to the process of historical mythologizing (and, indeed, de-mythologizing) is the creation of symbolic types – personages in whom character traits which are thought to be central in the generation of Australian society, and of history itself are gathered up and concentrated [see Klapp, 1962; Grathoff, 1970]. Like Weberian ideal types, of bureaucracy or religion, for example, symbolic types do not exist and have never existed in concrete and pristine 'reality'. They appear in myth, like Ned Kelly or Peter Lalor of Eureka, or Simpson of Gallipoli, and in legend, like the Man from Snowy River or The Sentimental Bloke or Ginger Meggs or, more recently, Crocodile Dundee, as potent and very real symbols of humanity, loyalty, courage and humour in adversity. The symbolic types of Stockman or Anzac, for example, draw to themselves wide-ranging personal characteristics which admirers and detractors alike can find to be significantly, even uniquely 'Australian.' What is significant about them is the way in which they present a multivocal focus of idealism, not their individual, corporeal existence. They symbolize egalitarianism, individualism, physical strength and skill, practicality and the triumph, even in the face of death, of the common man, the battler, over an oppressive and merciless reality beyond the ability of ordinary people to control. In Australia, that reality, symbolized by military chiefs, politicians, bureaucrats, the police, the 'illegitimately' rich (like *The Bulletin*'s archetype 'Fat Man': see Rolfe, 1979) and their lackeys, the bankers, was (and frequently remains) the state, against whom the people were implacably, if inchoately, ranged.

I have suggested that in capturing and holding the imaginations and loyalties of the people, myth-making converts personal biographies into social histories, drawing abstract lessons from the concrete events of a past era. The conversion of individual life stories into tales which point a moral still relevant to contemporary puzzles and problems has lately become something of an organized industry. The codification of 'national' heroes takes place at a time when modernist and individualist assumptions of linear progress are under examination, and when many more candidates for heroic status are presented from many more sources, for validation by scholars and lobbyists, and authentication by the members of those social groups they are thought to typify or to represent. No longer the subjects of balladeers and pamphleteers, the heroes of popular mythology are, in the process of nationalist image-making, sanitized, commoditized and re-presented to the people as object lessons in 'being Australian'.

As Australians seek to construct a distinctive national identity in a global context of competing identities, the creation of national heroes becomes an exercise not unlike the devising of a literary or artistic canon. Who has the authority to decide? Who should be included? Who should be dismissed? What are the criteria of greatness which suggest heroic stature for individuals? As positive or negative role models, heroes may have some commonsense pedagogic or demagogic value (*pour encourager les autres*, perhaps, as in naming the Australian of the Year), but as symbolic types, they achieve far greater significance in their gathering together of a multiplicity of images and symbols amenable to widely divergent interpretations, as well as to capture by the State, to be turned to the service of often shifting ideological ends.

A brief analysis of two works of secular hagiography which have appeared in the last decade-and-a-half may serve to illustrate some of these claims. The years leading up to the celebration of the bicentenary of British settlement in New South Wales saw an astonishing blossoming of interest in Australian history and historiography – astonishing, in that such interest had been infrequently cultivated in the schools of Australia or in the wider reading public. History has rarely been considered by Australians to have any relevance to their own lives or to the serious business of the contemporary world of getting and spending. But the advent of government policies focused on the mitigation of discriminatory practices - against Aboriginal people, against women, against people of non-English-speaking backgrounds - coupled with a desire for international recognition as a significant democratic polity, produced generous public and private support for the publication of numerous histories of business corporations, schools, minority ethnic groups, voluntary associations, personages neglected in the creation of national pantheons and styles of life held to have significant traditional virtue.

Not unexpectedly, the popular works produced at this time, works which often constituted desirable gifts of the coffee-table variety, placed their emphases squarely upon the parts played by individuals in the making of the nation. I discuss two of them here. One, Geoffrey Dutton's *The Australian Heroes: A Rousing Roll Call of 47 of Australia's Greatest Heroes and Heroines* [1981], presents the reader with an arguably idiosyncratic selection of vignettes of historical figures and symbolic types which he considers have had important impact on Australian understandings of greatness and heroism. The other was produced by an editorial board which comprised an Emeritus Professor of History and Deputy Chancellor of a university (Russel Ward), a Professor of Australian Literature (Leonie Kramer), a radio and television journalist (Ray Martin), a print journalist (Trevor Kennedy) and a publisher (Richard Walsh). The last two were both employed, as Managing Director and Editor-in-Chief respectively, by Australian Consolidated Press, Martin by Channel 9 television. Their work, *The Greats: Heroes, Larrikins, Leaders, Visionaries: The Fifty Men and Women Who Shaped Australia* [1986], was published by Angus and Robertson (the oldest publishing house in Australia, which also produced Dutton's book) in association with The Nine Network and *The Bulletin*, owned by Australian Consolidated Press.

I stress the provenance of these two works, one written by a poet, chronicler, critic and social commentator, an individual with an individual's viewpoint, the other by a committee of highly respectable academic and commercial people, an editorial board without a chair (perhaps the most egalitarian way of constituting a committee, though readers are not informed of the way in which the board was established, or at whose behest). It might not be too fanciful to suggest that Dutton's book speaks with the individualist voice of the people, while *The Greats*, as a collective work produced by academics and members of the mass media with the imprimatur of a powerful press empire, takes the even-handed tone of an ideological state apparatus. But because Ward, the historian, contributed the foreword (as well as a piece on Lachlan Macquarie) I will, for convenience, refer to him as the main author of the volume, while recognizing that this contravenes the egalitarian code within which the board and its forty-eight other contributors worked.

The two works have thirteen heroes in common. The Ward volume lists them chronologically, while Dutton places them into five of his nine specific categories. They are:

Ward et al.	Dutton
Henry Lawson (poet and writer)	Authentic hero
Nellie Melba (singer)	Authentic hero
Charles Sturt (explorer)	Authentic hero
Douglas Mawson (explorer)	Authentic hero
Caroline Chisholm (social worker)	Authentic hero
Albert Namatjira (artist)	Tragic hero
Ned Kelly (bushranger)	Villain hero
Daniel Mannix (Catholic Archbishop)	Love-Hate
Jack Lang (Premier, New South Wales)	Love-Hate
William (Billy) Hughes (Prime Minister)	Love-Hate
Robert Gordon Menzies (Prime Minister)	Love-Hate
Gough Whitlam (Prime Minister)	Love-Hate
Donald Bradman (cricketer)	Sporting hero

The determination of heroism exercises both Ward and Dutton. Dutton takes heroes to be those who have conquered fear while, more prosaically, Ward's committee agreed in the end that

> the fundamental criterion for inclusion should be the extent to which each person's life and work contributed to making Australia what it is, or more importantly is seen to be, today. . .. This criterion obviously places heavy emphasis on a person's 'Australian-ness'. That is why more artists, using that term in its broadest sense, find a place than do explorers, sportspeople, politicians, public servants, soldiers or business men. It is the business of writers, painters, sculptors, singers,

> architects, actors, journalists and intellectuals to record what is and what might be. [1986: Foreword]

So out of fifty 'greats', Ward et al. include fourteen artists (in a 'narrow' sense - painters, poets, storytellers, entertainers, film-makers), three journalists, two scholars and an architect - a total of twenty. Dutton, on the other hand, and in keeping with his conquering-of-fear criterion, lists only seven artists, but ten explorers or pioneers (to Ward et al.'s two). *The Greats* also include, despite Ward's disclaimer, thirteen politicians (five of whom are listed, perhaps unsurprisingly, in Dutton's 'Love-Hate' category) and five loosely defined 'public servants', only one of whom, Caroline Chisholm, finds a place in Dutton's work, as an 'authentic' hero.

Dutton's pantheon differs most from that of Ward et al. in the inclusion of a number of what Australians like to call *ratbags* - a term, usually of wry admiration, applied to cheerful rogues, flawed personalities who nevertheless command a certain amount of respect for their devil-may-care attitudes to the judgements of political, religious or moral authorities. Ned Kelly, classified along with two other bushrangers as a 'villain' by Dutton, is the only such personage common to both lists. Indeed, there is some significance to the dispute within *The Greats'* editorial board as to whether or not Kelly should be included at all, since some members argued that 'great' actually meant 'great and good.' Ward records,

> To some it seemed axiomatic that Ned Kelly led all the rest, but others . . . rejected him as nothing but a murderous thug. Should Hitler then be excluded from a book about the fifty greatest Germans? Since no one maintained that the Fuhrer was morally finer than the murderer of only three policemen, Ned finally made it, but only after spirited discussion. [1986: Foreword]

Dutton lists nine other ratbags in his compendium: seven 'collapsible heroes' - including Lola Montez - and two 'antiheroes' - Errol Flynn (screen star) and Barry Humphries (comedian). None of these finds a place in Ward et al.'s altogether more worthy tome. Neither do Dutton's animal heroes (Phar Lap, a racehorse, and The Dog on the Tuckerbox - also a notorious ratbag) nor his 'legendary heroes' - 'the digger, the outback woman, the bushranger, the horseman and the light horseman' and, the archetypal Ratbag, 'Ern Malley,' fictional perpetrator of a famous literary hoax in 1943.

The authors of both volumes try very hard to be fair in their selections and to give a balanced representation of the great and heroic. Dutton is apologetic that,

> Australia is so short of heroines that it is a shame that three of them, Eliza Fraser, Lola Montez and Daisy Bates, are distinctly collapsible. [1981: 6]

In other words, their 'status as hero is accepted, but [their] reputation turns out to be hollow' [1981: 5]. Ward et al. also argued among themselves whether

> each state (formerly Colony), even the most sparsely populated, should have some representation; but naturally or inevitably, identification of great Tasmanians proved most difficult. [But cf. Dutton's inclusion of Truganini as a tragic, and female, hero.] Similarly it was impossible to achieve any kind of balance or fairness between the sexes, hard though we sought to do so. [1986: Foreword]

The quest for balance and fairness is fundamentally an expression of egalitarianism. As such, while it is clearly much in the minds of the hagiographers, it runs up against their devotion to the events of *individual biography* as the definitive expression and evidence of greatness. Dutton produces the romanticized composite legendary heroes and enlivens his tales of Mawson or Bradman, for example, with personal reminiscences of his own; the editorial board of *The Greats* endeavours to maintain a strict devotion to historically validated fact, though their contributors' admiration for specific heroes occasionally borders on the sycophantic.

Within the kinds of egalitarian individualism favoured in Australian historiography and mythology, the fine line between sincere admiration and self-seeking toadyism is often blurred or transgressed.[2] So Ward et al. include a number of extremely wealthy businessmen in their canon on the grounds that in enriching themselves (for example, John Macarthur, Thomas Elder, Sidney Kidman, Hudson Fysh) they also founded important industries and/or opened up the country to commercial and industrial development. Similarly they include a number of lesser poets and writers (C.J. Dennis, creator of *The Sentimental Bloke*, and May Gibbs, creator of *Snugglepot and Cuddlepie*, and *Bib and Bub,*

The Gumnut Babies) in accordance with their belief that these artists contributed more greatly to 'the image of Australia' than others who might be thought 'greater' – 'if only because their popularity ensured they were read by more people' [1986: Foreword].

The populist strain of these observations is also evidenced in Dutton's work, though his own canon is at once more predictable and more idiosyncratic. It has the aura of an earlier age in its deprecatory, even cringing, judgements of literary merit, for example, and in his references to a 'search' for identity:

> Australians have not accepted many artists or writers as heroes. . .. It is partly, of course, a question of genius; Australia has not managed to produce a Shakespeare or a Dickens, nor a Rodin to sculpt a Balzac. Nevertheless, in proportion to time and population, the extent of the popularity of some writers – [Adam Lindsay] Gordon, Banjo Paterson, Henry Lawson, C.J. Dennis, 'Nino Culotta' – has been extraordinary. But all of those have distilled a heroic (or anti-heroic) myth, the Horseman, the Bushman, the Larrikin, the Migrant. [1981: 5]

Similarly:

> Perhaps the plethora of Australian heroes indicates the need for reassurance of a national identity in a colonial people. [. . .] It could be yet another illustration of Geoffrey Blainey's concept of distance; a reality here to compensate for the unreality of a distant world. It could be an instinctive reaction, especially in artists or writers, against the national egalitarianism, the cutting of tall poppies down to size. [1981: 1]

The decapitation of tall poppies is a cherished Australian practice. The expression 'we must cut the heads off the tall poppies' is attributed to Jack Lang, who as Premier of New South Wales in 1931, proclaimed that the reduction of government salaries during the depression was the way to a fairer distribution of wealth in hard times [Lang, 1970].[3] It has since come to be applied to any statement of deprecation, any egregious failure to recognise the achievements of another, any deflation of unwarranted pretension, and is usually flavoured with sour grapes. Dutton's assumption that artists and writers might be particularly sensitive to such egalitarian levelling reflects his own understanding that they are superior to other mortals and have a harder time of it in philistine Australia than in other cultural milieux where their work is more reverently valued.

The plethora of Australian heroes, and the size of the rogues' gallery within it, does indeed say something of egalitarian intent – as does the cutting down of tall poppies. What these discourses reiterate is an ideological statement of equality, phrased in terms of almost mathematical equals: every Australian is as 'good', as worthy a human being as every other Australian, within the limits set by fate, nature and custom. Those who achieve distinction are believed to do so by good fortune and the honing of natural talents – even, or perhaps especially, when those talents are not those which are admired and encouraged by the apparatuses of the state. By the same token, composite, nameless heroes of the kind lauded in Dutton's work can revive the flagging spirits of ordinary people in a way that is both more affecting and more effective than a retailing of the achievements of individual industrialists or politicians.

In this, Ward et al.'s 'greats' tend to be a much worthier group than the pantheon assembled by Dutton. Their inclusion of a career public servant, an economist still alive at the time of publication, indicates their care to be even-handed, to offend no one and demonstrate their support for a kind of demotic left-of-centre political rectitude:

> We took a punt on Nugget Coombs. All thought he deserved a guernsey, but doubted that any public servant's name could last long because of the square, grey, anonymous image of his tribe. [1986: Foreword]

Perhaps, as a powerful bureaucrat, Coombs could be thought of as quintessentially Australian, but this is not the line taken by his biographer, who rather stresses Coombs' humanity and his long support of Labor Party governments and Aboriginal land rights. But he is not a figure upon which to build heroic legends. *The Greats* is a work which treads a careful line between upholding traditional claims to fame and suggesting new arenas in which greatness might be discerned. Always, the heroes of this volume are those who, in the judgement of the editorial board, have made Australia what it is seen to be today – the 'greats' are the creators of Australian mythologies, gathered together by other mythologists who are perhaps too modest to include themselves. *The Greats* is a product of an ideological state apparatus, a work in which the exploits and activities of continually mythologized myth-makers receive the imprimatur of the mass media and the academy and are held up as exemplars of true Australian greatness in the service of the Nation.

The authority of the state and the autonomy of the people can be seen as in constant tension, and occasionally in open conflict. Mythical heroes can be pressed into the service of *either* the dominant ideology of the state *or* efforts to resist domination. Those who are reviled and officially condemned in one era may be celebrated and officially incorporated in another. That this is so tells us much of changing understandings of the worth of individuals and the comparative social standing of groups in egalitarianism. Indeed, so useful are the myths that they may be utilized at the same time, to present, for example, the image of an equal and co-operative society protected by law and good governance on the one hand, and an unequal and conflictful society ravaged by exploitation and corruption on the other.

Such a myth is the story of Ned Kelly, the bushranger, whose biography is presented below, with quotations from the *Dictionary of National Biography* [Stephen and Lee (eds) 1967–8, Vol. X: 1235].

Case 4. Ned Kelly: 'Almost Like Romance'

EDWARD (NED) KELLY (1854–1880), Australia's best known bushranger, was, with his two brothers, in constant trouble with the authorities for horse-stealing. In April 1878 the police arrived at the Kelly home to arrest Dan Kelly. In the ensuing fight, Ned shot one of the constables, and the brothers escaped, but their mother, brother-in-law and a second man were captured and sentenced to lengthy prison terms. The Kelly boys were joined by two others, Byrne and Hart, and the gang became 'the terror of the country'. In the unemotional words of the *Dictionary of National Biography*, 'some of their achievements read almost like romance', and

> their reckless audacity, their good fortune, and the fact that their murders were principally confined to policemen, their robberies to banks or government property, attained for them some popular sympathy, and they seem to have had no difficulty in obtaining provisions and intelligence in their hiding places in the mountains.

On 27 June 1880, the gang were surrounded in a shanty not far from Beechworth. The house beseiged and set on fire. All but Ned, 'who was outside and might have escaped, but that, with a courage worthy of a better cause, he refused to desert his brothers and comrades', were killed. His arms and legs, unprotected by his heavy iron armour, were badly wounded, and he was captured. On his recovery he was tried and convicted at Beechworth, and hanged there in October 1880.

The righteous rebellion of the free-spirited individual against the power of the State, especially when that power can be defined as resting upon the illegitimate usurpation of civil liberties and human rights, is a hallowed theme of Western democratic tradition. The Ned Kelly story has all the ingredients of myth, following a parallel path to that of Robin Hood, except that Robin Hood is an upholder of the legitimate monarchy, while Kelly is a champion of the people against what he and they take to be an illegitimate autocracy. His career was also contemporary with that of Jesse James (1847–1882) in the United States, who felt himself to be persecuted for his allegiance to a lost (Southern) cause. Kelly, son of an Irish ex-convict, wrote in his 'Jerilderie Letter' of 1879 of:

> Port McQuarrie Toweringabbie Norfolk Island and Emu Plains and in those places of tyranny and condemnation many a blooming Irish man rather than subdue to the Saxon yoke were flogged to death and bravely died in servile chains. [cited in Hughes, 1987: 444]

Where the outlaws of the American West had their genesis in the Civil War, the bushranging tradition in Australia owed its inception to the relation between convicts and prison-warders, escaped convicts and colonial police or 'troopers'. The surveillance of convict society by the military provided a framework for the foundation of a local constabulary, while the rules and regulations of the prison system were the foundation of the bureaucratic order of the State. Most of the convicts in Australia were what today would be classed as petty criminals, but tradition stresses the few who could be called political prisoners or prisoners of conscience: Chartists and Fenians, desperate parents and virtuous maidens. The loathing of the Catholic Irish for the Protestant ascendancy and of exploited workers for the combination acts was transported to Australia along with the felons themselves and found fertile ground in the new land. Ned Kelly and his family fit neatly into this tradition, encapsulating as they do qualities considered to be quintessentially Australian to this day: youth, audacity, loyalty, a care for the underdog, ingenuity, suspicion of authority, fatalism and a well-honed conception of social justice based upon complete equality before the law.

Craig McGregor, in his widely read *Profile of Australia* [1968], discussed what he called the two leading myths of Australian society, the Australian-as-bushman and the Australian-as-worker. He made much of their 'mythical' nature and proceeded, at least to his own satisfaction, to debunk these 'myths.' He wrote of the bushman:

> that mythical 'real' Australian which is known so well: a tall, lean, sun-tanned slow-talking character with a chip on his shoulder who hates authority, is loyal to his mates, stands up for the underdog and believes that any man is as good as the next, if not in fact a damn sight better. He is a seminal pioneering figure, and no doubt this is how many Australians like to think of themselves. [1968: 18–19]

And of the worker:

> Even more powerful than the bush myth. . .is that of Australia as the land of the worker. Ask most people to describe an Australian and they will probably reply in terms of a bloke with a sports shirt under his suit, a glass of beer in his hand and an accent a yard wide who is against the boss (he is never thought of as *being* the boss), gambles heavily, calls his wife 'the missus', was a digger in one war or another and is satisfied to be an ordinary bloody Australian. [1968: 21]

McGregor claimed that both stories were 'invalid as an explanation of contemporary Australian society' [1968: 22], in that, for example, they ignored the existence of women (though his own, statistically validated image of the 'average' Australian was still very much that of a man) and denied the complexity of contemporary urban styles of life. A quarter of a century later, McGregor's critique is, in general, even more real, but no more to the point. It is reiterated regularly, for example by Professor Donald Horne, one of the leading lights of Australian Studies and an accomplished mythologist himself. In his 1993 Elford Lecture at Flinders University, Horne raised yet again the question: 'How much harm was caused by the myths of the bush? And how is it being remedied?'

Horne's own answer is to suggest that the harmful nature of the bush myths is inherent in their obsolete assumption of a monocultural society, deeply racist and deeply sexist, and that the remedy lies in embracing the human cultural diversity that underpins policies of multiculturalism and is thereby antithetical to racist and sexist ideologies and practices. That this is no more a valid description of Australian social relations at the end of the twentieth century than it was at the end of the nineteenth might suggest to both the makers and debunkers of myths that the value of mythologies lies elsewhere than in their provision of a blueprint for social action.

All demythologizing exercises (and they are legion, as one might expect given the egalitarian furore for cutting heads off tall poppies, mythical heroes being by definition tall poppies) fail to take seriously the pivotal role of mythology and mythological practice in the creation, maintenance and re-creation of cultures, of ways of being in the world. They assume, as certain theories of ideology and false consciousness assume, that myths are in some deeply rationalist sense 'unreal' and thus to be contrasted with the hard 'realities' of everyday life. The debunking of long-cherished images of egalitarian mateship and justice by academics and journalists still has little impact on the way 'many Australians like to think of themselves', and indeed, may only serve to arouse their ire. Presumably, this is what Ward et al. (1986) recognize in their selection of the fifty men and women who shaped Australia: the one characteristic all fifty are held to have in common is that they provided a 'service' to the nation – or to the state. As such, they make excellent role models for aspirant 'greats', and as Ward concludes,

> If this process of compromise [in the selection of 'greats'] results in a merely popular, or democratically chosen, roll of 'greats', it will be, in the view of two centuries of stern, elitist, native and foreign critics, all the more truly Australian for that. [1986: Foreword]

Champions of the People, Enemies of the State

So why do these myths and stereotypes, democratically chosen or not, survive at all? Why, particularly, does a rationalist and prosaic age persist in remaking myths as fast as they are demythologized? It is certainly not enough to suggest, as Dutton does, that they are positive (or negative) role models of achievement, that they make (some of) us feel better about our lives, that they are vehicles for escapism, or that they are the expression of a collective conscience – though all this may be true to some degree.

Eric Hobsbawm remarks of a Balkan bandit: 'Nobody who is insignificant has several hundred songs made about him' [1969: 114], and it is this significance which needs explication. For the songs and ballads about Ned Kelly and other bushrangers are legion, while there is a dearth of songs about their enemies, the representatives of law and order, policemen, judges and other more respectable, if less romantic and heroic figures who showed a worthy dedication to the cause of the state. While there are statues of the latter, frock-coated and holding documents in speech-making pose, there are also statues of Kelly in his iron armour, as well as a series of paintings by the admired Sydney Nolan depicting his life and exploits and a ballet following his career (*The Outlaw*), while Ralph Boldrewood, pseudonym of Thomas Alexander Browne, based many of the incidents of his epic novel *Robbery Under Arms*, published in 1888, on the Kelly story. Kelly stands at the head of the roll of Australian folk heroes, a roll which includes numerous other bushrangers, famous 'gun' shearers and horsemen, and sporting heroes of prodigious skill and grace (Bradman the cricketer, Cazaly the footballer and, epitome of natural talent, the racehorses Phar Lap, Tulloch and Kingston Town).

There is a clue to the persistence of the Ned Kelly story as one of the foundational myths of Australian society in all of this. The bush or worker hero, of whom Kelly is the exemplar, is the hero of the people, not the official hero of the state or the history books. Unlike the Anzacs, heroes of the nation itself and recognized as such by the nation's elected and appointed leaders [see B. Kapferer, 1988], these heroes were ordinary people who lived and died in quiet desperation, not gloriously making the supreme sacrifice of their lives or health for the honour of defending a King and Country which most of them had never seen, or a state which, far from offering them protection and security, more often than not through its banks, police and imperial or national financial machinations had been the very source of their exploitation and misery.

Instead of eulogies in Parliament and obituaries in newspapers, these heroes – thieves, murderers, conmen, even enemies of the state – are remembered in songs and ballads. Traditional Australian folk songs, frequently set to Irish or Welsh tunes, are all about convicts ('Botany Bay', 'Jim Jones', 'The Plains of Emu', 'Moreton Bay') or escapees cocking a snook at their would-be captors, as in 'The Catalpa', which records the salvation of 'six poor Fenians' by an American ship off Fremantle. They are also about bush workers like shearers ('Widgegoara Joe', 'Tomahawkin Fred', 'Flash Jack from Gundagai', 'The Lachlan Tigers'), stockmen, drovers ('The Queensland Drover', 'Maranoa Drovers'), bullock drivers and cowcockies or small farmers ('The New England Cocky', 'The Old Bullock Dray'), and wanderers down on their luck but still insouciantly optimistic ('Dennis O'Reilly', 'Jog Along Till Shearing', and 'The Jolly Swagman' himself).

Notable in all these songs and tales are three themes: heroism, the scorn of authority and social position, and egalitarianism. The heroic dimension of activities not often considered to be noble – robbery, treason, insubordination – is intimately bound up with the objects of these crimes: these folk protagonists are resisting oppression and tyranny on behalf of the people, of those less able to stand up for themselves against the proud man's contumely, the greed of the rich and the indifference of the state. Jim Jones threatens:

> And some dark night when everything is silent in the town,
> I'll kill the tyrants one and all and shoot the floggers down.

Of Ben Hall it is sung:

> He never robbed a needy man, the records best do show;
> Staunch and loyal to his mates, and manly to the foe

and of Ned Kelly: 'Some say he's a hero, he gave to the poor.' Like the wild colonial boy, we are challenged to 'scorn to live in slavery, bound down with iron chains'.

The reckless scorn of authority and rank is evident in the lines:

> No brand of Cain e'er stained his brow, no widow's curse did fall,
> When tales are read the squatters dread the name of bold Ben Hall.

And, '"I'll fight but not surrender!" said the wild colonial boy' presaging the Jolly Swagman's leap into the billabong to escape the troopers: '"You'll never take me alive," said he' – epitomizing freedom, courage, stoic individualism and an audacious disregard for overwhelming odds. The end of the bushranger is likely to be the result of betrayal, like, but also unlike, the end of Jesse James, who was murdered by one of his old gang for the reward. Australian norms of mateship and loyalty do not allow for the celebration, or even the mention, of such a dastardly act, transgressing the norms of mateship. The deaths of bushrangers are otherwise, they die fighting for their freedom or are betrayed by police informers, as in the demise of Ben Hall:

> Then savagely they murdered him, those cowardly bluecoat imps,
> Who were led on to where he slept, by informing peelers' pimps.

The entire theme of the folk song 'Where's your licence?' is to derogate the licence inspectors – the 'traps' of the goldfields – and later songs echo the theme of ratbaggery and cheekiness, like 'The Woolloomooloo Lair', directed against the courts and the moralizing 'Salvos' (officers of the Salvation Army).

The characteristic deflation of class pretensions, the aggressive egalitarianism of these songs, like that exhibited by the unrepentant cattle duffer (thief) of 'The Eumeralla Shore', remains today as it did in the past in Kevin Carmody's bitter 'The Drover's Wife', Eric Bogle's 'Hard Times in the Lucky Country' and Australian Crawl's ironic 'Happy to be Australian.' The subjects of these songs are the poor and downtrodden, Aborigines, workers, the unemployed – driven to petty crime and desperate acts by the vicissitudes of life, but surviving with fortitude, even daring and wit. Ned Kelly was 'born in a ramshackle hut' and 'grew up with bad men and robbers and thieves', and city boys had similar unpromising starts in life: the Woolloomooloo Lair's father taught him how to swim 'when he heaved me off the pier at Wooloomooloo'. Yet they endure with cheerfulness and elan, like the Sentimental Bloke and his mate Ginger Mick fighting and romancing in the back lanes of late nineteenth-century Collingwood, or the council road worker in 'The Government Stroke', enjoying with wicked glee his ability to hold up traffic while he has his 'smoke-oh' or tea break.

This image of the cheerful rogue is in itself a mythologized understanding, a kind of metamyth, of the viciousness of razor gangs or the idleness of government workers, as the activities of the 'bloke' and the government worker may also be understood. But as Richard Quinney notes:

> The study of crime involves an investigation of such natural products and contradictions of capitalism as alienation, inequality, poverty, unemployment, spiritual malaise and the economic crisis of the capitalist state. [1980: 39]

The stories of worker-heroes, bushman-heroes and city larrikins of Australian mythology give point and force to this observation. There is, in effect, a dialectical relation to be discerned between domination and oppression on the one hand and accommodation and resistance on the other, and the recognition of this relation is at least a part of the explanation for the long-standing popularity of those heroes (and others like them today) who offend against the property and persons of the ruling class. For they are engaged in the kinds of active combat, with 'the natural products and contradictions' of capitalist enterprise and the repressive apparatuses of the state, of which others can only dream. The endurance of the tales of their exploits is iconic with the endurance of the thousands of unsung and unremembered actors on the stage of the everyday.

Such heroes as these may be seen as being engaged in what Hobsbawm calls 'social banditry'. They are

> peasant outlaws whom the lord and state regard as criminals, but who remain within peasant society and are considered by their people as heroes, as champions, avengers, fighters for justice, perhaps even leaders of liberation, and in any case to be admired, helped and supported. [1969: 13]

This is certainly the light in which Ned Kelly was regarded by the selectors of North Eastern Victoria, and there is some suggestion that Kelly, with his Irish background and American stepfather, may have been imbued with a number of dangerously subversive republican ideas [see McQuilton, 1979]. The Land Acts of the early 1860s produced much suffering for the selectors, in contrast with the squatters, and the arrest of Kelly sympathisers at harvest time did nothing to dispel local mistrust of police and legal authorities, as McQuilton makes clear. In one of his appendices [ibid.: 194–5], McQuilton reproduces the 1867 letter of a selector, one Thomas Carroll, to the minister responsible for the Land Act of 1865:

> Sir,
> I am the occupoyer of apoartion of lot 61 I errected my finces in as much as I knew anything of the Surveyor Mr Singer admits haveing made a mistake in computering a road on this lot which is the cause of not yate haveing this road finced Now Sir my little harvest is pressing on me and cant stind to the finceing Sir one hundred men cud scarcely erect this fince in 14 days Mr Bowing [the squatter] hoapes to foace us of the land if a baste belonging to any of us stand outside the fince to take a drink of water he drives it to the pound which costs 4 shillings and 9 pence perhead to get thim out by this means he sais he will drive us of the land he says he cares nothing about complaints Sir I now request an additional time I have no finceing stuff in hands as all the available stuff went to errect the finces after the heavy fluds Sir to erect those finces and collect my little harvest will at least take 4 mongths Sir Dam a poore man efforting to support eight in family. I will be drivin from the land if your Honour refuse me an additional time to errect the fince I trow myself at your feet and implore your well known humanity.

Hobsbawm proposes three major forms of social banditry – the noble robber, the primitive resistance fighter, and the avenger – and McQuilton presents a fairly satisfying case for Ned Kelly's career as expressing aspects of all three. It is clear, however, that the burgeoning State controls and bureaucratic repressions of nineteenth-century Australia give a particularly egalitarian slant to tales of resistance to the authority of the freebooting *laissez faire* capitalism of that state. Ned Kelly becomes, through the capture and destruction of his person by the state, much more than a social bandit. He becomes a symbol of resistance to oppression, and the image of his protective face-mask becomes stamped on the popular imaginary of just vengeance and the nobility of the common people.

Further, through an ironic inversion, this image is also captured by the state, most particularly in the twentieth century in the form of the Australian Labor Party, which for most of its existence has claimed to stand for all working people, for a fair go, a welfare state, equity and social justice. The conservative parties have also fostered an understanding of the state as a benevolent and even-handed protector. Like Ned Kelly, the state can thus be portrayed as the protector of the little people, the ordinary battlers, from the depredations of ruthless big business, foreign capital and foreign labour, from accident and catastrophe. But still, by a further twisting of icon and referent, that image can now be used to designate the state's 'bailing up' of the country, demanding the taxes and imposts which are beyond the abilities of the common people (now more frequently engaged in small businesses rather than being small farmers) to pay. State propaganda, meanwhile, insists that the nation is being held to ransom by unscrupulous and self-serving foreign interests – most often in terms of Australian free-trade policies *versus* foreign protectionism and subsidy of agriculture.

A right to the assumption of the mantle of Ned Kelly as protector rather than predator, as hero rather than villain, is thus constantly in question. In this process, Kelly becomes an ambivalent symbol, both good and bad, the embodiment of an oxymoron: a victorious victim. But as a symbol of the welfare state, protector of the poor and powerless, Kelly is stripped of his larrikinism and ratbaggery, thus losing much of his force and appeal as a popular hero. As Bernard Smith notes in his caption of Nolan's painting *Kelly and Horse* (1946) at Lanyon in the Australian Capital Territory:

> It is. . .by no means easy to decide whether Nolan intends Kelly to be read as a hero or clown and the ambiguity is well pointed, because Australians in general have never made up their minds either; he is an ambiguous figure, in the national imagination as in Nolan's art.

Visions of an Australian identity are always bound up with an understanding that such an identity requires historical validation and is thus in some sense unchanging. The characters chosen, whether by discovery or invention, to embody the virtues and qualities which mythology deems appropriately and authentically Australian are characters whose virtues are those of a past age, colonialist, imperialist, patriarchal, supremely confident. Those men whose bodies become captured by the repressive apparatuses of the state – bushrangers, swagmen, striking workers – are doubly captured when their very images are also appropriated by the ideological apparatuses of that same state to which their lives were so often forfeit. The enemies of the state, so designated precisely because they were champions of the people, are thus reconstituted as champions of the state, as if state and people were to be imagined *and practised* as indivisible. Such a double capture has the power to effect a further domestication of the wilder margins of the social formation in which they came to flourish. By such means as these, a tyrannous and autocratic dispensation can be reconstructed as benign and protective.

The Taming of Wild Women

> No convict ever got off Cockatoo
> Island by swimming except Thunderbolt.
> His lady, Yellow Long or Long Yella,
> whichever way the name points, swam
> the channel from Balmain before him
> bringing tucker and clothes, and she got
> him past the sharks when he swam for it.
>
> Les Murray, *At Thunderbolt's Grave in Uralla* [1991: 268].

It has been, and remains, far more difficult for women to undertake activist forms of resistance to the repressions of the State and the depredations of the rich and powerful, though Ned Kelly's mother and sister Kate are reputed to have sprung quite aggressively to his aid, bringing him and his brothers fresh horses, attacking policemen with shovels, etc. Women's roles in colonial society were strictly circumscribed within the bounds of support for men as good Christian wives and mothers, as helpers of the needy and distressed, or as illicit but necessary sexual companions.

The third of these roles offended quite as much against Victorian canons of propriety as anything that bushrangers or other rogues might do, and indeed went even further, striking as it did at the heart of the family as the foundation of society, and threatening the tenuous security and moral superiority of less adventurous or more fortunate souls. Such a character was Lola Montez, who matched, in her earlier years, the audacity and pride of the men who resisted the restrictions placed upon their freedom by the State, but never achieved the admiration of the People in anything like the same measure. A brief version of her story, with quotations from the *Dictionary of National Biography* [Stephen and Lee (eds.) 1967–8, Vol. VII: 1211–12], is presented here.

Case 5. Lola Montez: Countess for an Hour

MARIE DOLORES ELIZA ROSANNA GILBERT (1818–1861) 'dancer and adventuress', was known and is remembered by her stage name, Lola Montez. She was early and scandalously married in 1837, and divorced on the grounds of adultery in 1842. In 1843 she began her career as 'Lola Montez, Spanish dancer', and performed in Dresden and Berlin, 'dabbled in politics in Warsaw, was well received by the Czar Nicholas in St. Petersburg, and involved in a sensational duelling scandal in Paris'. In 1847 she danced in Munich and became the mistress of King Ludwig of Bavaria. On being created Baronne de Rosenthal and Comtesse de Lansfeld, she virtually took over the ruling of the kingdom. 'Her abilities were considerable, she had a strong will and a grasp of circumstances, her disposition was generous and her sympathies large.' The Jesuits and Prince Metternich became her political foes, and her patronage of a liberal student association called the Alemannen resulted in her banishment from Bavaria in March 1848 and the abdication of the king. She returned to England, appearing in 1849 in a drama entitled *Lola Montez ou La Comtesse pour une heure*. She remarried, was charged with bigamy, and fled to Spain, where her new husband was later reported drowned. By then she had repaired to New York, where she performed on Broadway in 1852, 'representing herself as the danseuse, the politician, the countess, the revolutionist, and the fugitive'. She moved via Philadelphia to California, where she married for a third time and subsequently divorced. In 1855 she performed in Sydney, and in 1856, in Melbourne, she horsewhipped a Mr Seekamp, editor of *The Ballarat Times*, 'on account of an article he had inserted in his journal reflecting on her character'. Other public disputes took place, although these did not appear to lessen her popularity with theatregoers. She returned to Europe and America, where she gave public lectures and published a book called *The Art of Beauty*. 'She wasted the greater part of the proceeds, and, shattered in health and deserted by her associates, she became the protegee of an old school friend and devoted the rest of her life to visiting the outcasts of her own sex at the Magdalen Asylum. After great suffering she died, sincerely penitent, in a sanitary asylum [in] New York in January 1861'.

Making allowances for the opportunities available to women in the mid-nineteenth century, the tale of Lola Montez is just as much one of derring-do as that of Ned Kelly. The two share a surprising number of characteristics: liberal, even radical political views, a strong sense of individual liberty and dislike of restriction, defiance of convention, and courage 'worthy of a better cause', which is to say courage which might have been less troublesome to the legal and moral authorities of the day if it had been channelled in the support of the social status quo rather than directed towards its overthrow.

But the career of Lola Montez is not one which receives even the grudging admiration which bourgeois morality can afford Ned Kelly. The characteristics for which the bushranger could be admired are still today considered in Australian cultural practice to be essentially masculine virtues. Montez' 'considerable abilities', her 'strong will and grasp of circumstances', could find no legitimate outlet in mid-Victorian societies which allowed women no voice or place of their own in public political life. The envy and suspicion of the Jesuits, of Metternich, of respectable married ladies and their menfolk were more than sufficient to keep adventuresses like Lola Montez away from the real centres of power in any role but that of courtesan. This role she played to the hilt, and it is this defiance of convention which made her notorious, rather than famous. As a role model, she falls more into the category of a bad example, though not irredeemably: she dies, after all, sincerely penitent. A Magdalen rather than a Madonna, a rose rather than a lily. If her 'generous disposition' and 'large sympathies' had always been directed to the care of fallen women and outcasts of her own sex, then her place in popular history would have been less significant and her place in society more secure, though less exciting. She would then have been like other women who spent a lifetime working to uplift the fallen, to ensure respectability for those women and their families, women like Caroline Chisholm, for example.

If Lola Montez can be cast in the role of damned whore, Caroline Chisholm, 'the emigrant's friend' who organized the emigration and settlement of hundreds of single women, wives of pardoned convicts, and children of transported parents – even going 'into the interior in charge of parties of women, and [seeing] them properly established' [*Dictionary of National Biography*, 1967–8: 260] as domestic servants, housekeepers and so forth – must be cast as an eminent member of God's police. Indeed, in the 1940s Australian primary schoolchildren still learned of Caroline Chisholm, along with Grace Darling, Elizabeth Fry and Florence Nightingale, as the pattern of the good woman, labouring mightily in the cause of family colonization and the protection of the virtue of single women. In her fierce championship of the family unit [see Kiddle, 1990], her spiritual descendants today swell the ranks of conservative women's groups around the country, groups like Women Who Want to be Women, or the Country Women's Association, as well as providing moral support to and occasional leadership of quasi-religious lobbies like Right to Life (anti-abortion) and the Festival of Light (supporters of a particular vision of the family and Christian values).

Women like these are secure heroes of the established order, and as such do not require capture by the state, or public rehabilitation as newly polished or refurbished symbols of state-endorsed virtue to be turned to ideological account. But the role of bad example is perhaps always required to encourage others in the paths of righteousness and morality supportive of the state. It is one which, in every generation, is forced upon women who dare to step outside the bounds of conventional morality and patriarchal protection. That those bounds are considerably wider now than they were a hundred years ago in no way suggests that they are any less significant or that those who might symbolize, for their peers and for succeeding generations, strength of will, nobility of character or independence of spirit can only do so within the constraints of currently dominant ideologies. Like Mae West or Madonna Ciccone, Lola Montez built her career on a certain kind of devil-may-care sexiness, outraging respectable public opinion, tantalizing and teasing private fantasies. What is more, she did this without the benefit of cinema or television image-making, without a Hollywood star system, commercial promotion or a sexual revolution which might have made her a role-model for thousands of aspirants to fame and fortune.

The symbolic type of 'larrikin' – cheeky, outrageous, youthful, energetic, iconoclastic, flouting authority and convention at every turn – has long been one of the most popular (in both senses of the term) Australian myths. Even Prime Ministers can be seen, admiringly, as larrikins, or derided for being too reserved and aloof, as not being of the people. Indeed, young criminals, to whom the term originally applied, are no longer generally called larrikins, so approving has the term become. Successful individual risk-taking in business and politics, especially when it is accompanied by well-publicized flamboyance or is seen to eschew old-style loutishness and thuggery, is the mark of the modern larrikin. But it is still only a term applied to men. If Lola Montez had been male, she might have been considered a larrikin – though it is, of course, highly unlikely that a life of philandering, as for example that indulged in by the swashbuckling film star of the 1940s and 1950s, Errol Flynn, one of Geoffrey Dutton's 'anti-heroes', would have evoked quite the same wholehearted enthusiasm, then or now.

That women are still not admired for larrikinism or ratbaggery but are still condemned for overstepping the bounds of moral rectitude, especially in relation to sexuality, tells us much about the relation between the sexes at all levels of Australian society today. The hegemony of so-called 'middle-class morality' (and the very real social, physical and economic dangers attendant upon affront to sexual mores) is such as to render the sexual liberation and concomitant social equality of women a disturbingly perilous prospect. And it is the mass media, most particularly women's magazines, which more than any other ideological apparatus of the state, work to guide women through the plethora of moral choices and physical adventures so greatly celebrated by the liberal capitalist state as the process of discovering the self and lauding the individual and her fulfilment – at home, at school, at work, at play, as a daughter, a lover, a mother, a companion, a friend. Despite vociferous objections to the notion of woman as a sex object, the women's magazines still find their greatest impact and greatest circulation figures in the depiction of proper female sexuality and the enhancement of contemporary understandings of sexual attractiveness and technique. The commoditization and technicization of human sexuality is the central concern of these magazines in all their variety, regardless of which age group they are targetting.

The relentlessly confident and frenetically boosterish tone of contemporary women's magazines and their own advertising offers a major buttress to the commercial ideal of maintaining high confidence in the technocratic marketplace. This is particularly noteworthy in the more traditional journals – *The Australian Women's Weekly* and *Woman's Day* (published monthly and weekly by Australian Consolidated Press) – which continue to present, as they have always done, a judicious mixture of articles directed towards women who are centrally concerned with families and 'home-making'. Regular articles are focused on fashion and beauty, craft, cooking, gardening and home decorating. Both magazines include, to perhaps a lesser extent than they did in a pre-television age, some fiction ('Great Reading'; 'Part three of a shocking new novel') and advice columns and fortune-telling pieces, often combined: 'Clairvoyant'; 'Your Stars'; 'The Moon and Your Moods'; 'Your Dreams'; 'Athena Starwoman'; 'Feng Shui'; 'The Toddler Tamer'; 'Dear Doctor'; 'Your Money'; 'Your Helpline'.

These journals are firmly focused on the solidly respectable Australian bourgeoisie and as such are creditable descendants of Caroline Chisholm's pamphlets. Their emphases on home-making and nest-building, food and family, are paramount and not unexpected, but in keeping with the times they are also required to accord more than a passing recognition to the overwhelming significance of sexuality, the successes of the women's movement and the paramountcy of the 'right' to independent choice in a freewheeling market-oriented social formation. And in keeping with their function as ideological apparatuses, the women's magazines also make clear the limits of respectability, the borders of sleaze and the territories of righteousness. In a shifting post-modern *pastiche*, these arbiters of sexual morality and 'family' values, though targetting different age groups and marital statuses (*Girlfriend* and *Dolly* for the pubescent, *Cleo* and *Cosmopolitan* for the nubile, liberated and aware single woman, *The Australian Women's Weekly* and *Woman's Day* for the harried housewife-and-mother, *Vogue* for the idle rich and those with pretensions to the trappings of the lifestyles of the rich and famous, and *Working Woman* for those 'ambitious' women who might choose a career unrelated to domestic work or family relations), nonetheless all circulate around a consensual individualist moralism which always stops short of radical non-conformism.

In so doing, they present a portrait of contemporary women as being as concerned with traditional 'feminine' activities revolving around home-making as with the newly liberated image of single women with careers and 'life-styles' which bespeak the contemporary or even the post-modern. The September 1993 issue of *Vogue*, for example, featured articles entitled 'Wild Women do, and they don't regret it' (a Jungian plea for a return to the instinctual) and 'Individuality: don't be afraid to express it' (a fashion feature introduced with 'I like clothes that say, "Look at me"' and 'I'll take the exception rather than the rule, any day' – all with clear undertones of Tom Wolfe's 'Me Generation'). 'In this, the International Year for the World's Indigenous People, *Vogue* salute[d] the natural beauty of our country' and featured 'the winning smile of Elaine George, *Vogue*'s first Aboriginal cover girl'. The October 1993 issue of *The Women's Weekly* featured 'Jackie O[nassis]'s White House Obsession' and 'Brooke Shields: My wonderful Aussie Lover', and in keeping with a long tradition of royalty-watching, displayed Princess Caroline of Monaco ('her heart set on a sentimental wedding') on the front cover. *Woman's Day*, a more breathless tabloid-style production, exclaimed on its cover of the 4th October 1993 issue: 'Jerry Hall's *amazing* body secrets'; 'Hot Pics: Brooke Shields [screen actor] rushes back to Richard Wilkins [television "personality"]'; 'Dying Twins: HORROR anorexia did THIS!' 'Sneak peek: Hoges' [screen star Paul Hogan] hot new movie' and 'WORLD EXCLUSIVE: We go inside the Skase fortress. Bitter brawls. Stolen treasures. Pixie's binges. TRUSTED "SON'S" SHOCKING EXPOSE AND TELL-TALE PHOTOS.'

In the melange of heath and beauty, diet and fashion, house and home, there is a clear taken-for-grantedness about what constitutes shocking behaviour, behaviour which may be admired and behaviour which is to be execrated. Execrable behaviour includes fiscal impropriety (as with the Skase family) and obsessive dieting to the point of illness. Shocking behaviour partakes of the titillating, or the mildly risqué: 'Fergie's "friend", John Bryan, has done more than any other individual to destroy her reputation and turn the royal family into a laughing stock' [*Mode* October/November 1993]. At the same time, sexuality is equated with physical attractiveness in a curiously *noli me tangere* style which has nothing to do with sexiness, with coolly unruffled models languishing on tropical beaches or colonial verandahs ('Indo Chic' in October-November 1993 *Mode*), the healthy, independent style of Freedom, Simplicity, Naturalness, Individuality, Reality, or the pale, thin waif-like image of 'Golden girl: Emma Balfour. . .the Australian model with the long cool looks [who] is fashion's real gamine' [*Vogue*, September, 1993].

The women's magazines take their roles as moral police and arbiters of feminine style very seriously. They pronounce on fashion not only in terms of clothing, cooking and decorating, but also in terms of values, opinions and tastes concerning family matters, health, childbirth and childrearing, finance, education and wildlife conservation. In doing so, they teach generations of women to seek constant slight changes in their lives and 'lifestyles', changes which bespeak the progressive and the modern, the fashionable, while maintaining the 'traditional' values of caution, moderation and dependability. Thus they produce style as substance, to an extent that it is sometimes difficult to tell where one ends and the other begins. Their treatment of scandalous public figures like the singer Madonna, for instance, renders female sexuality passionless, calculated and asexual, in parallel with the currently modish gamine little-girl helplessness of internationally renowned photographic models.

Even the more go-getting style of *Smart Woman* addresses questions of interior decorating, food preparation and fashion. In its advice to women who engage in the more up-market careers, such as finance, manufacturing, designing or the male-dominated professions, *Smart Woman* is still careful to stress 'the feminine' as, for example, assertive rather than aggressive, smooth rather than abrasive, quietly insistent rather than refractorily combative. The inaugural editorial statement of *Smart Woman* pointed out that

> The Superwoman's nineties counterpart is not the rare red-suited, silk-shirted species of a decade ago, she's a much more common-or-garden variety – like me, like my friends . . . like Mary Easson, who lost 10 years on her male parliamentary colleagues to devote herself to her family, but now uses her maternal skills to political advantage. . ..
>
> You see, women of the nineties just have to be smarter. Smart women are conscious of how to make the best use of their work, leisure and home time; smart women want the best for their families and know how to get the most out of their relationships; smart women keep fit and dress well; they are interested in issues that concern them [!] and enjoy reading about contemporary social mores and personalities. They work, in or out of the home, and keep up to date with finance and employment issues. [October/November 1993: 6]

The style of social interaction, 'networking,' time management and 'goal-setting' espoused by journals like *Smart Woman* is one which, its writers are careful to point out, is particularly effective in the contemporary business world. Which is to say it supports rather than undermines the operation of contemporary capitalist enterprise, utilizing all available talent and experience in the furtherance of commercial goals, while not allowing personal crises or difficulties to hinder productivity.

That the mass media are probably the single most powerful influence in the creation and reproduction of hegemonic understandings of femininity, female allure and womanly virtue is powerfully illustrated by the October-November 1993 edition of the bi-monthly *Mode*'s feature on 'The 10 most Fascinating Women in Australia' - as, according to the cover, 'nominated' by '40 celebrated men.' Not the ten most beautiful, or the ten best-dressed, or the ten most sexy, in the more usual style of fashion magazines or celebrity-chasing popular journals, but the ten most fascinating. The definition of what is 'fascinating', it should be noted in passing, is left extremely vague, as is the way in which the nominations took place:

> Coming up with a list of the 10 most fascinating women in Australia is no easy feat. To be completely objective, we asked a cross section of 40 men in the public eye to nominate their choice for the 10 top women from a list of 40. We salute those who appear on our pages, the fabulous females on our list, and you, the women of Australia, who make this country great. [1993: 65]

Readers are given no indication of the names of the other thirty women on the original list, and no criteria of fascination are suggested. But this is still hagiography of a kind, and indeed, we are given an object lesson in the skill of the mass media in instantly appropriating the images of well-known personalities to bear an ideological weight. While it is politically unsound for a magazine like *Mode*, whose target audience would appear to be the café society of the metropole, to push any line which might be construed as sexist, it is generally acceptable to celebrate 'fascinating' women as interesting people 'in their own right'. The 'cross section' of forty celebrated 'men in the public eye' is like a panel of judges in an athletic contest or an old-fashioned 'beauty contest'. They include sixteen men from the world of show business (the largest single occupational group): television presenters, fashion designers, pop singers, people in public relations, fashion photography; six (including the managing directors of two recording companies) from the upper echelons of business; five from the arts (opera, dance, drama, painting, film and stage direction); five sportsmen, four politicians including the incumbent Prime Minister, three journalists and one former chief justice. The bemused general reader can only assume that these men are qualified to judge 'fascination' because they constitute the late twentieth-century equivalent of boulevardiers, men-about-town. Like their assessors, the women chosen as the ten most fascinating fall into the category of 'celebrity', a peculiarly modern, even post-modern phenomenon. They are all well-known names, often because of their high-profile positions in the mass media, and are generally treated as worthy citizens. None labours under the stigma of notoriety or larrikinism, at least as far as general public awareness of them is concerned.

The most fascinating woman in Australia, at the end of 1993, turned out to be Senator Bronwyn Bishop, a Liberal (i.e. conservative) politician with ambitions to become leader of her party. The text accompanying her photograph compared her with Boadicea and Baroness Margaret Thatcher, erstwhile British Prime Minister.

Six of the ten most fascinating were women whose careers are intimately bound up with the mass media themselves: Judy Davis (cinema actress); Jane Campion (film director); Nicole Kidman (cinema actress); Elle Macpherson ('Australia's ultimate calendar girl'; 'international supermodel', 'The Body'); Magda Szubanski ('Australia's Queen of Comedy' and 'the cleverest, funniest, sexiest woman on Australian television'); and Liz Hayes ('the archetypal female Australian television journalist – warm, sexy, earthy, with a perpetual twinkle in her eye'). The remaining three nominees were Annita Keating, wife of the Prime Minister and 'one of the most beautiful women ever to grace the Lodge'; Blanche d'Alpuget, writer, biographer of and (since 1995) wife of former Prime Minister R.J. (Bob) Hawke, 'now in her late forties and still as beautiful as ever'; and Betty Churcher, 'a handsome, grey-haired woman', Director of the National Gallery of Australia.

Only two of the ten, Annita Keating and Elle Macpherson were not referred to by their surname alone (a sign of equality with men in the public eye, perhaps). One of the criteria of fascination appears to have been some character trait which has not, until very recently, been associated with interesting women: Davis is lauded for her 'ferocity' and 'intensity' and a 'fierce, edgy style'; Bishop is also characterized as fierce and implacable: 'Stone-faced, she just keeps boring in'; Campion is 'independent, forceful and utterly original'; Kidman brings 'intensity and passion to the screen' and exhibits 'a complete lack of pretension, a sense of humour and a highly developed sense of self'; d'Alpuget's work is 'acclaimed' and sometimes 'controversial'; the 'roly-poly' Szubanski 'exudes a considerable intelligence and a vast appetite for life'; Churcher cut staff at the gallery, 'but managed to turn the finances around' and organized a series of 'acclaimed' exhibitions.

Fascinating, as far as the outsider can judge, seems to equate with toughness of mind and independence of spirit, perhaps echoing some of the admirable characteristics of Caroline Chisholm, albeit characteristics renovated to suit twentieth-century capitalist tastes:

> The guardian angel of her helpless sex,
> Whom no fatigue could daunt, no crosses vex
> With manly reason, and with spirit pure . . .
>
> [Robert Lowe, 1846, cited in Kiddle, 1990: n.p.]

Nonetheless, fascination is still inseparable from beauty, stylishness and sexual appeal, the lesson incessantly hammered home by the women's magazines from *Girlfriend* to *Smart Woman*.

Snares and Delusions

The sexual and social liberation of women is often seen by the organs of the mass media as threatening to tear apart the carefully woven fabric of social structure, through the threat it presents to the family, as an economic unit of stable social and cultural production, reproduction, and crucially in late capitalist society, consumption. At the same time, however, that very liberation presents the mass media with a mine of information, strongly held opinion, titanic clashes of values and innane gossip, upon all of which popular culture thrives. The boldness, individualism and egalitarianism – the larrikinism – personified by a Ned Kelly combine to form a double-edged sword when they are applied to a Lola Montez. The capture of the feminine, therefore, is an imperative of advanced capitalist economies, a process in which ambitious and independent women are ultimately almost bound to collude.

> Feminism's political evolution has meant that in practice if not in theory, it successfully delivers the family type most suited to survival in contemporary capitalism – the affluent, dual-income, high-

> consumption family with self-fulfilment as the binding value, with functions once performed within the family contracted out. [Manne, 1995: 32]

For the manufacture of consent and the domestication of dissent require an always vigilant dedication to the understanding that what is in the best interests of a single individual is identical to what is in the best interests of the state. So all the ideological apparatuses of the state – the mass media, educational institutions, the public service – combine to ensnare individual citizens, however wary they may be, in a comfortable world of clichéd righteousness: user pays; cut your coat according to your cloth; no exceptions; no free lunches. The alternatives to entrapment – alienation, cynicism, poverty, ill health, even incarceration – are constantly paraded as *freely chosen*, wilful defiance of the tenets of the good life as arranged by the people and the state acting in harmonious concert. Thus in finally being captured by the state, fascinating women and larrikin men can come to stand as proud symbols of that very order of things which they once bitterly opposed.

Notes

1. The phrase 'damned whores' is attributed to Lt. Ralph Clark of the First Fleet, 'on sighting the *Lady Juliana* of the Second Fleet coming into Sydney harbour with over two hundred female convicts aboard. June 1790'. [Summers, 1975: 267] Caroline Chisholm, in her 1847 publication 'Emigration and Transportation Relatively Considered', claimed that 'all the clergy you can despatch, all the schoolmasters you can appoint, all the churches you can build, and all the books you can export, will never do much good without what a gentleman in that Colony very appropriately called "God's police" – wives and little children – good and virtuous women'. [cited in Summers, 1975: 291] Portia Robinson is critical of the works of Summers and others who make much of the language and sentiments laid bare in the Reverend Samuel Marsden's Female Register and of the efforts of governors, particularly Macquarie, to encourage female convicts to marry in order to hasten, in the words of Colonial Secretary Castlereagh, their 'Reformation [and] regular Settlement', to hasten

the day when New South Wales could no longer be conceived of as a place of 'Riot and Debauchery'. [cited in Robinson, 1988: 203] Robinson claims that many of the Catholic female convicts were unable to marry and that long-standing de facto relationships, frequently if belatedly regularised, had a stabilizing influence on the colony. That single women in the colonies were at the mercy of men, who vastly outnumbered them, is not disputed, least of all by Caroline Chisholm, who worked tirelessly to place single women as servants in 'respectable' family situations.

2. So, for example, Jill Bowen writes of Sidney Kidman, the 'Cattle King':

> Kidman was a controversial figure in his day. Many people resented the fact that he had climbed to success on the financial misfortunes of others. They also condemned him, out of envy, for holding so much land. He was also accused of either 'abusing' his land or not improving it with fences and additional water. He faced several commissions of enquiry, Royal Commissions and pastoral investigations and was frequently called upon to give evidence in matters relating to beef and land monopolies, pastoral taxation and management.
>
> Kidman emerged unscathed through these as a result of his constant claim that he would sell off or hand back any of his land to anyone or any government who would either take it on or do a better job! [in Ward et al. 1986: 136]

Kidman can certainly be counted as something of a ratbag: the press of the day apparently 'adored' his habit of 'plain speaking in colloquial terms' and his employees 'regarded him with a mysterious and even savage loyalty.' He had 'a lasting respect' for the Aboriginal people who called him 'Big pfella Kidman, King of all Adelaide'. He was frugal rather than mean, drank and smoked but did not swear [ibid.: 137]. Furthermore, his battles with government instrumentalities like the various Lands Commissions could be seen as an individual standing up for the rights of the individual against rapacious tax gatherers. On the other hand, refusing to allow the resumption of parts of his holdings for soldier settlement, on the grounds that 'the far out country should be left in big chunks since it could only be run by big men with big bank balances' [ibid.] might be counted by others as an act of extreme arrogance and tall poppiness [see note 3].

3. 'I referred to those being paid [more than 10 pounds a week] as the "tall poppies". . .. [In the Federal sphere] Mr. Justice Lukin, President

of the Federal Arbitration Court, publicly objected to the proposed 20 per cent reduction in his salary. As a Commonwealth judge, he was receiving 5,000 pounds a year and he was also receiving a pension of 1,000 pounds a year as a former Queensland judge. Yet he had been the judge responsible for the vicious attack on wage standards which caused the protracted timber workers' strike.' [Lang, 1970: 113] This, it might be noted, was a time when the federal basic wage had been brought down from £6.15s. a week to £3.19s.6d. [1970: 97].

CHAPTER FOUR

Cultural Space: The Production and Consumption of Symbolic Goods

At a time of globalizing transformations of the world economic order, social and cultural practices hitherto generally considered above or beyond pecuniary evaluation and state control are inexorably drawn into a multinational web of fiscal manipulation and national economic planning. At such a time questions of cultural identity take on a new and sometimes sinister urgency. The impulse to claim a widening range of everyday activities and beliefs as constitutive of specific cultural traditions and heritages is testimony to a number of conflicting tendencies discernible in Australian cultural politics.[1] Such tendencies accept, even demand state support of particular traditions as an egalitarian and democratic right, but they also seek to make those same traditions exclusive, partial and fracturing of the universalist rhetoric of the national state.

Contemporary social and cultural convention places ideological soundness, or what in recent years has been called political correctness, at the centre of discussion about culture; political rectitude largely constitutes the boundaries of taste, while moral righteousness moulds the critical trajectory of much currently fashionable debate, in the academy and the marketplace, about the relevance, ownership, preservation or destruction of cultures.

The elements tradition-heritage-culture have become inextricably linked in these debates, at least partly because of a well-developed understanding of conservationist attitudes, as well as, on the other hand, an urge to avoid transgressing culturalist mores or offending the custodians of sub-cultural purity. In such a situation, the definition and protection of cultural heritage focuses on the question of ownership, possession and the right to speak for any particular cultural tradition. Outsiders are easily characterized as trespassers or exploiters, and the matter of cultural preservation and renewal is frequently construed as a sacred trust passing from one generation to another. There are dark intimations here of race memory and collective consciousness, both of which sit uneasily with the ideals of tolerance and openness to change which are thought to characterize liberal democratic societies. Indeed, the understanding of we-ness which is at the heart of expressions of national identity and nationalist sentiment is constantly threatened by racist, ethnocentric and exclusivist interpretations of *Geschlecht*, as Derrida [1987] points out.

Cultural exclusivity is essentially a political ploy utilized by members of subordinate cultural groups in an attempt to counteract the exclusionary practices of those dominant social strata which arrogate to themselves the power – through schools, through arts funding bodies, through the mass media – to evaluate and judge all cultural practice. In what Bourdieu [1993] calls the field of cultural production, such dominant groups are landowners whose dominance allows them to act as rentiers of less important fields, while they and their agents maintain control of the marketing and distribution of symbolic goods.

I have argued that understandings of national identity and cultural heritage must constantly be learned. The construction of secular hagiographies, the creation and popularizing of national heroes and a few heroines is, I have suggested, a major means of entrapping nationalist or communitarian imaginations in the service of the nation state or a designated community. But such hagiographies have been accompanied by the recognition that cultural heritage consists in much more than a few legendary heroic tales. The continued celebration of a heroic past and the assumption of a noble future also require the construction of secular shrines, 'temples of culture' wherein icons and artefacts may be arranged and displayed for the edification of their inheritors.

This is a time-honoured practice, as much within 'new' or revolutionary societies as within 'old' and stable ones. The old Union of Socialist Soviet Republics was swift to convert the churches and palaces of the Czarist *ancien regime* to the secular uses of communist society, for example. The Carnavalet Museum in Paris is dedicated to the recording of the domestic everyday lives of Parisians (both aristocratic and bourgeois) in the eighteenth and nineteenth centuries, as well as documenting in grand paintings and tawdry souvenirs [cf. Horne, 1984: 81] the events of the Revolution itself. Georg Mosse [1975] recounts the building of shrines to national socialism in the Third Reich as a further example of the ways in which groups with particular political and social visions of their world invent, rediscover, manufacture the events and circumstances of a previous golden age in order to emphasise the renewal of that age under the aegis of a new dispensation.[2]

National museums and art galleries throughout the world form repositories of the material cultural wealth of nations. The evidence, record and celebration of valorous deeds and momentous occasions are to be found within their walls, as well as the treasures of mundane existence, the tools and utensils of everyday life and the implements and relics of ways of life long past. National collections of these kinds are of far more than antiquarian interest, especially at times of heightened concern for the nature of national identity. Indeed, the universalizing tendencies of a world economy have been accompanied at every turn by an increased scrutiny of particularist identities defined in national, regional or communitarian terms. At the same time, in egalitarian societies peculiarly sensitive to charges of elitism, a plethora of smaller sub-groups has achieved the means of displaying to themselves and others the central understandings of their own past as a particular, distinctive social group.

In immigrant societies like Australia, with a multicultural history often bloodied by violence towards the indigenous people, great efforts have been made in recent years by the state, and more recently still by minority ethnic groups and Aboriginal people themselves, to establish insider portrayals of minority histories and cultures in modern Australia by means of ethnographic museums and, in conjunction with interest groups and voluntary associations, other specialized museums like the Workers' Heritage Centre in Barcaldine. These latter foundations have been able to escape at least some of the strictures of critics like Clifford [1988] or Sahlins [1985] in that they are the work of insiders themselves, work which, moreover, has at its heart the overcoming of that very alienation which official ethnographic museums are likely, even if unwittingly, to dramatize.[3]

My purpose in this chapter is to address some of the social ramifications of the development of a market for symbolic goods, a development attendant upon the increases in material wealth and the spread of popular education which have been a hallmark of twentieth-century experience in the industrialized world. Cultural production and cultural consumption have become sites of contestation in which the commercial value of symbolic goods – Aboriginal rock paintings, for example, or ecologically vulnerable wilderness, or beachfront property, as well as 'high' cultural productions in art, literature, music, dance and design – threatens to overwhelm their pristine cultural value. At the same time, however, the marketing of cultures has come to constitute a discourse of identity which also risks spilling over into a number of radically differing, often oppositional sub-discourses which find no necessity in state control, state support or state intervention.

The commoditization of symbolic goods and the discourses of identity which accompany it are perhaps no more clearly displayed than in the development of certain kinds of (surely politically correct) tourism: eco-tourism, cultural tourism, heritage tourism. These tourisms lack the stigma of unreflective sensation-seeking, insensitive sight-seeing and uninformed souvenir-hunting characteristic of 'mere' holiday-making; they have much more in common with the altogether worthier aims and styles of the study tour, the journey that focuses on the increased understanding of the social worlds of otherness. The study tour finds its ancestry in the Grand Tour of young eighteenth-century European noblemen, its most recent form being the motivating force for (all-expenses-paid) 'fact-finding missions' on behalf of official instrumentalities. What has changed is the ease of access to such a style of travel: increased leisure time, financial independence, improved transport and communications, a more wide-ranging education and greater expectations on the part of youthful travellers especially have combined to bolster the enormous development of those 'tourism and hospitality industries' upon which national governments like that of Australia place so much economic reliance.

These 'niche' tourisms can have the effect of overcoming a certain reluctance in puritan-capitalist societies to admit to wasting time and enjoying it: 'mere' holiday-making. Eco-tourism, for example, allows for both a serious study of the natural environment and the security of knowing that one's tour will not have harmful effects on often fragile eco-systems. Also, such tourism is most frequently undertaken by groups of like-minded travellers, thus ensuring a level of compatibility which other packaged tours might not provide, as well as fellow enthusiasts with whom to discuss the day's discoveries. In similar vein, heritage tourism, which focuses upon the built environment and material culture, brings together travellers with similar interests and purposes which can broadly be thought of as educative. (Still other kinds of holiday, which emphasize adventure, the learning of new skills or the practice of old ones, sports or health-improvement, while similarly educative, are less to be thought of as tourism, in that they mostly lack the element of movement from one site to another.)

The pedagogic aspect of eco-, heritage and cultural tourism is clearly discernible in the didactic tone of tour guides and guidebooks, enhanced by the sensation of being a member of a school class on excursion. This ambience is achieved not only by having one's attention drawn to signs instructing visitors to keep off the grass, keep up with the main body of the tour group, and so on. In Parliament House, for example, the guide inquires of the mainly adult tourists, 'Who can tell me why the kangaroo and emu were chosen for the armorial bearings of the Commonwealth?' Grown men vie with each other, thrusting their hands in the air, to gain the guide/teacher's attention and be permitted to give the answer. At other venues, school excursionists form the central body of the tour group, and the guide's questioning and commentary are perforce oriented towards them. It is observations such as these which have formed my understanding that cultural heritage has to be taught and learned as much as picked up at the elders' knees.

Meaghan Morris has remarked, in her discussion (after Baudrillard) of the ways in which television actually destroys the capacity for imaginative interpretation, that 'historical sense is weakening and critical distance is diminishing in contemporary culture' [1988: 163], something also noted by Frederic Jameson [1984]. Australians have lost, Morris says, the 'space of splendid isolation' which was available to them in the 1930s.

This was a space which allowed the freedom to discover, interpret, create, rework and above all put to personal, everyday use a chaotic variety of meanings, understandings and knowledges of ways of being, traditions, heritages and cultures. These individual acts of cultural consumption permitted and encouraged parallel acts of production, mundane and parochial in many, perhaps most instances, but acts, productions and meanings more nearly within the control of their producers than seems conceivable today. For the cataloguing and classifying of cultural heritages has led, no doubt inevitably, to a kind of commoditized pre-packaging and 'quality control' which permits of no deviation from a sanitized, politically and commercially acceptable standard. 'Campbelltown Welcomes You', proclaims a prominent billboard; this hospitable sentiment is illustrated with a universally recognized logo of golden arches and the information that 'McDonald's open 6 a.m'. Heritage tourism and international fast food merge seamlessly to promote each other.

State organization and subsidy of Australian arts and crafts, while undoubtedly a more egalitarian method of supporting the production and consumption of symbolic goods, replacing consumer patronage with state mediation of the arts, is also likely to encourage certain kinds of politically and commercially preferred production over others. While artists and professional cultural producers of all kinds are painfully aware of this phenomenon, the lack until very recently of a significantly and reliably wealthy ruling class in Australia has slowed the private patronage of the arts, and Australian industry has long proven extremely reluctant to engage in corporate patronage.

There are signs that this situation may be changing. As tourism becomes a major source of foreign earnings and as governments become less able and/or less willing to provide funds for public services – in health, education, welfare, crime prevention, transport and garbage removal, as well as for community and individual arts and crafts projects – so private enterprise is increasingly looked to for providing such funding and, tellingly, for the efficient management of all these 'industries.' The diminution of the role of the state meshes with the augmented freedoms of transnational corporations and local big business to override old labour legislation as inefficient, for example, and to replace it with 'enterprise bargaining'. Yet the rolling back of state control has not bestowed greater power upon individuals and communities to run their own local services. On the contrary, the way is opened for a corporate takeover of these services, as noted by Julian Cribb in *The Australian* [6/4/94: 34].

> Earthwatch, a private foundation characterized by a 'radical blend of business-led environmentalism', is supported by Australian corporations because, its president Mr Brian Rosborough claims, 'it is not adversarial'.
>
> In future, he predicts, private enterprise will end up managing most

> of the big global resource and environment issues because it is equipped to do so.
>
> '*Too many of the Earth's resources are unowned, unpriced, or priced too low. Too many are owned by governments who don't understand the economics,*' Mr Rosborough says. (my emphasis)

Earthwatch's emphasis, Cribb reports, has been on equipping 'private-sector personnel. . .with new disciplines for prudent business practice in an age where resource management will determine both commercial and environmental success.'

Leaving aside the fascinating question of what constitutes 'environmental success' in anything other than commercial terms (perhaps the phrase refers only to an absence of environmental disaster?) one is forced to Al Capp's cold-war conclusion, suitably updated and 'greened': What's good for the environment is good for the economy. Or vice versa. By the same token, young people are being taught that the economic survival of their country depends upon their own (voluntary and unpaid) efforts to ensure the attractiveness of the environment to potential tourists, who will in turn provide jobs in the 'service industries' for those who cannot find employment elsewhere. Economic survival – even success – within a world constantly threatened by ecological cataclysm thus becomes the responsibility of a rising generation, drawn into clean-up campaigns by altruism, and into low-paid work by desperation.

Thus Morris notes that 'nationality [I would say, rather, nationalism] is not here the object of a quest, but a field of big-business philanthropy' [1988: 182] and goes on to mock 'the space of "our" national debt, "our" credit rating, and "our" need to please the consumer'. Yet the extent to which ordinary people can be suborned into thinking like managing directors or even shareholders remains a matter of conjecture. There are numerous indications of the ways in which people can, within the spaces and interstices of big business and cautiously sycophantic government, construct their own individual or communal ways of converting technocratic imperatives into enlightened and personally satisfying cultural practices which may *also* serve some economic purpose. It is particularly in the blossoming of cultural and heritage tourism (as well as in eco-tourism) that examples of this phenomenon abound.

Blood on the Southern Cross: Heritage and the Hyperreal

Throughout the country, a wide range of reconstructed and renovated 'pioneer villages' and pioneer townships exists with a twofold purpose, to attract tourists, and to teach Australians something of their history. At such places visitors are invited to 'step into living history' (at Old Gippstown, Moe, Victoria) or 'Come share our heritage' (Kapunda, South Australia). At Echuca Wharf, the 'historic riverport museum,' visitors are encouraged by the tourist brochure to

> Explore the illegal underground bars of the Star Hotel and hurry through an eerie escape tunnel to avoid the police constables.
>
> On the massive redgum wharf, wander round the old railway station, where you can relive the romantic hard-working days of rail, boats and steam. View life-like dioramas of the old Port in the Cargo shed and sit on wool bales and listen to an old riverman's tales of his adventure on the paddlesteamers.
>
> Regular demonstrations of working steam engines and traditional boat-building recreate the romance of this exciting era.

What these re-created colonial pasts have in common is an understanding of history and heritage as the story of ordinary people, merchants, storekeepers, miners, small farmers eking out an existence in a harsh environment and protecting themselves as best they can against the depredations of oppressors both 'legitimate' (tax collectors, bureaucratic inspectors, profiteering merchants, merciless banks, greedy neighbours) and illegitimate (outlaws, escaped convicts). They celebrate an existence which can only be rendered 'romantic' or charming through the safe distance of a later time, a welfare state, modern sanitation and technological progress.

Whether the pioneer village is the work of a municipal council or a state tourism commission, supported by private enterprise, or of an individual or small unofficial group, the results tend to differ only in so far as the former, with greater financial backing, are more elaborate, better advertised and more profitable enterprises. Thus the privately owned and operated Sandhurst Town's brochure can proclaim

> Sandhurst Town is one family's tribute to their Australian heritage.
>
> Isolated in the Whipstick bushland near Bendigo, the Green family

> have celebrated two momentous times in their history in Australia the glorious days of the 1850s Gold Rush, and the battling years of the 1920s and 30s.
>
> And you are invited to share their experience.
>
> All aboard the Red Rattler train for a ride through the Black Forest back to 1852. Beware, the bushranger 'Mad Dog' Mitchell often preys on this train.
>
> Gold Wash Gully is Australia's largest and most authentic recreation of its type. Here the diggings become a massive stage for Sandhurst Town's famous street theatre. . ..
>
> The Sandhurst township is typical of rural Australia in the 1920s and 30s. In fact most of the buildings and equipment have been re-located from original sites.
>
> You'll take a leisurely ride on a wagon pulled by a Clydesdale, to the 'Fair Dinkum' Eucalyptus Distillery.
>
> Although they were hard years in the country, there was also a quality of unhurried friendliness, and this is one of the main features the Greens strive to preserve at Sandhurst Town.

The Sydney Cove authority, on the other hand, as manager of The Rocks, takes quite a different tack with its brochure: more sophisticated, less didactic, more oriented towards tourists with money to spend on having a good time:

> Nestling beside the great arch of the Sydney Harbour Bridge, and overlooking the famous sails of the Opera House is The Rocks, a unique 19th century village. . ..
>
> The Rocks has been witness to much of Australia's turbulent history since [first New South Wales Governor] Phillip's arrival. But now it offers much more than haunting reminders of the past. . ..
>
> A sensitive conservation program has preserved the area's character and heritage.
>
> Restored to its early charm, the area is a hub of culture, of history, of business, social life and relaxation. . ..
>
> Many of The Rocks' pubs offer live music – jazz, folk and pop. On weekends, outdoor concerts fill the streets. And throughout the year several annual festivals centre on The Rocks bringing days of banners and balloons and a lively parade of people.
>
> These events complement the galleries, museums and craft centres permanently housed in the district's historic buildings.
>
> Shopping in The Rocks is a fascinating experience.
>
> Be it a gallery of fine Australian craft housed in the cells of the old sandstone police station. Or a boutique in a restored warehouse. Or a specialty shop in a colonial cottage. . ..

But for those who enjoy the thrill of being preyed upon by 'Mad Dog' Mitchell at Sandhurst Town or being pursued by the constabulary through the tunnels of The Star at Echuca Wharf, the privately operated and completely fabricated 'Old Sydney Town' ('one hour north of Sydney – 200 years back in time' and also 'available as a unique wedding or function venue') allows the thrill of a number of attractions which the recreated 'original' village at The Rocks skirts quickly around:

> The Greatest Adventure in Living History
> Unique experiences you'll always remember
> * See soldiers on parade and hear the thunder of the daily cannon salute.
> * Thrill to the excitement of a pistol duel or boxing match.
> * Be part of a typical trial of the day as colonial justice takes its course in the magistrate's court. See convicts tried and [for the bloodthirsty!] punished.
> * Take a leisurely ride around 'Sydney Cove' to the animal park on a bullock waggon. Hand feed the kangaroos and emus.
> * Chat with the townspeople as they go about their business.
> * Browse through authentic stores of the period and choose from a wide range of craft products.

Much of the enjoyment to be had by tourists, especially at those sites which perform re-enactments of scenes from the daily life of a bygone era, comes from watching and indeed taking part in those activities. The ride in a Cobb and Co. coach at Sovereign Hill, the bullock dray at Old Sydney Town or the Red Rattler train at Sandhurst Town, though unexpectedly uncomfortable, the visit to the colonial schoolhouse with Victorian schoolmaster and children dressed in the costumes of another age, engaged in recitation and painstaking handwriting lessons, all serve to remind tourists that the past is not so distant, that their own grandparents and great grandparents more than likely lived that world. It also serves as an ideological bonus for the state in giving a reminder of the vast improvements in the quality of life enjoyed by most Australians since those pioneering times.

A further ideological spinoff results from the heavy emphasis on 'family entertainment'. Like regular tourist and holiday resorts, many of the recreated colonial and pioneer villages offer 'fun and adventure for all the family', with special concessionary rates for family groups, children's meals and children's activities. There are also frequently group and club booking concessions, which enable both 'senior citizens' and school children to join with others in the appreciation of cultural heritage and folk history. Activities are often centred upon the family group, as in the very popular sepia-tinted photograph of the family dressed in Victorian finery: instant ancestry. The didactic tone of tour guides to which I alluded earlier lends an air of moral probity and wholesomeness to the entire excursion, a tone welcomed by parents, teachers and local business people alike.

Such wholesomeness extends to the participation in making or using the artefacts of an earlier era and the subsequent purchase of folk crafts produced by local residents. Leather-working, pottery, lace-making, boomerang-throwing, poker-work, wildflower-pressing, fly-tying and tie-dying are all represented as authentic regional arts and crafts. Visitors are also encouraged to join with the locals in square dancing, country dancing and/or the choruses of old (now folk) songs like *Botany Bay* or *Click Go The Shears*, with both school children and elderly people seeming equally amenable to the lessons offered in learning the steps or the words.

What saves these images of the past from a certain po-faced mawkishness are the constant reminders of a raffish cops-and-robbers existence assumed to have been the dominant *modus vivendi* of the nineteenth century. While it is only comparatively recently that respectable middle-class Australians have been proud to claim convict ancestry (and in truth, only a very small percentage of the population can actually do so), re-enactments of floggings, the ghostly moans of convicts housed at Hyde Park Barracks in Sydney, the overlay of Irish nationalism evident in the accents of actors in the sound and light shows of the pioneer villages and the reconstructed prisons, all combine to produce an image of 'agin-the-government' to which many Australians are easily sympathetic. There is a kind of ahistorical simplicity in the adoption of such views, a simplicity much played upon by the producers of the sound-and-light shows and the offers to step back in time, and one which ignores, where it does not deny, the existence of multicausality and multi-meaning in the events of the past.

The valorizing of a rebellious past which pitted the little battler against the overweening powers of the colonial state – the imagery of the Kelly legend – is all the more potent when the battle is depicted as being between entire groups representing the people and the state, as the Sovereign Hill Tour brochure suggests by comparing the Eureka Stockade battle with the storming of the Bastille and the Battle of Gettysburg: 'Out of each [event] a new nation grew'. So visitors to Sovereign Hill at Ballarat in Victoria are introduced to the spectacular evening *son-et-lumière* performance of Blood on the Southern Cross, a re-enactment of the miners' rebellion at the Eureka Stockade in 1854. This short-lived and unsuccessful rebellion has little of the swashbuckling associated with events like the Boston Tea Party, though its long term results were important for the establishment of democratic rights in the colony of Victoria.

> Some 22 diggers and three soldiers were killed. . .
>
> By 1 April 1855 [all those arrested] had all been freed, no jury willing to convict them.
>
> But although the diggers lost their battle at the Stockade on that fateful December morning, they eventually emerged victorious. By June 1855 new legislation was set in place by the Victorian government which abolished the Gold Licence system, allowed miners to frame their own mining laws, and gave them the vote and representation in Parliament.
>
> Many say that this was the beginning of democracy for all Australians. [*Blood on the Southern Cross* brochure, and text of the performance]

The miners' grievances centred on the issue of the compulsory purchase of miners' licences and the harassment of raids by the licensing police, the 'traps,' in search of unlicensed miners. The Ballarat miners had no representation in the colonial parliament, and the corruption of government officials made their livelihoods – and sometimes their lives – tenuous and difficult.

The re-enactment of the miners' twenty-minute defiance of the forces of law and order in the goldfields is the centrepiece of the eighty-minute show in which spectators are exhorted to 'use their imaginations' in order to help re-create the events of Sunday 3 December 1854. There are two, sometimes three performances a night, with the first beginning at around 6.00 p.m., and the audience being transported around the performance sites in open-sided tramcars which stop at strategic points to allow for transfer to bridges, hillocks and finally an auditorium from which particular events can be viewed. There are no actors involved, although the costumed tour guide's peroration from the balcony of the restored United States Hotel takes its words and style from the rebellion's main leader, Peter Lalor. The soundtrack of the events includes the murmurs of protest, the warning cries of 'Joe!' to alert miners of the approach of the traps, the shouts of men, the sounds of battle. Above it all, the recorded voice of a narrator tells the tale of the abortive uprising.

Blood on the Southern Cross is also, and importantly, a technological *tour de force*, of which its producers and sponsors are very proud:

> This totally automated show takes place across 25 hectares and below ground are enough electrical and control cables to stretch from Ballarat to Melbourne.
>
> At the beginning of each show the Guide presses a remote 'start' button, and five computers run the programme with ten compact disc players producing 17 channels of multiphonic sound through scores of loudspeakers. The computers also control 400 major lighting sources and almost 1000 peripheral lights through 256 lighting channels, in synchronization with the sound.
>
> A surprise moment is the sudden appearance of the 20-metre long Stockade. This runs along small wheels along a sunken track, and is programmed to be hauled into position hydraulically.
>
> The burning of Bentley's Eureka Hotel is a visually dramatic point in the story. Propane gas creates 3-metre-high flames leaping from each of the 12 windows. These flames generate so much heat that water is programmed to pour down the facade of the building both before and after the burn. . ..
>
> Perhaps our greatest challenge was to preserve the integrity of our Red Hill diggings, so that, to the daytime visitors, they still appeared to be of the 1850s era. Our imaginative staff have hidden 100 lights and 15 speakers in this area without destroying the period atmosphere.

Sovereign Hill and *Blood on the Southern Cross* achieve an immediacy and a kind of authenticity which is lacking in other, less technologically sophisticated re-creations of pioneer settlements and re-enactments of past events. Not only is 'the period atmosphere' – the costumes of the daytime worker-performers at the *Ballarat Times* printery, the foundry, the pottery, the schoolhouse, the very real aroma of carriage horses and the clang of the working forge – convincing. What is more important is the way the past is brought into our presence, and our present, by a combination of sound and lighting effects and the absence of modern amenities (motorized transport or street paving, for example) at the site itself. The site and the performance thus themselves become a discourse on the nature of Australian democracy and egalitarianism, without presenting any undue challenge to beliefs in the unilinear progress of history, for example, or even faith in the triumph of right over might. It is the experience of 'being there' which discovers for many Australians their roots in colonial settlement and in rural working-class struggle. The hyperreality of the re-enactment of old battles, old victories and old defeats, the shock of recognizing those old events as personal, as the works of forebears, however distant, is what gives potency and immediacy to heritage tourism.

Spatial and Symbolic Practices of Power and Resistance

The cultural productions of everyday life consist largely in '*ways of using* [consuming] the products imposed by a dominant economic order' [de Certeau, 1984: xiii, original emphasis]. 'These "ways of operating" constitute,' according to de Certeau [1984: xiv] 'the innumerable practices by means of which users reappropriate the space organized by techniques of socio-cultural production', and are enabled to utilize those very techniques to exclude or to threaten others (I am thinking here of the layout and decor of, for example, shopping malls, car parks, bars or music performance venues, and the practices of crowding, graffiti-writing and auditory assault).

Aboriginal cultural centres reappropriate the space of the museum or the pioneer village (perhaps the archetypal artefact of the conqueror) by taking a more overtly didactic line than that espoused by other centres of cultural/heritage tourism. These centres, of which there are an increasing number around the country as Aboriginal groups re-discover and re-vitalize, even re-invent [see Michaels [1988] on 'bad Aboriginal art'] their cultural roots, set the parameters within which identity claims can be made, understood and sustained. Furthermore, the frames of mind within which outsiders generally orient their own discoveries of Aboriginal history and culture are deeply affected by understandings of racism, genocide and collective white guilt, to the extent that a visit to an Aboriginal cultural centre takes on something of the flavour of pilgrimage to the religious shrines of an alien society. At the same time, a dominant cultural conviction of the essential nobility of the underdog, a culture of suffering and victimage, resonates clearly if somewhat shame-facedly with the dreadful history of black/white relations in this country and Aboriginal land claims and demands for compensatory treatment.

So a visit to the Brambuk Living Cultural Centre at Budja Budja (Halls Gap) in the Gariwerd (Grampians) district in south-Western Victoria not only introduces non-Aboriginal people to a wide range of the arts and crafts, clothing, weapons, tools and foods of five Koori communities in Gariwerd and the Wimmera, with fine examples for sale. The centre itself, and particularly its guidebook, pricks the conscience of white people while asserting a politics of identity compounded of the recognition of a horrendous past, the slow piecing together of half-forgotten ancient customs and the possibilities for a productive and distinctive cultural future.

The Brambuk guidebook, *A Journey Through Time*, takes the assertion of Aboriginal identity as fundamental:

> The most sacred right of humanity is to be ourselves and to be in control of the making of ourselves.
>
> The word 'Aborigine' is a European word for 'native of the land' and as such has no meaning in the vocabulary of the indigenous peoples of Australia.
>
> In Western Victoria we prefer to be called by our traditional language groupings. . .or by a clan name associated within each language group.
>
> However Koori (or Koorie) is sometimes used as a collective name for our people in South-eastern Australia.

The refusal to be named by the representatives of an invading and conquering force enables Kooris to make a principled stand against the defining of their situation by others who have no knowledge or experience of it. Those who have in the past been defined almost entirely in negative terms, with 'European' or 'white' as the benchmark, have come to be heard with care and respect since some pathbreaking political decisions concerning land rights. But in many respects, this turn of events has also produced added difficulties for Koori people unfamiliar with their own pasts and traditional ways. Indeed, it might be suggested that white Australians have constituted Aboriginal Australians as the conscience of the nation, requiring them to bear the moral meaning load and material burdens attendant, in a rationalist and often puritanical society, upon poverty, disease, criminality or plain despair. Like Caesar's wife, prominent Aboriginal people – successful artists or athletes, public servants or elected spokespeople – are expected to display the greatest probity and the success in their dealings with, for example, Aboriginal health and housing, education and welfare. In fact, the expectation is that such people will act as the very pattern of integrity and honour, setting an example to other public servants and politicians whose everyday venalities and shady dealings are popularly taken for granted.

Sites like Brambuk, then, gather together an ensemble of meanings which serve a multiplicity of purposes. On the one hand, Aboriginal people are enabled to discover and explore a past with which they have had only the most tenuous connections; the consciousness of Aboriginal identity is raised, and white outsiders are taught something of Aboriginal custom and belief. The guidebook teaches:

> This is the land that supported our people both physically and spiritually. Its earth, water, plants and animals gave us physical strength, while its rocky peaks and deep valleys and all things connected with the land became the resting places for our creative and legendary heroes. . ..
>
> In the numerous rock shelters of Gariwerd we gather to talk, yarn, sing and dance. We teach our children and pass on our knowledge. . ..
>
> We hunt and gather the abundant food in the area by various methods such as netting, spearing and digging. . ..
>
> Life is thus sustained in an orderly, balanced manner according to the laws of Bunjil.

On the other hand, non-Aboriginal visitors to Brambuk (and to similar sites in other states) are apprised of the agonising past of European settlement ('the killing times') and the horrible effects of shooting, massacre and poisoning, smallpox, influenza and measles. . .[and] starvation. The guidebook cites the report of Commissioner Watton in 1842:

> Mr Robinson. . .had sent away into the bush to some natives. . .a quantity of what was supposed to be flour. Of this they partook, and were immediately seized of burning pains in the throat, excruciating pains in the stomach, vomiting. . .and on the following morning 3 men, 3 women and 3 children were dead. I also find that a few months ago Mr Robinson received from Port Fairy two pounds of arsenic.

The special relationship of Aboriginal people to the land is foregrounded everywhere at Brambuk. The approach to the

Centre's award-winning building follows a 'journey pathway' along which a wide variety of plantings demonstrates the scope of the local ecosystems, and the everyday uses to which native plants are adapted, for food (bush tucker) and medicine:

> *Acacia melanoxylon* Blackwood Wattle
> The wood is very hard and was used for making spear throwers and shields. An infusion of bark was used to bathe rheumatic joints.
>
> *Eucalyptus viminalis* Manna Gum
> This tree had many uses. Flat shields and coolamons were made from the bark. Manna, the sweet, sugary secretion made by a tiny lerp insect, was scraped from the leaves and eaten. The leaves were used to smoke out fevers and the flowers, called korr, were used for magical purposes.

The didactic urge which is always close to the surface in so much of heritage tourism is repeated throughout the centres of Aboriginal cultural renaissance. So, for example, the Ngarrindjeri people offer one- and two-day tours of the Coorong wetlands in South Australia, an 'adventure with purpose' which, according to their brochure, 'provides a fascinating insight into one of Australia's unique environments and allows you to share an authentic cross-cultural experience'.

> The Ngarrindjeri were one of the largest groups of Aboriginal people in South Australia and there is a need to talk about the history, heritage and culture of these people who occupied the land surrounding the Coorong. With this is mind the Ngarrindjeri people of Meningie decided to establish a Race Relations Cultural Education Centre called Camp Coorong, to teach about Aboriginal History, culture and their perspective of the Coorong, river and lakes environment to groups. The centre has a cultural Museum where arts, crafts and history are displayed, and features modern hostel-style accommodation. The Ngarrindjeri people are now working in partnership with Osprey Wildlife Expeditions to interpret and share their wisdom and culture in unique cross-cultural experiences.[4]

Similarly, if rather less elaborately, the members of the Wallaga Lake Koori Community on the New South Wales south coast conduct Umbarra Cultural Tours to 'local Koori sites such as Gulaga (Mt. Dromedary), Mumbulla Mountain, Mystery Bay, Fairhaven Point'. The Community also offers talks on Dreamtime stories, bush tucker and medicine and local Koori history, and 'hands-on' lessons in boomerang- and spear-throwing, painting with ochres and open-fire cooking.

The Yuin people, who form part of the community at Wallaga Lake, have only begun to formalize and codify their knowledge of their own recent past in the last few years. Collections of old photographs have been made, for example, showing nameless young Koori women dressed as domestic servants on the sheep stations of the Monaro – a complete and thoroughgoing obliteration of cultural identity. Other photographs depict children or old men, often posed in studios but demonstrating scarification, or the breastplates which conferred the title 'King' upon Aboriginal elders. The filling of gaps, the collection of wordlists of all-but-forgotten languages, the painstaking process of piecing together shattered pasts and teaching them to the dispersed descendants of dispersed forebears is a process which is shared around the country, as new generations of Kooris begin to discover their historical, spiritual and mythic antecedents. At the same time, at celebrations like Aboriginal Family Day at the Adelaide Festival Fringe, young children and adolescents engage in contemporary song and dance performances which stoutly oppose the unhappy victim image of earlier times.

The changing orientation of and to the artistic productions of Aboriginal people is displayed in numerous specialist theatres, museums and galleries – at the Araluen Centre for Arts and Entertainment in Alice Springs, for example, the Tjapukai Dance Theatre in Kuranda, or the Tandanya National Aboriginal Cultural Institute in Adelaide. It is in places like these that cultural tourists can begin to see the differences between the folk cultures which provide the themes and materials of the instantly recognizable 'Aboriginal art' of the dot-painted Papunya style and the desert-hued screen-printed tea-towels and T-shirts on the one hand, and the pathbreaking contemporary 'high culture' styles developing out of ancient ceremony and modern interpretations of millenial traditions on the other.

Such an exhibition at Tandanya in March 1994, *Moving Sands: Forward Momentum,* was comprised of four large sand sculpture/paintings or 'installations' telling of natural features of the land, connections with ceremonial events and connections with the land itself. These were highly complex works, requiring a large degree of concentration on the commentaries provided by some of the artists, some appreciation of the advantages and difficulties of the medium employed, and some knowledge and understanding of Aboriginal mythology and religious practice – and all light years removed from the banalities of souvenir art, or the easy sentimentalities of habitant poetry and prose.

The State and the Arts: National Identity, Commercial Investment and the Control of Cultural Space

The discourses of identity gathered into sites for the marketing and consumption of symbolic goods, the analysis, interpretation and critique of elements of a cultural heritage, become, in the process of their consumption, *capitalized*, and even over-capitalized. The transformation of an artefact, a custom, a value of cultural significance into something of commercial value renders that thing at once more highly valued in monetary terms and more open to the vagaries of market forces, changing tastes and fashions, questions of authenticity and problems of over- or under-supply. Indeed, it is this process of transformation that constitutes goods as symbolic – they are simultaneously commodities *and* symbolic objects. As Bourdieu [1993: 113] points out, the cultural and commercial values of the symbolic good commonly remain relatively independent, though economic sanction may come to reinforce cultural consecration.

The production and consumption of symbolic goods has fallen increasingly under the control of the state, as the ideological benefits of the distribution and sale of works of art are recognized, or the defining elements of distinctive cultural formations receive the imprimatur of style arbiters, trendsetters and spin doctors. The cultural apparatuses of the state, and most particularly the sponsors, financiers, competition judges, reviewers and critics of commercial cultural productions – in film, television, crafts, design, dance, drama, the fine arts, music and publishing – have as one of their major socio-political functions the bolstering of the legitimacy of the dominant culture. It is their choice of productions thought to be worthy of support, the criteria, terms and languages in which and grounds on which that support is justified, which bestow a kind of secondary legitimacy upon the art and craft works of minority, regional or mass cultures.

This is by no means a haphazard or capricious choice. It is the social and political content of popular and folk cultural productions (epitomized in the artefacts, activities and meanings of cultural or heritage tourism) which gathers to them the approval and support of arts funding bodies like the Australia Council or the accolades of Tourism Australia awards. In a hierarchized class society, dominated by commercial values and vehemently stated respect for the commonsense materialism of ordinary people without pretensions to or interest in 'high' cultural tastes, it is most commonly competence, craftsmanship and collective 'production values' which find favour over the arcane creations of individual talent.

So, for example, the Greenway Gallery at Sydney's restored Hyde Park Barracks houses 'a timely programme of temporary exhibitions about history, ideas & culture'. The 1994 programme included exhibitions of The Australian Scarf, The Domestic Revolution ('Discover the feminist fight for efficient kitchens & the origins of the humble billy can!'), Gold Fever ('diaries, drawings & letters' of the 1850s), Wool in the Australian Imagination ('connections between wool and Australian creativity, science and language') and Harold Casneaux – Photographs:

> Fun Parks, the Australian outback & the construction of the Sydney Harbour Bridge – photographer Harold Cazneaux focused his camera on the world around him. This exhibition explores Cazneaux's world, the people, places & events spanning the first half of twentieth century Australia. [Historic Houses Trust of New South Wales, brochure, 1994]

This last exhibition, while focusing on the works of a single artist, presents him as centrally a recorder of the mundane and the everyday, one who was, significantly, a photographer, not a painter.

The right to speak, write, paint, sing, dance, design and compose – to depict, represent or express a shared experience or practice on behalf of those whom one takes for granted as fellows, like-minded members of one's *Geschlecht* – is crucially a political right. Subject to continual prohibition, expectation or mandate, and closely bound up with questions of *personal* identity, it is a right which is granted on tenuous grounds, often enough through the agreement of an immediate circle of influential sponsors like the Office of Equal Opportunity in all Australian states, the Ethnic Affairs Commissions or the Australia Council. It is also a right which becomes legitimated through the familiarity bestowed by the mass media's use of 'experts' and spokespersons. Transformations of understandings of personal identity (as in the 1970s slogan 'the personal is political') into beliefs about *group* identification become established through periods of struggle with dominant cultural fractions, and as such are made respectable and legitimate through the good offices of the very state instrumentalities and apparatuses they once opposed. Black power, grey power, gay power movements have been born in public, sometimes violent confrontation with the taken-for-granted power bases of political and economic domination. That the demands of formerly oppressed, suppressed or merely ignored groups have gone beyond earlier and relatively simpler calls for, for example, equal opportunities within meritocratic formations is indicative of the ways in which such demands are, through democratic political processes, constituted as cultural and collective rather than psychological, personal or individual, and the votes of perceived 'blocs' are solicited.

Such an outcome is no more than might be expected in a society where individualism and egalitarianism are so precariously balanced. Where each is considered equal, in nature, with all others and is thereby granted equal social and political opportunities, all are assumed to have *the same* social, political and cultural needs and desires. The dilemmas of personal taste and individual preference are resolved by referring to them as just that: matters of *mere* personal choice, but choice nonetheless constrained within the bounds of collective understandings of what were once called, by writers in the field of multicultural studies, 'core values'. That such 'core values' sit so well with the meanings and actions of a dominant socio-cultural fraction, with the power of definition firmly in its control, provides further evidence of the way in which the cultural apparatuses of the state are crucial in the moulding and remoulding of group identities as if they were nothing other than personal identities writ large.

By the same token, the cultural and collective can also be re-construed as individual and personal. In Australia it is not uncommon to hear the members of minority racial or ethnic groups addressing audiences of others in terms of *my* culture, or *my* heritage. This development is parallelled by an equal and opposite force which focuses on a single defining characteristic, most often an ascribed one like sex, ethnic background or skin colour as a sufficient indicator of other achieved cultural characteristics. What is happening here is the rebirth of those essentialist theories which stressed an almost genetic (and mystical) relation between culture and temperament, in effect suggesting the heritability and inevitability of what are otherwise thought to be learned or chosen personality traits. But at the same time, the easy slippage between ascribed and achieved characteristics and the identification of individual with collective does have the potential to transcend the Them/Us opposition which feeds the rhetoric of nationalism and the discursive practices of inclusion and exclusion.

The mechanisms whereby individual and collectivity become interchangeable are central to the cultural practice of contemporary Australian social formations. Several consequences follow from this interchangeability and its encouragement within those social structures and discursive practices which buttress the late capitalist state. I mention briefly here three such consequences, and others at greater length in succeeding chapters. The consequences I discuss, I hasten to point out, carry with them no particular value judgement of good or bad at this stage; I mention them largely to illustrate the claim that cultural action undertaken by highly diverse social groups has widespread and often unintended ramifications.

The common egalitarian refusal to attend to 'otherness' in terms of difference and a corresponding emphasis upon the problems attendant in egalitarianism on the virtual fetishizing of *individual* differences produces a perhaps peculiarly Australian understanding of natural equality in a culture where the individual is held to embody the social. Individual persons are frequently thought to act as representatives or archetypes of the social groups to which they belong, whether those groups be based on ethnicity, race, gender, class, religion or occupation. In effect, the very individuality of persons is denied in the process of their being created as typical. That this is not an outcome confined to Australian social practice is shown by the way in which social prejudices are expressed in a variety of cultural formations which claim to be liberal, democratic and egalitarian [see, for example, Sartre, 1970].

The interchangeability of collective and individual which enables the sliding between My and Our in the discussion of culture and heritage is also a product – perhaps an inevitable product – of a capitalist culture in which possessive individualism is so greatly admired and where autonomy, independence and self-sufficiency are so highly valued as personal characteristics. In a context in which individual property ownership is held to be an ideal, it is not surprising that culture also comes to be understood as the property of individuals, with consequent questions about trespass, exclusivity, inheritance and the right to speak as a member of a specific cultural formation:

> I once asked an African-American lesbian student what she thought about the politics of identity. With a little smile she said that after she heard Ishmael Reed say black women didn't have the right to write about black men, she threw in the ideological towel. [Edmund White, *Sydney Morning Herald* 23/12/93: 9]

The practice of naming something as one's own, of depicting it in terms believed to have a particular and special resonance for specific cultural groups, constitutes an act of symbolic appropriation. Such an act is an element in the accumulation of cultural capital by individuals and by collectivities; and where, as in Australia, the greatest economic good lies (and has long done so) in the ownership of land, and the greatest cultural good has increasingly been conceived of as the land itself, it is likely that artistic as well as political, legal and economic attention will continue to focus on the land and the varying relation of its inhabitants to it.

So Australian literature is liberally endowed with works entitled *My Country* [MacKellar, in Mackaness and Mackaness (eds.) 1934]; *My Place*, the latter tellingly promoted by its American publishers as 'The Australian *Roots*' and acknowledging the financial assistance of the Aboriginal Arts Board of the Australia Council and the Australian Institute of Aboriginal Studies, as well as support from the Fremantle Arts Centre Press, the Literature Board of the Australia Council and the Western Australian Department for the Arts [Morgan, 1987]; *South of My Days* [Wright, 1971]; and *Poor Fella My Country* [Herbert, 1975]. Parallelling this kind of possessive singular nomenclature are works stamped with an individual's personal interpretation of place but clearly influenced by the works of others. Here might be included the hazy Golden Summers impressionism of the Heidelberg School (Roberts' *Mentone 1887* and *Holiday Sketch at Coogee 1888*; Streeton's *Sirius Cove 1890* and *The Purple Noon's Transparent Might 1896*; and Conder's *Coogee, 1888* and *Holiday at Mentone 1888*); the more primitivist style of the Brushmen of the Bush (Absalom, Hart); the modernist outback landscapes produced by Drysdale (*The Rabbiters* 1947) or the traditional watercolours of Namatjira (*Mangeraka*

Gorge 1950). All such works of landscape painting, and many others besides, can come to be constituted as part of Our (Australian) cultural heritage, whether they be in private collections, inaccessible board rooms or public galleries.

There is an aspect of egalitarian thought which finds expression and comfort in belonging to a clearly designated cultural group, in having a common culture and taking for granted shared understandings of being in the world. Where culture is understood to be simultaneously the property of individuals and collectivities (ethnic, national and so on), it is likely that democratic egalitarian societies will require the protection and preservation of symbolic goods – cultural property – by the state. The national state is seen to guard not only the jointly owned land (as symbolic capital or as a real financial asset) and the rights of individual citizens to own private property; it is also expected increasingly to act on behalf of both individuals and collectivities in disputes between and among them over economic *and* cultural goods. And this it largely does, not only in germinal land rights cases like *Mabo v. State of Queensland* [see Stephenson and Ratnapala eds., 1993], but also (less spectacular but more far-reaching) as a consequence of the enactment of laws and the establishment of administrative bodies dealing with, for example, racial vilification, sexual harassment and so on.

The seeds of these laws and administrative bodies are to be found within a context of egalitarian individualism which produces the demand for and the fact of the interchangeability of individual and collective. Concomitantly, the globalizing of world economies is accompanied at every turn by an adaptation of local practices and discourses of identity in a process whereby difference becomes smoothed over and identity becomes sameness. Such a process feeds the marketing and worldwide distribution of hitherto local cultures and heritages, commoditized and sanitized for ease of consumption. The price to be paid for uneasy individualists is that cultural production also becomes subject to the same global market forces which have turned it into an industrial process:

> Though it attracts far less attention, tourism shopping earns as much foreign currency [$1.5 billion] as better known export industries such as crude oil ($1.8 billion) aluminium ($1.7 billion) or lead and zinc ($1.4 billion). [A. Joel, 'Bourne to Shop', *Good Weekend* 30/4/94: 49]

So the streams of cultural capital emanating from metropoles, ebbing and flowing through global currents, invade the backwaters and confluences of smaller tributaries. Gathering to themselves the style and substance of nationalist imageries already formed from the expression of sectional identities, they participate in particularist discourses of identity and finally redirect them to universalist statements of what it is to be in the modern world.

Notes

1. One might note in this context a number of claims made in terms of the relation between Aboriginal cultures and 'European' cultures [see Symes and Lingard, 1988] or the relation between patriarchal and feminist aesthetics, the production of works by members of minority ethnic groups or of 'street poets' or others constituted as in some sense marginalized as well as the bureaucratic surveillance exercised by funding bodies and other patrons of the arts. Lippmann, writing of the United States Congress in the 1920s, may easily be paraphrased to apply to cultural production in contemporary Australia:

   > What patronage did to attach political chieftains to the national government, the infinite variety of local subsidies and privileges do for self-centred communities. Patronage and pork amalgamate and stabilize thousands of special opinions, local discontents, private ambitions. . .. [T]he degree to which the material for a common consciousness exists determines how far cooperation will depend upon force, or upon the milder alternative to force, which is patronage and privilege. [1965: 184]

2. See, for example, the plethora of works addressing the 're-writing' or reinterpretation of history over the last decade or so: Bodnar, 1992; Gillis (ed.), 1994; Kammen, 1991; Lowenthal, 1985; as well as an increasing number of works addressing the 'heritage values' of widespread material manifestations of 'the past': e.g. Hewison, 1987; McBryde (ed.), 1982; Uzzell (ed.), 1989; Vergo (ed.), 1989; Wright, 1985.
3. Nonetheless, 'Western' traditions of museology remain dominant, and indeed without them the chances of government support and funding would be slight. As Clifford remarks,

> The distinction between historical and ethnographic practices depends on that between literate and oral modes of knowledge. History is thought to rest on past – documentary, archival – selections of texts. Ethnography is based on present – oral, experiential, observational – evidence. Although many historians and ethnographers are currently working to attenuate, even erase this opposition, it runs deeper than a mere disciplinary division of labour, for it resonates with the established (some would say metaphysical) dichotomy of oral and literate worlds as well as with the pervasive habit in the West of sharply distinguishing synchronic from diachronic, structure from change. [1988: 340–1]

The space within which cultural heritage centres can operate is limited by the knowledge of dependence upon government support, but it is also liberated by the risk-taking knowledge of deep cultural differences which are now widely celebrated in Australian historiography and ethnography.

4. Since 1989 a number of Ngarrindjeri women have been engaged in an ongoing battle with property developers who are proposing to build a bridge from the mainland to Hindmarsh Island. The women are adamant that a bridge would intrude on a sacred site which would thus be open to the depredations of ignorant tourists and vandals. Despite the intervention of the Commonwealth Minister for Aboriginal Affairs, the affair still lurches from one crisis of interpretation to another. See Partington, 1995 and Fergie, 1995 for two opposed views.

CHAPTER FIVE

A Fortunate Style of Life: The Accumulation of Symbolic Capital in Suburbia

In a society as aggressively egalitarian, as vigorously individualist as that I have argued for Australia, it can come as no surprise to discover that one of the most widespread of everyday debates and disputes, in both public and private arenas, turns on matters of taste and distinction.

Australian sociology has long argued for the kind of class analysis which relates the emergence and maintenance of a ruling class and its elite fractions, and a ruled class and its fractions, to the economic and industrial transformations of a capitalist order. This has sometimes been contrasted with or opposed by a more conservative social stratificationist tradition and a popular discourse which assumes that elite membership is self-evidently the product of (achieved) economic and political power. As Connell and Irving put it, the largely stratificationist study of elites (class analysis focussing, until quite recently, on the study of the poor, the oppressed and the working class) has been a matter of 'making social structure and politics basically a contest of Who's Who versus Who Isn't' [1980: 17]. This sort of analysis, still very much dominant in those academic circles which seek to supply government and commercial interests with the demographic data which allow for a more efficiently targeted manipulation of masses of voters and consumers, is grounded in a deeply entrenched understanding of Australian social structure as a meritocracy, with upward social mobility being achieved through hard work, brains and a modicum of luck.

It can be argued, I think, that since the economic upheavals of the 1980s and the rise of cultural studies with a post-modernist bent, the two kinds of analysis have come closer together. Empirical cultural studies in Australia have tended to deemphasize questions of class, focusing instead upon those of status and style of life, with gender and ethnicity as powerful structurating principles. Along with such studies has come a perhaps belated recognition that the objectivation of class relations misses, because it counts as trivial the routine daily practices of human beings whose actions and interpretations of it actually do reflect and structure the social world (social history, for example, as tales of 'child-rearing and church-going, crinolines and corsets' in Connell and Irving's [1980: 14] phrase). The fundamental economic conflicts of capitalist social formations find their counterparts in hundreds of mundane expressions of hostility, anxiety, envy and resentment.

That Australians are as able as anyone else to discern degrees of status as manifested in social surveys and that they do evaluate their fellows in hierarchical terms by no means negates their everyday concern for strict equality of treatment for persons considered to be of equal worth. Elite status is rarely granted and (with one highly significant exception) is never referred to as such, being considered synonymous with the very pejorative term elit*ist.*[1] Thus trainee teachers may use the term 'elitist schools' to refer to those long established, non-government high fee-charging institutions of secondary education which are not open to the general public as of right and are popularly referred to as 'exclusive.'

It is characteristic of egalitarianism within contemporary social formations of a liberal democratic kind to be deeply conscious of the minutiae of status markers, while steadfastly denying their relevance for daily social intercourse and laying claim to a state of classlessness. This is commensurate with the increasingly battered but still hegemonic principles of meritocracy, even while merit is constantly redefined and renegotiated to produce a new class with a new style.

What I want to outline in this chapter are some of the ways in which status is inscribed in a society which simultaneously professes egalitarianism and individualism in like measure. For it is in the everyday discourses of status that we can trace not only the legitimation of the social structures of late capitalism, but also the constitution of a fundamental moral order which underpins, develops and maintains those structures. Social status in such a society is most clearly manifested in those situations where sizeable private capital investments are placed on permanent public display, as status benchmarks by which individual worldly success can be judged and aspired to in concrete terms: in short, in the dwelling places of the social elites.

Public Myth and Private Practice

The opposition between town and country is a venerable theme in Western cultures. From at least the time of Hesiod, in the ninth century BC, as Raymond Williams [1975] notes, the myth of a pastoral Golden Age had taken hold of the imagination of writers, artists and commentators upon social life. Hesiod posited a first Golden Age wherein, 'remote and free from evil and grief. . .[mortal men] had all good things, for the fruitful earth unforced bare them fruit abundantly and without stint' [cited in Williams, 1975: 24]. That age was long gone, however, by the time of Hesiod's writing. It would seem, indeed, that it is a human trait to imagine that earlier ages were free from the unremitting toil and pecuniary exploitation that always characterize the present. In Judaeo-Christian cultures this long perspective upon human ease and human suffering finds its genesis in the Garden of Eden, and it is this garden, and the fall from grace, which provides the foundation for all our later myths of the innocent pastoral and the counter myths of the evil city.

But if it is to be effective in ideological formation and maintenance, contemporary myth must always speak to the circumstances of its time and place, from one context to another. The Australian pastoral is as likely to focus upon the harshness of rural life as upon the benevolence of the land; it is less allegorical, more literal. Its central concern is not the bounteousness of nature but rather the struggle to survive in the face of maleficent and relentless natural forces. It is *human* nature which is celebrated in Australian pastoral mythology. The Drover's Wife and the Sick Stockrider, Hanrahan and the Man from Ironbark, their fortitude and laconic composure, courage and humour lie at the heart of the Australian pastoral tradition, and it is their dauntlessness in the face of flood, fire and famine which is mythologized, not the land itself.[2] This archetypal rural dweller finds no resonance with the nineteenth-century European image of a lotus-eating South Sea idyll. Australian heroism is grounded in that same Protestant ethic and spirit of capitalism with which the country was settled and came to twentieth-century nationhood.

The Australian city, on the other hand, founded as an outpost of the industrial revolution, as a repository for crime and viciousness and a trading station for British exploitation, is conceived of, mythologically, as a sink of degradation. Like industrial cities the world over, Australian cities are seen to breed venality and corruption, physical and mental disease and illness, violence, greed and sloth. This is where the bloated capitalist and the envious worker, the larrikin youth and the brutal state face each other in an incessant battle for supremacy and machiavellian schemes are hatched to suborn the hearts and minds of the people. In song and story, the urban hero is at best an impudent scrounger, the young Sentimental Bloke or the Woolloomooloo Lair, raffish and disreputable. The suburbs of Australian cities, however, like the early twentieth-century garden cities and new towns of England, offer the chance of combining the best of both worlds. As Gilbert says in discussing Henry Lawson's *Faces in the Street*, perhaps the best-known nineteenth-century statement of anti-metropolitan sentiment: 'The city was a practical necessity, the 'bush' an idealized dream. This made the suburb a marvellous compromise' [1988: 35].[3]

Australian social commentary is replete with attacks upon 'suburbanism' and apologias for it. Rural dwellers tend to speak of the city, the Big Smoke, as encompassing the suburbs (it's either Sydney or the Bush) and, with the town planners, bewail urban sprawl and unfettered development. A sense of neighbourhood and locality is found to be wanting in suburbia, but so also is a city-fostered spirit of adventurousness and cosmopolitanism. Despite occasional forays into writers' or painters' camps or rural convention centres for business people, *la vie Bohème* and the risk-taking, innovation and creativity of art and science, trade and finance, the intellectual life of the nation, are all unrelentingly centred on the city. The suburbs are thus thought of as little more than dormitories, suited neither to sturdy agricultural production nor to the excitement and intrigue of the marketplace and the academy, but only to the placid daily routines of housewifery and childrearing. That is to say, the suburbs, haunts of women and children, are both trivial (or trivialized) and banal. They are banal in Baudrillard's sense, as popularised by Meaghan Morris [1990], the common experience of the everyday.

So the suburbs are also conceived of as the worst of both worlds. But this is the shifting and contradictory nature of the myths I wish to explore here. In 'a culture increasingly dominated by space and spatial logic' [Jameson, 1984: 71], the ways in which space, and particularly dwelling space, is owned, controlled, shared and distributed have significance well beyond what such arrangements say about capitalist accumulation in the late twentieth century – though, of course, they do this as well. The connections between space and time, between physical and psychic space, between the dream of community and the dream of continuity, strike to the heart of human understandings of ends and beginnings, of 'the tyranny of distance' between geographical locations and in social life.

The questions I want to focus on here are about habitation, space and spatial relations and what they tell of the social arrangements of those who create and live them. They are about the languages of egalitarianism and individualism inscribed in cultural space, the accumulation of symbolic capital, the ways in which exteriors and façades may be used to hide interiors and inner lives, as well as to advertise them; house and garden as text:

> Houses live and die: there is a time for building
> And a time for living and for generation
> And a time for the wind to break the loosened pane
> And to shake the wainscot where the fieldmouse trots
> And to shake the tattered arras woven with a silent motto.
> [T.S. Eliot [1959] *East Coker*]

The complex of house and garden continues to be a crucial site for the construction, maintenance and refraction of those hegemonic home and family mythologies which undergird and express dominant cultural understandings of 'the good life' in late twentieth-century Australia. These mythologies, fashioned by dominant groups in their own image, illustrate what Bourdieu [1984: 101] calls 'the structure of the symbolic space' and 'the systematic nature of life-styles and. . .the whole set which they constitute'. But more than this, the analysis of habitation offers a direct insight into the way in which social practice and social situation are mutually reinforcing, proclaiming and supporting styles of life taken for granted as appropriate to certain ages and conditions of being.

In late as in early capitalism, the consumption, whether conspicuous or otherwise, of highly valued goods and services provides an index of social class and symbolic power[4] which is assiduously fostered through the mass media, particularly through women's magazines, the social pages and gossip columns, and a ceaseless emphasis on fashion in food, clothing, decor and *lifestyle*. The development and understanding of such an index is crucial to our comprehension of the ways in which social actors place themselves and others within a social field, with important consequences for social relations.

It is within the forms of popular culture that we can best see the power of one social fraction, what we might, with Gouldner [1979], call the cultural bourgeoisie, to shape understandings of taste and distinction. Notions of correctness, propriety and fitness always underpin judgements of style and fashion and enable interpretations of an ensemble of styles which 'go together' to produce a convincing and authentic 'image'. In an age of hyperreality, where image is after all often of greater import than substance, people can recognize like-minded others, and advertisers can obtain 'profiles' of their likely markets through a scrutiny of the choice and adoption of certain styles of life, of flamboyant opulence, commercial upward mobility or solid citizenship and conservative 'family values.' Nowhere is this better illustrated than in the complex of house and garden.

While the house-and-garden complex presents to the outside viewer a simultaneous advertisement and protective shell, both proclaiming and shielding its inhabitants to and from inquisitive strangers, it has the further mythic function of providing warmth, shelter and escape for those within its walls, beyond the public gaze. This the outsider also recognizes, but cannot see. Despite horrific tales to the contrary, we persist in endowing the home with the values of tranquillity, nurturance and safety which Bachelard [1969] attaches to the lighted hut in the forest. The secrets and intimacies of childhood and family life are secluded within the quiet corners of the garden and the drawers of the wardrobes.[5]

So on the one hand, the house-and-garden complex presents a public façade from which passers-by may read off indications of wealth, status, age, interests and priorities. Is the garden neat and bare, overgrown and luxuriant, filled with 'native' flora or exotics? Are there swimming pools, tennis courts, aviaries, statuary, swing and sandpit, clothesline and compost heap? Is the exterior of the house carefully maintained, tidy? Lavishly embellished or strictly plain? Is there more grass than concrete? Are the curtains drawn, does the complex lie behind high walls and fences? Is it open to the street in the American style? Or is it entirely hidden from view? On the other hand, the outsider's reading can tell nothing of the passions that simmer behind the façade, the heartbreaks and happinesses of the family members. Above all, the suburban house and garden respects privacy.

In any social formation, the ownership and control of physical space is a prime indicator of class and status. (It is also, but in a different way, an indicator of psychic security, as Virginia Woolf made so clear in *A Room of One's Own* [1929] and as Bachelard develops in his discussion of the poetics of space.) Australia's earliest ruling groups, high government officials and squatters, made this quite obvious in their construction of large houses in the wilderness surrounded by broad tracts of productive land and 'signed' by gatepost names announcing origins, connections or pretensions: 'Glenview', 'Riversleigh', 'Cressbrook' or 'Isis Downs' cheek by jowl with 'Wongwibinda', 'Burrabogie' or 'Tilbaroo'. It is not, of course, ownership of just any space which confers distinction; there are the 'prestige sites', 'blue-chip precincts' and 'dress-circle suburbs' beloved of real estate advertisers and the productive pastoral lands which form the basis of old wealth in Australia, to be contrasted with the weatherboard cottages of country towns and the narrow terraces of the inner city. What I want to argue here is that in terms of housing styles, the more closely a dwelling approximates to the traditional colonial homestead, the more desirable and prestigious it is conceived to be, even if (or perhaps particularly if) that dwelling happens to be in the city – incorporating, for example, both open fires *and* reverse-cycle air-conditioning: tradition without the inconvenience.

The Rural Homestead: Property, Heritage, Productivity

> 'Belaradah' Mudgee. Magnificent residence minutes from Mudgee and set on 32 acres of good grazing country. This exceptional property boasts luxurious accommodation for 10 persons and includes floodlit tennis court, pool with cabana and kitchen. 'Belaradah', the subject of several magazine articles, presents the opportunity to acquire a unique rental investment or a truly gracious lifestyle. [*Sydney Morning Herald* real estate advertising, May 1990]

> 'Purrumbete'. One of Victoria's most prestigious historic homesteads [. . .] Set amongst English Oaks and Elms in spacious parklike gardens, the magnificent Historic Homestead demonstrates classic Victorian architecture which offers a gracious way of living with four formal rooms and ten bedrooms. The hall, two formal drawing rooms and the dining room are spacious and provide outstanding entertainment facilities enhanced by a turn-of-the-century charm of exquisitely carved screens and staircase. . .. [estate agents' brochure]

The rural homestead has the capacity to signify the self-sufficiency, independence, security and stability which are mythologized as the true yeoman virtues of an arcadian past. Tradition and heritage are signified in the age of building materials, in well-worn pathways and ancient trees, ennobled through long use and inherited familiarity, legitimating the rise of the squattocracy and its primary role in the making of Australian wealth. Today, when Australia no longer rides on the sheep's back and wealth is generated in cities and conurbations far removed from the bush, the possession of rural land and country estates and the ease of old wealth still act as crucial indicators of the *right* to riches and power, the just reward and proclamation of financial success.

Length of settled ownership is probably the single most important indicator of legitimate wealth and social status. 'Old' families are distinguished from others (presumably equally long-standing) by their possession of the same large landholdings over many generations. While a pioneering background is considered unquestionably meritorious, however, it is also possible that a convict or bushranging forebear, especially one whose descendants maintained and increased the family wealth, has, by a peculiarly Australian inversion, the added cachet of ratbaggery and anti-authoritarianism [see, for example, Rolls, 1981]. There is an almost aristocratic thumbing of the nose at bourgeois convention and bureaucratic caution to be discerned here; but no matter how the family's fortune was originally obtained – by crookery, chicanery or honest labour and luck – the important thing about it is that the wealth is now sanctified by its longevity.

Almost as important is size, though as an indicator of legitimate wealth and status, size is a double-edged sword. While a great fortune, much land and a grand house are necessary for granting legitimate membership of the ruling group, they are not in themselves sufficient. The sources of capital, whether it be inherited or earned, have vital import for the justification of wealth, as does the style of expenditure. As Veblen [1899] long ago pointed out and many others, including the writers of handbooks on etiquette, have since demonstrated, the definition of ostentation and pretentiousness rests with those whose social power is most securely grounded and whose high social rank is of longest duration. It is according to their lights that styles of life, tastes in material goods and preferences in work and leisure activities may be accepted as appropriate or derided as inappropriate to membership of elite circles.

It is above all the women of the ruling group who orchestrate, arbitrate and, as in Veblen's time, demonstrate dominant understandings of distinction in any social formation. And it is in their traditional sphere of control, that of home and family, house and garden, that their judgements of propriety and taste are most clearly observable. Antiquity (of ownership, of cultivated surroundings, of furniture and durable goods like silver or jewellery) forms the basis of the determination of distinction, but it is juxtaposed, in a time and place where domestic service is rare, with ease and convenience (of household appliances, water supply, heating, cooling, lighting, access) predicated upon the possession of ultramodern sophisticated equipment. Distance from city centres is reduced by the possession of a light aeroplane; ducted air-conditioning mitigates the rigours of Maranoa summers or Monaro winters.

Such luxuries are more important, and more dearly bought, in thc bush. This is one reason why the rural homestead achieves its status as the benchmark of housing distinction. The other is the control of large tracts of expensive space. In the city, where space is at a premium and can indeed generate further income, even the wealthiest do not take up huge acreages as their own private demesne. The freedom from being 'overlooked' by neighbours, the sense of proprietorship engendered by longevity, expansiveness and privacy, comes most easily to the rural rich.

The distinguishing characteristic of the ideal typical rural homestead is its spaciousness: both house and garden are generous, rambling, with hidden nooks and broad vistas. (A 'view' in the city – of the harbour, the river or the gulf – comes at a high price. It may be noted in passing, too, that real estate advertisements are fond of the phrase 'commanding views,' thus implying superior control of one's situation.) The rural garden is productive, with compost heap, woodpile and tool and machine sheds, windmill, clothesline and barns. Fencing is likely to be utilitarian, designed to keep out animals, not people. The boundary between formal garden (flowers, trees, lawns) and 'working' garden is blurred, unlike the suburban garden, which distinguishes clearly between front garden and back yard or 'utility area'.

As with the grounds, so with the house. The house is not only the dwelling place, it is also the business centre of the agricultural enterprise. Rural families 'live over the shop', as the Prince of Wales once noted of residence at Buckingham Palace. The office is the hub of the family enterprise, often designed to act as a storefront, with a separate entrance for visitors calling on routine business. This is where the family 'does the books' in the evenings and where records are kept, telephone and computer assisted livestock management deals transacted. Often adjacent to it is the kitchen: large, central, designed for the eating of hearty meals and the discussion of the family's daily round. This is the domain of the country wife, with an enormous, slow combustion stove (now largely obsolete, and being replaced with an electric model), freezer and separate tap for rainwater. The focal piece of furniture is likely to be the kitchen table, used for both the production of meals and their consumption. It is this dovetailing of the family's activities that so bespeaks the past, the living at the workplace, the partnership of husband and wife, the slowly changing division of labour which now has the wife in formal partnership with the husband for financial reasons, rather than the informal partnership which sprang from the situation of the rural family as a unit of production. Now the country wife gives her occupation as grazier, where a generation before she was a 'housewife'. Little has changed in terms of the work in which she engages on a daily basis. The new nomenclature merely reinforces the understanding of the rural family as a single productive unit.[6]

The furnishing and decoration of the ideal typical rural homestead echo the style of the house and garden: traditional, functional, conservative. Antiques are most likely to be English, expressing the solidity of the Victorian era, rather than the delicacy of, say, eighteenth-century France, and they are most likely to have been inherited. Paintings are usually original Australian landscapes, watercolours rather than oils. Books are not greatly in evidence, colour schemes reflect the need for coolness or warmth, soft furnishings are in serviceable patterns and materials, especially in those houses where log fires, productive of ash and soot, are still in use. While contemporary interior-decorating magazines like *Country Style* and the manufacturers of kit homes are fond of utilizing nineteenth-century American styles as appropriate to a rural setting – a plethora of crafts, Shaker furniture and log cabin – these tend to be taken up in new housing in the bush rather than by residents of long standing.[7]

The family farm has fallen into rapid decline since the 1980s, and with it the dreams of a country estate for struggling land-owners. Now, more commonly than not, the homestead has become the property of a giant pastoral company inhabited by an employed manager and his family, rather than by those who, having been born in the house or one very like it, expected their children and grandchildren to follow them. Yet the myth of the family farm, of the productive, self-sufficient household, lives on in suburban developments around the country.

The Suburban Family Home: Fences, Privacy, Security

> A distinctive mansion of exceptional elegance, quality and superb positioning with dual access to New South Head Road. Featuring traditional craftsmanship and materials of a quality no longer available. Harbour views. Extensive grounds. Landscaped gardens. Saltwater heated pool. Gelosa kitchen. Magnificent entrance hall. 33ft. ballroom. Formal drawing room. Open fires. Grand dining room. Large family living/dining room featuring vast Georgian styled floor to ceiling windows looking out to harbour. 5 bedrooms, main bedroom with own sitting room. Ducted central heating (convert to air conditioning). Double garage plus level parking for up to eight cars. Full security. [*Sydney Morning Herald*, May 1990]

> 6 Room, 2 Storey Family Residence Plus Granny Flat, 4 Bathrooms, s/ Pool, Corner Allotment. This 3 yr old Residence offers flexibility in floor plan to suit 2 family accommodation or large family. Features 8 main rooms, Granny Flat, inground swimming pool and spa, double garage and beautifully maintained grounds. Excellent location near schools, short distance to shops and transport and few minutes drive to Marion Shopping Centre. [Adelaide *Advertiser*, May 1990]

> YOUR KIDS WILL LOVE IT! Brand new carpet throughout is a feature in this beautiful colonial-style home consisting of three bedrooms, lounge/dining, modern kitchen with built-in dishwasher and heaps of

> cupboards. A family room with air-cond. opening to a patio area – ideal for entertaining. A small easy-care pool and sep. rumpus room a bonus. The double garage and ample car parking is just the go for the tradesman. [Adelaide *Advertiser*, May 1990]

I have expatiated upon the rural homestead at some length because of my contention that it is, like English stately homes or French chateaux, the benchmark whereby other, less expansive styles of house and garden are to be judged as signing something of national character and aspirations – of independence, self-sufficiency and the importance of private, familial ties in a world perceived as increasingly regulated and rationalized by impersonal bureaucracies, often corrupt State instrumentalities and powerful economic forces. A world where governmental disdain for the common weal breeds a familial privatism of the *j'y suis, j'y reste* type which brooks no interference from officials or inquisitive neighbours.

McQueen points out (1988: 36): that 'As a state of mind and a way of living, suburbia is not confined to certain geographic areas. . . [but] still aspires to the ways of living that are most completely realized by nuclear families on garden blocks with detached houses'. And as Short observes of the fuzzy boundaries which are constantly being redrawn between inner city and suburbs, and, we might add, for Australian cities 'outer suburbs,' these terms are 'general mythological entities' [1991: 50]. Suburbia is a state of mind, an organizing myth of an urban society standing between the other very Australian organizing myth of the bush and the universal myth of the city.

The open, haphazardly placed trees and winding dirt roads of the bush give way in the suburbs to mellow avenues and carefully tended lawns, paved roads and 'nature strips': a profusion of trees and greenery is one of the signs of suburban affluence. Sheds and outbuildings are replaced by carports or garages, and wire fences by more substantial structures, often bearing signs conveying the message that the property is electronically protected.[8] There is little indication that the residence has any connection with its inhabitants' means of getting a living. Indeed, the suburban house is above all a domestic arrangement, the place of the family. The work that is done there is 'housework' or 'homework' or 'household chores', activities connected with the maintenance of a style of life and the socialization of the young. It is where city workers retire at the end of the working day for recreation, revival and reproduction of the health and strength required to go on working. As such, it represents a unit of consumption rather than of production, and its fences signify a careful division between public and private life.

The suburban house suggests Australians' ambivalent relation to the natural environment of the bush, or in conservationist parlance, the wilderness. Banjo Paterson's romanticism notwithstanding, 75 percent of all Australians live, as they have always done except in the gold-rush era, in the towns and cities of the coastal belt, 40 percent of the total in the conurbations of Sydney and Melbourne. The sunlit plains are, more often than not, considered boring, to be traversed as swiftly as possible by plane, train or car, and the starlit night is faintly sinister, haunted by the spirits of the dreamtime. Productive they may be, or ecologically sensitive, but vast areas of land, the Pilliga Scrub or the Mallee, for example, hold little attraction for the holidaying tourist or those seeking a place to settle. Australians seek the comfort and convenience of gas and electricity, mains water and sewerage, paved roads, shopping centres, propinquity and clearly defined boundaries between themselves and their neighbours.

> The single detached home on the quarter-acre block is one of the most striking visual symbols of urban Australia. Roughly three-quarters of dwellings are of this kind. Flats, terraces, low- and high-rise apartment blocks characteristic of European cities are relatively rare even in the more dense urban areas. In outer Brisbane and Melbourne over nine in ten households live in separate houses. A far cry from Berlin, Paris, Amsterdam, Athens, Rome, where only the rich and outer suburban dwellers have a garden or front door of their own. [Watson, 1989: 73][9]

The high priest of suburbia in Australia has been Hugh Stretton, a historian who, in 1970, undertook the rescue of the preferred style of life from the scorn of social and cultural critics like Robin Boyd [1963] and the derision of comedians, notably, perhaps, Barry Humphries in his manifestation as Edna Everage, the archetypal suburban housewife from Moonee Ponds. Stretton is largely correct when he points out that most Australians 'choose' to live in the suburbs:

> Most of the best poets and painters and inventors and protesters choose it too. It reconciles access to work and city with private, adaptable, self-

> expressive living space at home. Plenty of adults love that living space, and sub-divide it ingeniously. For children it really has no rivals. [1970: 20–21]

Gilbert's 'marvellous compromise' again.

But 'choice' is not quite the appropriate term to explain the concentration of Australians in suburbia. Stretton's easy usage of 'the best' to describe poets, painters, inventors and protesters suggests why this is so. The ability of the well-to-do to choose their residence blinds them to the constraints placed upon others who must take what they can get. It is significant that, in his encomium on suburbia, Stretton lauds the affluent and antiseptic *banlieux* of Canberra rather than the inner reaches or the vast outer suburbs of the big cities as the archetypal suburbia. Families do not so much *choose* to live in the latter but rather are forced to do so for reasons of cost and proximity to schools, transport and other facilities. The 'best' people are not so constricted. There is a world of difference between the luxurious mansions of Toorak, Vaucluse or Dalkeith and the crabbed and crime-ridden laneways of Darlinghurst, Fortitude Valley or Clifton Gardens, or the featureless tracts of outer suburban developments like Morphett Vale or Mount Druitt – areas which are becoming more and more the habitation of the unemployed, the low-paid and the uncared-for.

In a word, that difference is class: ownership and/or control of the means whereby surplus value is produced in capitalist society enables the purchase and maintenance of a style of life which valorizes and advertises the benefits of free enterprise and bourgeois morality to every passer-by. The wide, shady lawns and water views, high fences and quadruple garages of *haute* suburbia proclaim the wealth and power of their owners. On a lesser scale, the double or triple fronted brick-veneer bungalow, with trim hedge and neat front garden, announces the prudence and respectability of the petty bourgeoisie and the virtuous working class. This is so despite controversial exposés of high suburban styles of life (in the 1992 ABC/BBC 'reality' television series *Sylvania Waters*, for example) which periodically disturb the widespread public complacency of suburbanites, uneasy with the interrogation of moralities and lives generally believed to be private and inviolable.

The suburbs, whether prestigious or merely worthy, opulent or unassuming, articulate the social conscience and cultural imperatives of the middle class: canny, provident, morally upright. The concerns of suburbanites revolve around provision for the future, the family, capital appreciation, domestic discretion and civic pride. Striving, sometimes desperately, to avoid the loss of esteem consequent upon financial problems, suburban dwellers shelter behind a façade that announces their ability to raise, or at least maintain, their social status:

> The Powers' garden and landscaped surrounds are scrupulously maintained. As Bob Power said: 'People who live here are conscious of keeping their properties the way they should keep them. You don't want some guy living next door who doesn't give a stuff about his house – that detracts from the value of your own'. [Horin et al., 1985: 2]

Such a status-conscious view contrasts with, but does not negate, the views of a less affluent and a less outspoken era:

> The most marked characteristic of the Australian taste probably was its unashamed superficiality, a result of the Australian national tendency to place an unusual degree of importance on small incidental details. . .. There was a sort of earthy functionalism about this national style. Red bricks were favoured because they required no maintenance. Cream paint did not show finger marks as readily as white. A floral pattern on the carpet disguised dirty footprints. . .. [Boyd, 1978: 234–5]

But the stultifying private life behind the closed front doors takes its toll of relationships and family harmony. Sophie Watson, erstwhile urban housing activist, claims that she lost her sense of self in suburban Canberra:

> I had always seen my room as my sanctuary. A place to be, to write and do wood engraving, to make a fire, to invite friends. I'd grown accustomed to communal living. The lack of my own space, the suburban box, the long empty streets, the difficulty of meeting people, the social life based on couples, the lunchtime affairs, the absence of community and local politics, the overpowering dominance of one homogeneous world of work and politics beside which all other work seemed a pale reflection – that was Canberra. [1989: 10]

The profusion of housing styles in the suburbs reflects changing fortunes and changing fashions. It also reflects a desire, assiduously cultivated by the specialist architectural press and the weekend magazines, to be different, distinctive, individual – though without too much transgression of local laws of 'taste' – impressing the neighbours, but not offending them. Convinced that the resale value of their house is ultimately paramount, owners are expected to maintain and improve their property by ensuring that it 'fits in' with local mores; lawn-mowing and exterior painting therefore receive major attention, as an act of civic duty and personal morality:

> Behold the man – the Australian man of today – on Sunday mornings in the suburbs, when the high decibel drone of the motor mower is calling the faithful to worship. A block of land, a brick veneer and the motor-mower beside him in the wilderness . . . [Ashbolt, 1966: 373]

And,

> The popularity of the tile roof was largely due to the fact that it looked heavy, imposing and more expensive and therefore a better investment than other rooves. ... Any addition that made the house look more expensive was worthwhile, for the Australian breadwinner tended to plan not so much for his own enjoyment, or even to excite his neighbour's admiration, as for eventual sale. Any small extras spent on the roof or front porch could be classed as a good investment, because they could be counted on to raise disproportionately the offers of potential buyers. [Boyd, 1978: 235]

As Polly Adler, a notorious Chicago madam of the 1930s observed, 'a house is not a home', a dictum long taken to heart by real estate agents and upwardly mobile suburbanites. The dwellings for sale are never characterized as mere houses: they are cottages, villas, bungalows, mansions, residences, duplexes (i.e. semi-detached) and, more than anything else, homes. In the inner city, where the absence of gardens and 'outdoor entertainment areas' and triple garages precludes the nomenclature 'home', dwelling places are called, predictably, homettes or home units, maisonettes or town houses, or cheaper and less attractive flats and shared accommodation – i.e. boarding houses.

'Homes' advertised for sale represent a plethora of styles, some of which are perhaps a little incongruous in the context of Australian suburbia. In a two-week period (May 1990) the following styles were listed in *The* (Adelaide) *Advertiser:* French Provincial,

Spanish Mission (white stucco, archways, terracotta roof tiles and guttering, supernumerary shutters), Cape Cod (steep gables, dormer windows, shutters), Tudor (faux half-timbering, mullioned windows), Mediterranean (in the words of Sydney journalist Paola Totaro, describing the Italianate suburb of Haberfield as ABBAfield: 'All Bloody Balustrades and Arches'), Victorian (iron lace), Georgian, Colonial and, current nostalgic favourite, Federation, featuring fretted verandah posts and rails and elaborate timber finials.

Many of these homes will be 'architecturally designed' if they are of recent construction, or will express 'the charm of yesteryear' or 'the character of a bygone era' if they are over eighty years old and well kept. Many will also be situated in 'a botanic setting' (meaning that the garden is planted with 'natives' rather than exotic flora which require constant maintenance and produce excess water rates charges). Old houses will have their stained glass or lead lighting, their 'elaborate cornices', 'ornate fireplaces' and 'ceiling treatments', their wide hallways and double doors lauded; newer constructions will have their patios, pergolas and gazebos paraded, especially in terms of their suitability for outdoor or 'al fresco' entertaining and 'family living'.

As with exteriors, so with interiors: electicism reigns. It is not unusual to come across a bluestone cottage with lead-lighting, wide hallways and the charm of yesteryear, featuring an 'art-deco high-tech kitchen' or a 'cosy country-style [or "farmhouse"] kitchen with high-tech convenience'. For $710,000 (at a time when around 10 per cent of the labour force was officially unemployed, and the average weekly wage was $490, the poverty line at $169) one is invited to purchase 'Sophisticated Georgian Spendour. . .some nine principal rooms, three bathrooms, stunning Roman courtyard'. Post-modern bricolage and pastiche are also invading the suburbs, featuring Beaubourg style high-tech exposed pipes and hard-edged geometrics transposed into the residential mode, with – in a single building – triangular, circular, semi-circular and even rectangular windows (dressed, in one case with which I am familiar, in heavily ruched Austrian blinds), minimalist gardens, a garage or carport screened by latticework, and the whole painted in 'Federation (or "Heritage") colours' – salmon pink, mustard, pale apricot. Colours, according to one paint manufacturer, are particularly important in expressing the personality of the householder:

> Your colours are you! You don't get many chances in a lifetime to make a statement about yourself as enduring as changing the look of the world around you. [sales brochure]

As a microcosm of Australian society, the suburbs present a vision of a liberal democratic workers' paradise to the world outside, a powerful image in Australian political and economic rhetoric. Despite social conformism and aesthetic populism [Jameson, 1984: 14] and the stress engendered by sustaining at least the outward trappings of family harmony and occupational success, upward striving and fear of social failure, the suburban home is still conceptualized as enshrining egalitarianism, individualism and that freedom of choice which is believed (in discussions about the privatization of utilities, schooling or medical services) to lie at the very heart of a liberal capitalist democracy.

And yet, as Wilkes remarks of the works of those playwrights (Williamson, Buzo or Hibberd, for example) who pillory the philistinism and bourgeois pretensions of middle-class Australians with their roots deep in suburban soil, 'the effect is still celebratory' [1981: 122]. Wilkes indeed discerns a reassertion of idealism in Australian literature expressed by 'an often passionate concern for human values in the conditions of ordinary living' [ibid.: 134], and it is this very *ordinariness*, this mundanity and conventionality, that encapsulates the appeal of suburbia to the average householder, the seeker after Lasch's [1977] haven in a heartless world. It is also, however, the mediocrity, conventionality and averageness, the anti-intellectual, penny-pinching self-righteousness of the suburbs that forms a constant counterpoint to this picture of comfortable cosiness and the basis for the anti-suburbanism of those who would consider themselves to be cosmopolitan citizens of an intellectual, political and artistic world unbounded by bourgeois, parochial concerns of getting and spending [see, for example, Robin Boyd's 1960 [1980] attack on 'featurism' and 'Austerica' and the strictures of Vance and Nettie Palmer cited by Rowse, 1978]. As Corrigan remarks, in a peculiarly self-deprecating passage, a revelation of Australian egalitarian-individualist thinking: 'The values of the bourgeois Australian dream. . .offer no social redemption, but at least they are ours' [1985: 22].[10]

Both views of the suburbs, the celebratory and the minatory, find resonance not only in Australian literature, but also in the actual daily lives of suburban dwellers. Here, at least in theory and sometimes in practice, ordinary people can enjoy (thanks to homely technological developments) domesticity without exploitation, privacy without loneliness, security without regimentation. They are also enabled and indeed encouraged to express what interior decorators are fond of calling their 'individuality' and Stretton calls their ingenuity, though always within the boundaries of their quarter-acre block, without undue aural, visual or olfactory impingement upon their neighbours.

The suburban family home provides the site of what Bachelard [1969: 12) calls 'the domains of intimacy' in a crowded world. It provides the venue and occasion not only for intimacy, but also for the kind of free, secure and self-directed sociality which is impossible within the public domains of city streets and parks and buildings. The dangers and excitements of the industrial and commercial world are excluded by gates and doors which open only to the members of the household and their associates. Protection and security are vital to the careful householder in any sphere, but nowhere more so than in the suburbs. In the bush, protection is generally thought to be needed against the elements and afforded by deep verandahs; in the inner city, double-locking and spy-holes are reminders of the heartless world beyond the thresholds of flats and units and shared houses. But in the well-to-do suburbs, high fences *and* complicated locks *and* alarm systems *and* remote controls are not enough. Here, the early morning tranquillity is disturbed only by the discreet whirr of reverse-cycle air conditioners or the frenzied baying of assorted alsatians, dobermans and rottweilers alerted to their guard-dog duty by an innocent but promptly terrorized stroller or jogger.

The garden, too, and the 'nature strip' act as a kind of mini greenbelt, sheltering the house from the fumes, bustle, noise and pollution of the street. The suburban front garden is as much a part of the façade of the house as the exterior walls themselves. Typically, it is smaller than the back garden (or yard), more formal and symmetrical, a buffer zone in which family activities such as barbecues, games or summertime entertainments do not take place, while the evidence of domestic activities (clotheslines or the ubiquitous Hills Hoist, the incinerator, the tool shed, the vegetable garden, the swing and sandbox, the occasional chook pen) is hidden from view in the back yard. In the more affluent suburbs, it is still likely that the tennis court, swimming pool, croquet lawn and garages which are separate from the house (not 'u.m.r.' or under main roof, in advertising shorthand, the favoured space-saving style of newer houses) are to be found at the sides or back of the house, rarely at the front [but see Dovey, 1994: 135–6, for a discussion of the changing use of backyard space].

The disposition of space within the suburban family home reflects the owners' understandings of privacy, intimacy and sociality, and their financial ability to provide specific zones within the house for activities centring upon these psychic needs. Newer houses are designed to include 'children's areas', 'entertainment areas' or 'family rooms' to answer to sociality needs, and 'granny flats', parents' or teenagers' 'retreats', or master-bedroom-with-en-suite-bathroom to cater for solitude and privacy.

Such a disposition also tells much of hegemonic Australian understandings of the family, of individualism and moral duty. The separation of generations is a case in point. Suburban houses, even relatively new and inexpensive ones, reflect the (outdated) understanding that the mother will be at home raising the children, at least when they are at the pre-school stage. Her operational headquarters is conceived of as the kitchen, and thus the children's 'play area' must be situated where it is easily surveyed by her, without the children's 'getting under her feet' – annoying, and dangerous. As a slight acknowledgement that contemporary women may wish to, or actually do, work outside the home, in paid employment – that they are not solely household skivvies – the disposition of space may also provide for a place where the mother (or the 'principal care-giver' in correct welfarespeak) can remove herself (sometimes himself) from the scenes of her/his household responsibilities. The erstwhile 'den' or 'study' of the 1950s, the retreat of the *pater familias*, has given way to the parents' retreat or has disappeared altogether – again, perhaps, an acknowledgement of a changing division of labour within the household. But, like Sophie Watson in Canberra, she may still not be able to find a room of her own. For, as Rowse points out: 'The negative image of suburbia is often equally a negative image of women. A rough equation that seems to be employed is: women + domesticity = spiritual starvation. (Men + wide open spaces + achievement = heroism of the Australian spirit) [1978: 13].

The Inner-City Zone: Commerce, Progress, Corruption

> Adelaide. U41/19 South Ter. INNER CITY LIVING. 1 b.r., b.i.r. Freshly painted. No pets. $85.
>
> Adelaide. 2 bedroom b.i.rs., R/C air cond., w.w.c., phone, (optional undercover) off street parking, adjacent parklands. $125 p.w.
>
> Keswick. Nice upstairs unit 2 b.r., b.i.r., 5 mins city, ex/security. Value $85 p.w.
>
> Adelaide. Working, responsible person to share older style furn. 2.b.r. mais. Own unf. rm. $70 + 2 wks. Bond.
>
> North Adelaide. Person to share 3 b.r. house, must be clean, reliable, emp./student. Close all facs. $65 p.w. + Bond. [*Advertiser*, May 1990]

If the suburban house is central to the mythology of harmonious hearth-and-home family life in Australia, signifying the warmth, security and unity of the nuclear family, other urban styles of life present a darker image. Outer suburban public housing, the institutionalized dwellings of the aged and/or indigent[11] and inner urban rental accommodation all throw into high relief some of the most pressing human and material problems of the late twentieth-century Australian state: homelessness, pollution, decay, loneliness, poverty, alienation, anomie and physical and symbolic violence.

There is, of course, nothing new in the juxtaposition of urban vice and rural virtue, as I have observed. Short [1991] uses it as the basis for his distinction between wilderness, rural and urban myths, and Williams remarks that Quintilian made the contrast between town and country his first example of a stock thesis [1975: 61]. He cites Juvenal's *Satires* as addressing not an idealized rural economy, 'but a purchased freehold house in the country, or "a charming coastal retreat" or even "a barren offshore island".' This, then, he adds, 'is not a rural but a suburban or dormitory dream' [ibid.: 62]. The same might well be said today of the way in which the rural homestead is eulogized as the epitome of a gracious and even aristocratic way of life.

The inner city zone, those areas surrounding what 1980s town planners took to calling the 'central business district' as it emptied of dwelling space, filled with often untenanted high-rise commercial buildings and choked with traffic, represents the polar opposite of the rural farmstead as a place for human habitation. Daylight, greenery and fresh air are banished, towering steel, concrete and neon replace lowslung timber, stone and sunlight; the dull roar of cars, trucks, vans and public transport punctuated by the wail of emergency sirens replaces the sound of birdsong, distant thunder or the solitary tractor. Carbon monoxide and rotting garbage substitute for the aroma of eucalyptus and freshly tilled (or fertilized!) soil, while far horizons are blotted out by smog and human scale is erased by the commercial and industrial imperatives of the Big Smoke.

But this too is myth, as the facetious parentheses above imply. And the distance between the arcadian freedom of the bush and the satanic degradation and exploitation of the city has been one of the most enduring bases of Australian ideologies of self-sufficiency, mateship and egalitarianism. The settler population of Australia has, with rare exceptions, always been resolutely urban. The movement of peasant farmers to the cities, characteristic of the industrial revolution in Britain and Europe, was reversed in nineteenth-century Australia as pioneers moved out of the cities into the bush to make their fortunes. But these never constituted more than a fraction of the population, and in the late twentieth century, with the breakdown of the family farm and of agricultural export markets, the children of farming families are once again moving to the cities in search of training, employment and income. That the bush and its settlement was characterized as much by tedium, brutality, venality and grinding poverty as the city has been conveniently forgotten in the welter of nationalist myth-making and the hagiography of The Man from Snowy River and Clancy of the Overflow that continues to this day.

Like the bush and the suburbs, the city transmits conflicting messages. As a zone of danger, it is also a zone of excitement, the hub around which not only trade and industry revolve, but also a centre for the arts and entertainment, sports festivals, intellectual life, fashion, finance, social services and government. The city provides both a market and an audience. But as the Australian economy shifts inexorably from a comfortable and longstanding dependence upon broad-acre primary production to globalized high technology and service industries, so the city also becomes the centre of production.

Where do these producers live? Increasingly, blue-collar workers are exiled to the outer suburbs as are the 'non-productive' – single-parent households, the unemployed and pensioners. More than any other locus of habitation, the inner-city zone is notable for the social heterogeneity of its residents. It is home to an enormous range of classes, creeds and ethnic groups. Where the bush is the domain of men and the suburbs of women, the city is truly heterosexual, with men and women, straight and gay, bi- and transsexual thrown into a multi-cultural, multi-gendered melting pot. Here the young and reckless, the old and toughened, thrusting 'management trainees' and junior executives, pimps and prostitutes, students, artists, standover men and derelicts, small shopkeepers and bartenders, chefs and waiters mingle on the streets, day and night, with transient holidaymakers, foreign tourists and suburban diners and theatregoers. It is indeed on the streets and in the bars and coffee shops that inner-city dwellers conduct their social lives; unlike the careful suburbanites, they do not lock themselves and their children (if they have them at all) away at the end of the working day. For them, the working day stretches into the night, when it does not actually begin then, and small children and animals (except for the ubiquitous and appropriately sinister cat) are conspicuous by their absence.

There is a consensus, reflected in constant sensational exposés in the mass media, that the inner-city zone is not a suitable place for child-rearing. Drunks and drug addicts, police, social workers, sex-industry workers and strip-joint bouncers accost every passer-by; 'adult' bookshops and sex-shops and nightclubs with names like 'The Pink Pussy Cat' and 'The Love Machine' parade their wares with little regard for the tender sensibilities of the young. The congested traffic is frenziedly bad-tempered, garbage overflows on to the streets and gutters. Moral and physical peril lurk, and 'traditional family values' are assaulted, at every corner and in the tiny patches of greenery optimistically labelled 'parks'.

Yet this is where the action is, the bright lights, colour, movement, urgency and noise. The sense of moving forward, of making one's way, of being at the centre of things is what lures the ambitious country youth and young suburbanite out of their predictable and cautious routines into the stimulation and adventure of the inner city. The anonymity of the street affords freedom from the surveillance of family and neighbours; and having a place of one's own, despite (or because of) its being shared with like-minded age-mates, provides the sense of independence and self-sufficiency that in an earlier era came from the actual physical production of food and shelter or the receipt of a private income.

Property ownership in the inner-city zone is differently constituted from that of the suburbs or the bush. Since all but the accommodation of the very rich is rented, the land, bricks and mortar of the flat or shared house belong to and are the responsibility of another. The state of repair of the building, its plumbing and wiring, and the condition of the interior paintwork and 'fixtures' (curtains, floor-coverings, cookers, bathrooms) are not the concern of the tenant who, almost by definition, is a temporary resident – which is why so many rentiers insist on a bond. In such a situation, ownership devolves upon portable goods: kitchenware, linen, bric-a-brac, books, electronic equipment and items of furniture. For all but the down-and-out, individual taste and social status are exhibited less through decor and a style of life that revolves around house and garden, hearth and home, than through personal possessions (especially clothing) paraded in public and leisure activities carried on in public places – the cafe, bistro, pub, beach, disco or street. This is where the rising generation goes to see and be seen by others who can recognize them as fellows on the path to fame and fortune. It is also where the desperate go in search of succour from worker-priests or local dealers.

In the inner city, the suburban supermarket and rural general store give way to the kerbside stall, the early-morning produce markets and the delicatessen. The privatized activities of the suburban or rural householder give way to the communal activities of the city tenant: people meet, combining domestic chores with social intercourse, at the laundromat, the newsagency, the street stall and the deli, and their proprietors come to know their regular customers by name. It can be argued that the sense of community is stronger in the crowded city neighbourhood that it is in the primly privatized avenues and impersonal shopping malls of suburbia.

The apochryphal borrowing-of-a-cup-of-sugar is the act of a city dweller, beneath the dignity of the suburban housekeeper, unnecessary for the provident country cook. The sharing of a household, with all members contributing an equal share to rent and expenses, engenders a spirit of (sometimes belligerent) collective enterprise and egalitarianism. Such people are not at all like Ashbolt's suburban man, who 'has never seriously considered the possibility of joint ownership of a motor-mower with, say, twenty of his neighbours. The pride of personal property is too strong. The motor-mower has become to him an assertion of democratic rights, an expression of power, an object of reverence'.

[1966: 373] The only motor mowers in the inner city are publicly owned, the property of the municipality, used in the care and upkeep of the city's parks and gardens. But inner-city flatmates and neighbours may and do, often of necessity, share watering cans and trowels as they tend their windowboxes, pot plants and balcony herb-gardens. Convenience and ease of care characterize the private gardens of inner urban dwellers, but they are nonetheless frequently lovingly cultivated, perhaps in an atavistic attempt to re-create one aspect of the style of life of imagined agrarian forebears without the back-breaking labour and mind-numbing precariousness of dependency on variably fertile soils and capricious climatic conditions.

A zone of excitement, the inner city is also a zone of speed. Events, all of seemingly universal importance, succeed each other with dazzling rapidity and anything-can-happen unpredictability. Materialism and hedonism, the fast-paced rhythms of urban life, the society of the spectacle [Debord, 1970] all preclude the solitary contemplation of growing things and the wonders of nature. The few parks ('do not walk on the grass') are locked at night or taken over by the nefarious or the foolhardy; the stars pale into invisibility before the glow of the city lights. The cut flowers have no scent. Both time and space are expensive commodities in the city and both are carefully husbanded, with an eye to maximum profit.

Ease of care and low maintenance are the watchwords of the urban tenant, and the disbursement of space in inner-city dwellings reflects its cost. The emphasis in interior decor is upon compactness and duality of purpose, with the bed-sitting room standing as the archetype of inner urban living, the convertible sofa-bed and the drop-leaf table as its central furnishings. Scaled-down furniture and light colours and fabrics are utilized to create the illusion of space in what are often extremely cramped quarters, as perusal of any number of interior decorating magazines will demonstrate. The kitchen (or 'kitchenette') is more likely to reflect the tight convenience of the ship's galley than the expansiveness of the farmhouse, the dining room is non-existent, the bathroom severely utilitarian. The accessibility of a 'view' – usually only from the summit of tall buildings – raises the rent to commensurate heights.

Those who actually choose to live in the inner-city zone can be conceived as doing so not so much *pour épater le bourgeois* (though they may certainly do that) as to escape from the stultifying confines of a world where many people – family, neighbours, school teachers and schoolmates – have known them since childhood. The anonymity and egoism, the sheer size of the city, confer freedom and space to experiment with styles of life which are unavailable or disapproved of in the suburbs and country towns and districts. As such, the inner city is also a zone of transition. Those who have the choice will more than likely return from whence they came, or to something very like it, when a slower pace, children or a mortgage come to have an appeal which once seemed improbable.

The Australian Dream: Urban Pastoral

> Individuality, individualism, unique identity. Notions of private ownership, private access, private control as the ideal – have shaped Australian urban policy. Business interests, transnational and monopoly capitals – the hidden hands. Public transport. 'We'll provide a little.' But not enough. 'It's not economical. It's too impractical. Everyone's too spread out. Use the car.' Private buses to service the suburbs. Rare and expensive. Use the car. And the woman stuck at home in the one-car family, the old and the frail, the teenage kid looking for the action? Trapped. No metro. No autobahn. No underground. No trams. [Watson, 1989: 139]

Both critics of and apologists for the suburbs seem to agree on one thing: suburban living is quintessentially Australian – or Australian society is quintessentially suburban. The metonymy is exact, but it is so broad and all-encompassing that it can accommodate a wide range of contradictory and complementary messages, mythologies to suit rich and poor, young and old, boss and worker, man and woman. The suburbs enable safety and security, privacy and community, convenience, comfort and self-respect: a style of life of which millions can only dream. They are also a wasteland of philistinism and conformism, apathy and fragmented social relations, status-seeking materialism and narrow-minded nosiness. Rowse [1978] characterizes the suburbia debate as separating the private and domestic from the political realities of working life, as fragmenting and atomizing social relations which might otherwise be solid and supportive of collective rights. The suburbia argument is couched in apolitical terms which lull all parties into the comfortable belief that *this* is the real world, not the world of the workplace and the marketplace. The ideology of suburbia, in both its positive and negative forms, is an ideology of self-serving conservatism.

This ideology has much in common with what Aitkin reminds us was called 'countrymindedness' in the late 1920s and early 1930s [1988: 51], a slogan which he characterizes as a 'tribal chant' of the Country (now, significantly, National) Party, an ideological stance firmly focused upon the political. But Aitkin thinks that this ideology is 'finished,' dead, and indeed it may well be, if it is to be seen as merely the political perspective of a rapidly dwindling sectional minority. But what I have tried to show is that 'country-mindedness' lives on, not as a narrow party political slogan, but as the cornerstone of a nationalist ideology, at once atavistic and forward-looking, sanctified by both tradition and progress. 'Suburbanism' too lives on, again not as a party political platform, not even as a clearly formulated ideology, but rather as the taken-for-granted preferred mode of existence for millions of ordinary Australians.

For mythologies of everyday life form the bedrock of widespread understandings of national identity in any social formation. The intersubjective construction of styles of life and the conduct of social relations as expressing distinction, status, class membership or ethnic affiliation is instrumental in creating and sustaining currently hegemonic conceptions and practices of what it is to be an Australian. It is in everyday patterns of existence, in what Bourdieu [1990: 131] calls 'the habitus, the mental structures through which they apprehend the social world', that people construct their understandings of the world they inhabit. And, as Bourdieu is quick to insist [ibid.: 130]: 'No doubt agents do have an active apprehension of the world. No doubt they do construct their vision of the world. But this construction is carried out under structural constraints'. It is these constraints (manipulated to a greater or lesser extent by the ideological state apparatuses, particularly the mass media) that so greatly influence the meanings Australians attach to their dwelling places. And it is the mythology of the pastoral, encompassing both history and legend, which most profoundly undergirds those dominant and highly conservative ideologies of hearth and home, family life, probity, self-respect and social esteem which find expression in the Australian house and garden.

Even in the inner city, the site of artifice and legerdemain, the rural homestead is quoted, however tenuously, in the seeking of spaciousness and natural light, in the cultivation and taming of nature in street plantings and parks and indoor plants. But this homage to the pastoral idyll finds its apotheosis in the suburban villa. Here, in 'bushland settings' and 'farmhouse kitchens', the idealized Australian family is encouraged to enact – in so far as its circumstances, both material and spiritual, permit – the Australian dream of private property ownership and egalitarian social relations, the best of both worlds.

Notes

1. The exception to the charge of elitism is to be discerned in the case of champion athletes, or 'elite sportspeople' as they are often called. Global economic competition has its counterpart in global athletic contests – Olympic Games, World Championships and lesser events like the Commonwealth, Asian or Pan-Pacific Games. The financial impact of these events is immense (in television rights and perceived tourism benefits, for instance) particularly when coupled with the 'professionalization' of sport, and, on an individual plane, with product endorsements and commercial sponsorships. The concatenation of individual athletic prowess and objectively measureable achievements of individuals has the effect of ratifying success on behalf of all those who share a common national identity with their hero. But more than this, the successes of individual athletes and whole sporting teams are now understood as a global (cultural and commercial) phenomenon, with, for example, Australian youth being avid supporters of US football teams or basketball players and of their perceived styles of life.
2. In this, as in so much else, white Australia is at odds with black Australia. The concept of partnership with a nurturant land is not one which sits easily with the thinking of those who would expropriate its riches for capital gain.
3. And not only for home buyers. Hoskins makes the point that urban social reformers before the Great War thought so too, and brought their theories to bear in the formation of 'garden suburbs' like Daceyville in Sydney. 'Within the discourse of this period, the "model" or "garden" suburb became the idealized material spatial form, while assuming a metonymic place in ideological representations of identity. . .the ideology of the modern suburb became

indelibly linked to an Australian identity' [1994: 4].

4. Veblen's 1899 classic, *The Theory of the Leisure Class*, one of the most swingeing critiques of the styles of the *nouveau riche* remains apposite today: the legitimation of social and financial power through the establishment of a pecuniary culture and pecuniary canons of taste, displayed through conspicuous consumption and conspicuous leisure, is as much a feature of late twentieth century Australian society as it was of late nineteenth century America – though there are, of course, important differences. As C. Wright Mills remarked succinctly, in his preface to the 1953 edition of Veblen's work, 'Prestige buttresses power, turning it into authority and protecting it from social challenge' [1970: xvi]. That is, prestige *legitimizes* power.
5. Christopher Lasch's *Haven in a Heartless World* [1977] is probably one of the better known statements of the role of the family in the protection and nurturance of the human psyche, much as it is counterbalanced by works such as Kerreen Reiger's *The Disenchantment of the Home* [1985] and other feminist critiques, such as David's [1980]. But it is popular women's magazines, and not only those directed at imaginary archetypal 'housewives', which most vigorously foster the image of the home as statement of self and of the family's social status. I have drawn extensively on these magazines and their close relatives, the interior decorating magazines, in adducing evidence for many of the points made here.
6. This is so even when the country wife does not engage in income-producing work outside the farm, either as an employee or the proprietor of a small business. In good times, her income is most usually used to pay for extras and luxuries. It is only in increasingly frequent bad times that the family may become totally dependent on her earnings.
7. Journals like *Country Style* constantly promote a nostalgic image of rurality which centres upon age and solidity: antiques, quilts, solid fuel stoves and so on. There is a parallel to be found with the vogue for the 'Aga-Saga', novels eulogizing English village life in the 1990s. All of these present 'country style' as quintessentially warm, welcoming and hospitable, a boon to advertisers of farm holidays and rural 'inns' or 'convention centres.'
8. The cost of fencing can be exorbitant. It ranged, at a time when the average weekly wage was $490, from around $45 per metre for simple metal fencing to $500 plus per metre for stone walling. Even the household boundaries can be used to suggest the social status and pecuniary rank of the members of the household behind the fence.
9. Of his proposals for the suburb which was to be named for him, New South Wales' first Labor Colonial Secretary, J.R. Dacey declared in 1912 that 'The day is past when free Australians were content to be

herded together in terraces of mere dog boxes. In some of the suburbs they are compelled to herd together like flies, and the time has come when we should create a garden city' [cited in Hoskins, 1994: 7].

10. Cf. Corrigan's fellow Melbourne architect Epaminondas Katsilidis' statement: 'Suburbia is neither city nor country. It's terrible, vacuous, isolated, awful lack of information and interaction; suburbia is based on real estate and the construction industry'. [*Good Weekend* 3/6/95: 28]
11. I do not address here the housing styles and control of dwelling space permitted to the poor in Australian society. My concern is to delineate the *preferred* styles of social elites and of those who would emulate them.

CHAPTER SIX

Power, Knowledge, Practice: Common Sense and Received Wisdom

> When our elders, the castes who live by delegation,
> turned in, like unlicensed guns, imagination,
> thoughts, spirits, ideals to the all-wise University
> there were aspects of learning they did not foresee
> like being called The Masses, Funny Little Men
> who live in the suburbs and resemble Eichmann.
>
> Academe is the class struggle, and whatever side
> prevails will be hers.
>
> Les Murray, *Sidere Mens Eadem Mutato* [1991 [1974]: 114]

Serious discussions of class, status and party, of material wealth, social distinction and political power and their interconnections, are fraught with peril in pragmatic, egalitarian societies like Australia. Accusations of elitism, snobbery and affectation abound, along with heated disputes concerning the degree to which individuals may actually be said to deserve the material advantages they have amassed. Even more dangerous, however, are analyses of *non-material* distinction which, being not amenable to quantitative measurement, is popularly understood to be (a) trivial, and (b) a matter of mere taste or opinion. Nowhere is this more true than in the arenas of commonsense knowledge and expert knowledge and the relations between the two in contemporary egalitarian society. For, as Hobbes long ago [1651] observed in his *Leviathan*,

> Nature hath made men so equall, in the faculties of body, and mind; as that though there bee found one man sometimes manifestly stronger in body, or of quicker mind than another; yet when all is reckoned

> together, the difference between man, and man, is not so considerable, as that one man can thereupon claim to himselfe any benefit, to which another may not pretend, as well as he. For as to the strength of body, the weakest has strength enough to kill the strongest, either by secret machination, or by confederacy with others, that are in the same danger with himselfe. [. . .]
>
> For such is the nature of men, that howsoever they may acknowledge many others to be more witty, or more eloquent, or more learned; Yet they will hardly believe there be many so wise as themselves: For they see their own wit at hand, and other mens at a distance. But this proveth rather that men are in that point equall, than unequall. For there is not ordinarily a greater signe of the equall distribution of any thing, than that every man is contented with his share. [1970: 63]

I quote Hobbes at some length because his characterization of human equality is very close to the meanings constructed in Australian cultural practice, most particularly in the fields of education and intellectual endeavour. The concept of equality of opportunity, enshrined in educational policy, is premised upon this understanding that everyone has the capacity to achieve, with time and application, the same learning as everyone else. Common sense, being equally available to all through experience, is thought to be equally distributed in fact. But expert knowledge is the result of one person's voluntarily choosing to spend greater time and effort on some specialized field which may or may not have practical relevance in everyday life. Thus the social role and political influence of the intelligentsia of the academy is, in general, of peripheral interest and value to others outside it. But the activities of those whose expert knowledge can be seen to have material benefit for the society at large – those whom Gouldner [1979] termed the technical intelligentsia, and those 'experts' whose services are sought and paid for by non-experts in that one field – these can be seen as of vital concern to the prosecution of everyday affairs, and as such deserving of respect and admiration.

Indeed, the very terms, intelligentsia and intellectuals, produce a nervous *frisson* amongst the materialist and pragmatic members of a cultural milieu which still fosters the belief that the academy is an ivory tower remote from 'the real world' of industry and commerce and getting a living. Those who in other cultures might be respected as gurus or scholars are derided as pundits or boffins or, most pejoratively, academics, whose scale of values is gravely distorted and, worse, whose labours, financed by the taxpayer, cannot be turned to the immediate and visible economic benefit of the common weal.

'If men,' proclaimed W.I. Thomas in 1928, 'define situations as real, they are real in their consequences.' This maxim, a fundamental tenet of both symbolic interactionism and ethnomethodology, echoes, if perhaps in a more positive tone, Hume's aphorism: 'We are no sooner acquainted with the impossibility of satisfying any desire than the desire itself vanishes' [cited in Bourdieu, 1977: 77]. And,

> The moment we perceive the falsehood of any supposition, or the insufficiency of any means, our passions yield to our reason without any opposition. I may desire any fruit as of an excellent relish; but whenever you convince me of my mistake, my longing ceases. [Hume, 1911: 128]

Engaging in their simplicity and commonsense, these assertions may be interpreted in either an optimistic or a pessimistic light, depending on where one stands in relation to the definition of the situation of reality or impossibility or mistake. And this is why they are so fraught with problems for the social scientist that, in the end, they become little more than quietist '*che sera, sera*' justifications of the status quo, accepting all, explaining nothing. In this, as with Hobbes, they are deeply ideological. For what they assume is that it is equal individuals in face-to-face interaction who make things happen, while ignoring the fact that these same individuals bring to any context of social interaction a vast array of meanings and understandings, possibilities and constraints, the product of past experiences, any of which may or may not be shared with the interacting Other. Further, and even more significantly, they fail to take account of the social structures within which even the slightest of everyday interactions takes place and which themselves structure those very interactions.

The most obvious of these structures are those which designate relations of power and authority in any particular historical social formation, for it is the power to define situations as 'real', to deny 'possibility' or convince of mistakenness, which, tacitly understood as modifying or qualifying these statements, lends them their initial force and plausibility. It is characteristic of naive individualism to conceive of power in interpersonal relations as a property of individual persons, any one of whom may 'possess' more or less of it than any other. While some social interactionists [e.g. Blau, 1964] have recognized that power is an 'emergent property' of social situations and social relations, they have not in general gone so far as to embrace the kind of structuralist analysis which recognizes the structures of power as determinant of the relative strengths and weaknesses of social interactants.

On the other hand, as critiques of the works of structuralists like Althusser or Lévi-Strauss have demonstrated, the over-determinacy which is a feature of the most stark structuralisms leaves little space for the kinds of human agency which the symbolic interactionists and ethnomethodologists sought to present as central to the outcomes of human negotiations and the social order itself. Structuralism is charged with the denial of free will in the same way as interactionist analyses are accused of blindness to the social.[1]

What is required for an analysis of the cultural role of intellectual elites in egalitarian society is a theoretical approach which utilizes the insights of structuralism without succumbing to its determinist and defeatist implications. Such an orientation may allow for the explication of on the one hand, the ways in which the ideas of the ruling class are maintained as the ruling ideas and existing relations of production reproduced [Althusser, 1971], and on the other the ways in which these ideas are also and at the same time modified, displaced, resisted and even transformed. Despite the pointers to deconstruction (of the discursive practices of everyday life) and a continuing goal of de-mystifying structures of power, this is not really a post-structuralist position. Rather, it is one that engages a somewhat older sociological tradition, deriving from Weber but articulated most famously by Mannheim in *Ideology and Utopia* [1968; first published in England in 1936] and lately somewhat neglected in cultural analysis – the sociology of knowledge.

While the post-structuralist analytic framework allows for an escape from the essentially pessimistic positivism (or what some call scientism) of structuralism, it retains the parent theory's ahistorical and anti-humanist perspectives, as Milner [1991: 76] points out. But this need not necessarily be the case, especially if it is borne in mind that the vitality and fruitfulness of any theory rests in its power as an analytic tool. Theorizing for the sake of theorizing has tended of late in the social sciences (and the humanities) to produce little more than critiques of the critics, without maintaining a focus on the phenomena to be explained and analysed. Hence the charges of theoreticism and scientism. If theory cannot perform its function as an analytic tool, it degenerates into the very kinds of mystificatory babble that the original theorizers sought to dispel: an unceasing round of ultimately sterile disputes about what Derrida, or Foucault, or Althusser, or Marx *really* meant.

Mannheim's concern to explore the possibilities of a science of politics produced the recognition that the driving force of democratic political action springs from the interests and values of opposed social classes. Those who articulate these interests and values are rarely, however, those who are active in the political process. Rather, they are conceived of as being above the battle, detached from the immediacy of everyday class struggles and attached instead to a rationalist, 'scientific' and holistic mode of thought.

> Such an experimental outlook, unceasingly sensitive to the dynamic nature of society and to its wholeness, is not likely to be developed by a class occupying a middle position but only by a relatively classless stratum which is not too firmly situated in the social order. . .. This unanchored, *relatively* classless stratum is. . .the 'socially unattached intelligentsia' [Mannheim, 1968: 137]

or, in Alfred Weber's famous phrase, from which Mannheim borrowed, the 'free-floating intelligentsia' (*freischwebende Intelligenz*). This socially unattached position produces, according to Mannheim, a dilemma for intellectuals, who are conceived of as engaged in 'endless wavering'. They have taken, he suggests, one of two ways out of this dilemma. The first has been through their largely voluntary attachment to 'one or the other of the various antagonistic classes' – usually, 'the class in need of intellectual development'. The second, less frequently observed, consists in 'scrutiny of their own social moorings and the quest for the fulfilment of their mission as the predestined advocate of the intellectual interests of the whole' [1968: 140].

While 'endless wavering' almost exactly describes Australian understandings of the activities of academics and those few intellectuals who, in Australia, are not attached to the academy, it also describes that set of attitudes which are generally characterized as tolerance for other points of view. But as Barrington Moore [in

Wolff et al., 1969] points out in a famous essay, tolerance is too often the mask of indifference for this kind of dismissal of the intellectual world (or any other unfamiliar world) to be taken on trust. It is when the socially oriented activities and the socially critical products of intellectuals begin to be felt in arenas beyond the academy that derision or bemusement becomes suspicion and even open hostility.[2]

Attachment to the political interests and values of the working class, or more specifically to the concerns of relatively powerless social groups, is fraught with difficulty for intellectuals who in Australia are still largely drawn from the liberal bourgeoisie or have been co-opted into it. Not only are the objects of their attempts to support the oppressed wary of them as patronizing aliens, but so are those in government, business or in education itself who see such support as a kind of *trahison des clercs* and a possible threat to the ideological bases of their own power.

At first sight it would seem that Gramsci's [1971] argument for the formation of an intelligentsia which is organic to its class (i.e. to the peasantry and working class, for he was in agreement with Mannheim that this was the class most 'in need of intellectual development') provides a way in which a hitherto subordinate class might produce and succour its 'own' understandings of the world, understandings which might then be turned to the political benefit of powerless groups:

> The mass of the peasantry, although it performs an essential function in the world of production, does not elaborate its own 'organic' intellectuals, nor does it 'assimilate' any stratum of 'traditional' intellectuals, although it is from the peasantry that many other social groups draw many of their intellectuals. ... [1971: 6]

Australian egalitarians would be in fundamental agreement with Gramsci's statement that 'All men are intellectuals. . .but not all men have in society the function of intellectuals' [ibid.: 9], though they might not take to his homely example: 'Thus, because it can happen that everyone at some time fries a couple of eggs or sews up a tear in a jacket, we do not necessarily say that everyone is a cook or a tailor' [ibid.: 9f.]. At any rate, they would agree that *Homo faber* cannot be separated from *Homo sapiens*. Recent changes in the Australian education system as a whole bear witness to the general agreement (with important modifications concerning the changing nature of industrial and technological practice) at all levels of society that 'In the modern world, technical education, closely bound to industrial labour even at the most primitive and unqualified level, must form the basis of the new type of intellectual' [1971: 9].

It should be clear, however, that both Mannheim and Gramsci in their different ways idealized the intelligentsia as, at least potentially, a coherent and a highly influential group *in its own right*. That is to say, Mannheim's relative classlessness and Gramsci's organicism both underplay, though they do not ignore, what Mannheim called the specific class backgrounds of the currently active intelligentsia. These are conceived of by both writers as capable of being overcome or turned to account through the processes of education, as if these very processes themselves were not deeply implicated in the production, maintenance and the reproduction of the structures of class power. Thus Mannheim's second route out of the intellectuals' dilemma, the mission of the advocacy of 'the intellectual interests of the whole', runs aground on the shoals of defining what, if anything, answers to the intellectual (or any other) interests of 'the whole,' of assuming agreement among the intellectuals, and even, in class society, of reaching a coherent view about what that whole might be.

For the intellectuals are not as socially unattached, nor as altruistic, as Mannheim had hoped. Nor are they so averse to the comforts and privileges of the academy and the liberal professions in bourgeois society as Gramsci wished. Indeed, rather than forming a separate and powerful stratum, let alone a class, in their own right, the intellectuals of the twentieth century, in Australia as elsewhere, have become increasingly enmeshed in the moral and political projects of either the revolutionary left or the radical right. That is, when they have not become enthusiastic and unquestioning promoters of consensual political and social thought.

Theories about the formation of a New Class of intellectuals (and its project) have been advanced since the nineteenth century. Bakunin envisaged a ruling class with a monopoly of knowledge, forming governments which administered the masses not only politically, but also economically:

> It will be the reign of *scientific intelligence*, the most aristocratic, despotic, arrogant and contemptuous of all regimes. There will be a new class, a new hierarchy of real and pretended scientists and scholars,

> and the world will be divided into a minority ruling in the name of knowledge and an immense ignorant majority. [1966: 87]

Szelenyi and Martin [1988] characterize the earlier theories of the new class (Bakunin, Mannheim) as being most concerned with agency and with proposing the rise of an intellectual class, while ignoring the structural position of the intellectuals as a group. The second wave of such theories (Burnham, Veblen) in the mid twentieth century promulgated a bureaucratic, managerialist and technocratic ruling class assured of a strong position within governing structures, but was little concerned with the types of knowledge that such a new class would monopolize. The third group of new class theories, advanced in the 1980s, of which Konrad and Szelenyi's [1979] work and that of Gouldner [1979] are taken to be representative, pays close attention to the types of knowledge monopolized by what Szelenyi and Martin call the 'knowledge class', while remaining weak in its structural position.

Gouldner's theory suggests the rise of two fractions within what he calls the 'new class' – the intellectuals, and the technical intelligentsia. The former are the old-style 'humanistic' intellectuals, the latter the managerial, administrative and scientific personnel of business, government and the institutions of higher education. Both fractions subscribe to what Gouldner calls a 'culture of critical discourse', a speech community whose expansion has been coterminous with increased access to education in Western societies since the French Revolution.

Szelenyi and Martin suggest that the intellectuals of the late twentieth century could achieve greater power for 'the knowledge class' through bureaucratization, thus achieving the structural position they currently lack, but at the price of endangering their current privileges of academic freedom. They pose the following question, and suggest a possible answer:

> Would the intellectuals and the highly educated knowingly and willingly forgo these privileges just to exercise [political and economic] power? [. . .] Intellectuals, by resisting the temptation of class power may actually gain a different type of power, namely 'symbolic domination'. [1988: 664]

Utilizing Gouldner's distinction between intellectuals and the technical intelligentsia, and noting that in Australia the latter are already held in high regard, one must concede that at least the technical fraction of the nascent 'new class' is well advanced along the road to political power in late capitalist societies like Australia. Furthermore, consequent upon changes in industrial production and managerial style, reforms in education over the last decade have produced the kind of situation in which the Australian technical intelligentsia may be seen to be attaining political and economic power, as well as symbolic power, through being co-opted by, and co-opting, the old dominant class and its structural position.

Althusser's [1971] description of education as the dominant ideological state apparatus of the twentieth century provides a starting point for the analysis of how this situation has come about. Australian history and everyday discourse attest to Australians' pragmatic and materialist respect for the exemplars of successful capital accumulation, whether 'legitimate' or otherwise. Conversely, the mistrust of those who fail to produce material goods and practical services – philosophers, scholars and teachers, theologues, artists, writers, critics and politicians – is deeply rooted. Even teachers are fond of quoting Shaw's aphorism, 'those who can, do; those who can't, teach.' At the same time, the mistrust of bureaucrats, generated from the settlement of the Australian penal colonies at the end of the eighteenth century, is constantly directed 'out there,' as if those who do the mistrusting are not also those who are mistrusted. This is particularly clear in a context in which roughly one in five employed adults can be classed as public servants, and many more as being engaged in those professions and occupations which plan, administer and execute 'services' to the nation; that is, all those who maintain and benefit from and legitimate the capitalist hegemony, whether by force or ideology. These are the 'deputies' of the ruling class who in Gramsci's terms mediate, and exercise the subaltern functions of, social hegemony and state domination [see 1971: 12–13]. They are the active functionaries who make Althusser's ideological state apparatuses work.

Hegemonic Common Sense, Expert Advice and Legitimation

A democratic welfare state like Australia operates at least as much to serve the state itself as it does to serve the people. It is in the interest of that state and of its ruling class to ensure that all citizens are provided with the basic minimum necessary to sustain and reproduce existence, to ensure the maintenance of economic stability and social order, and to protect and maintain the legitimacy of the form of government. Moreover, maintaining the legitimacy of the form and personnel of government is not only dependent upon the provision of material benefits for a needy population, it also depends crucially on winning the hearts and minds of those who might otherwise begin to question legitimacy and subvert authority. It is in this arena that the ideological state apparatuses are required to exercise their powers in the production of that cultural capital which defines certain kinds of knowledges and meanings as correct, just and appropriate and others as mistaken or dangerously seditious.

Here, it is the discursive practices of ruling groups which achieve hegemony (though not without difficulty in a liberal democracy). For the later nineteenth century, and for most of the twentieth in Australia, that hegemony has been little threatened by opposed traditions and practices. The advent of mass schooling in the 1870s, the enactment of progressive welfare legislation, the long economic boom of the mid-twentieth century, the taming of the mass media, have all combined (notwithstanding honourable exceptions) with the ideology of egalitarian individualism to suppress dissent rather than encourage critical reflection. For the culture of the intellectuals and the technical intelligentsia (Gouldner's culture of critical discourse), where it does not produce quietism and withdrawal from public affairs, may be turned *either* to a radical critique of the socio-economic context in which it is embedded *or* to an expert apologia for the status quo.

It is the third of these alternatives I address here. As mediators of the ruling ideas of the ruling group, it is those highly educated and trained 'experts' – teachers, social workers, psychologists, economists and health workers – who convert their expert knowledge into common sense and continually re-establish the material and ideological domination of the capitalist class. Nowhere is this more evident than in the control and management of the family. As Engels long ago recognized, the holy family is a central icon of capitalism, condensing within itself highly specific understandings of power and authority, private property and inheritance, duty and affection.[3] The ideal family in capitalism is the microcosm of the ideal capitalist State.

Case 6. Expert Advice and the Management of the Family

Of all the public exponents of correct family practice in the welfare state, social workers play a pivotal role not only through the operation of powerful regulatory bureaucracies dealing with the societal problems of age, illness, crime and poverty, but also, and more extensively, through their professional control over definitions of economic morality under capitalism. In this they are ably supported by the mass media, with its voracious appetite for 'human interest' stories.

In May 1987 *The* (Adelaide) *Advertiser* published a front-page description of the plight of a young woman, her husband and five children under the age of seven, who were having difficulty managing their existence on welfare.The first public responses to this story were sympathetic. The family was offered food, child care and money by individuals; others wrote to the paper (May 5):

> It really must be a nightmare for those parents to live. . .seeing their children like that.
>
> What an innately selfish and insensitive society we are.
>
> What have we become? What should we all be doing?

The next day saw a change in tone:

> Ann M's letter. . .made me so furious I just had to write. . .. What the hell is wrong with you if you can't feed and clothe your children on $160 a week? [. . .] I draw only $145 *from the business* to feed and clothe my husband, myself and our three children. . .. I am in a position where I could offer you a job. . .. However I do not feel inclined to offer it to you, for I know from past experience that people who cannot make the best of what they've got. . .are not good workers either. [my emphasis]
>
> I am sick and tired of reading stories about *so-called families* trapped in a life of poverty. [. . .] Go to the Riverland and pick grapes and oranges. [my emphasis]

And on May 7:

> [The children] should be taken away from their mother. . .. They have been brought into this world without any thought by their parents as

> to their future. . .. By the standard she has *chosen* for herself and her children she has condemned them to the bottom rung of society, forever. [my emphasis]
>
> A welfare officer should investigate this utter lack of *basic family management*. . .. I have less income with four children but with two loan commitments from a failed business. . .and my family have all [necessities]. [my emphasis]

Eleven of the fifteen published letters to the editor were severely condemnatory. None was from a person or body professionally involved with social welfare provision, and this is significant, demonstrating the hegemony of ruling-class views of individual responsibility for moral and financial defeat or victory, and God-helps-those-who-help-themselves among the 'respectable' poor. The moral justification of welfare provision in Australia rests squarely upon notions of 'the deserving poor', harking back to the Elizabethan Poor Law and the Speenhamland system. 'Innocent victims' – political (but not economic) refugees, haemophiliac (but not homosexual) AIDS sufferers, for example – are readily accorded support, sympathy and sustenance. The children of the poor and those who have fallen on hard times through the injury or death of a wage-earner are seen as deserving assistance, but not feckless youth or idle vagrants. Moreover, it is not only the poor who are placed in the position of depending upon the state for confirmation of the righteousness of their family practice. The mass media are replete with journals which give advice on the care and raising of children, and adult education classes on parent effectiveness training are readily available. While much of this advice concerns everyday questions about sleeping hours, dietary habits, illness and disease, much is also concerned with moral judgements of manners and morals.

The expert advice circulated in the child-rearing manuals and magazines is almost invariably proffered by trained experts – paediatricians, psychologists – who are also 'ordinary parents'. *The Australian Women's Weekly*'s resident expert, 'The Toddler Tamer', in May 1987 was Dr Christopher Green, Head of Child Development at the Children's Hospital, Camperdown. His rather mealy-mouthed discussion of 'Nasty Habits of Nice Children' mentions bad language ('possibly an older child might need cautioning or Dad should return to finishing school'); masturbation ('playing with the "naughty bits"); nail-biting and people-biting; head-banging and nose-picking; 'fighting, whingeing [complaining], lying, stealing, thumb-sucking, breath-holding and. . .vomiting on demand' – some of which might be seen as rather 'nastier' habits than others.

In March 1987, the Toddler Tamer's views on 'Bonding: The Tie That Binds' [p.231] included the following homily:

> I can't help thinking that there would be fewer marriage bust-ups and disturbed children if parents were to make a solid commitment to give of their best and see it through. This happy-go-lucky feeling that you can walk away from a situation which you no longer fancy is a major contributory cause to family disintegration and the traumas that brings.

Such a seemingly commonsensical observation is given heightened authority by the writer's medical qualifications, the suggestion of underlying specialist research knowledge ('a major contributory cause') and the magisterial resonance of phrases like 'give of their best and see it through,' reminiscent of school teachers' admonitions to pupils falling by the moral wayside. In such ways does expert knowledge in diverse fields give added force to the everyday discursive practices of dominant groups, producing their meanings and understandings as pragmatically efficacious and morally proper.

The earnest liberal and humane intent of many of Australia's experts in what are called 'the helping professions' (and the widespread appellation 'professional' is indicative of increasing status and influence) is continually subverted by the moral economy of capital accumulation. Economic and technocratic pressures to ensure budgetary prudence and individual responsibility for problems which are socially generated undermines egalitarian and humane sympathies. Possessive individualism and the public upholding of private property and freedom of choice as moral and civic rights and duties both underlie the morality of social welfare. In blaming the victim, the individualist nature of Australian egalitarianism is made abundantly clear.

But at the same time, individualism is placed under threat by those very economic and technocratic pressures which deny equitable treatment in the field of social welfare. In the name of egalitarianism, individuals are besought to repress any thought of personal benefit in deference to the common weal. Where real economic benefit might accrue from the actions of individuals, the agents of capital – listed companies, entrepreneurs, the state itself – are quick to intervene.

A case in point is the practice in institutions of higher education of designating the products of scholarship (ideally disinterested) as the 'intellectual property' of the university or the employing institution of the scholar concerned. This is part of a wider strategy to draw educational institutions into a competitive commercial and industrial marketplace in what the state designates as 'the national interest' [see especially the Commonwealth of Australia's Schools Commission's 1987 document, *In the National Interest: Secondary Education and Youth Policy in Australia*].

Case 7. Higher Education and the National Interest

The following statements and phrases are drawn from an 'intellectual property policy' document produced by one Australian university in 1989, and much revised since to excise loopholes. What is most notable about them is the way in which they express the intense commoditization of knowledge which has taken place over the decades since the Second World War. In Australia, this has meant the formation of numerous institutions of higher education and their subsequent amalgamations and mergers to form a 'unified national system' of universities, and the expansion of their interests to include subjects and disciplines originally beyond their purview and control (such as journalism, nursing, business management, and hospitality and tourism). In this process, the state, which funds the universities, may be seen as exercizing a new intellectual dominance with the help of those intellectuals and academic bureaucrats who have chosen to throw in their lot with the projects of business, industry and a transnational economic order:

> [The University and its entrepreneurial arm] have jointly incorporated a company. . .to develop commercially the intellectual property of the University. A 'Joint Venture Agreement'. . .sets out the terms under which the parties have agreed to establish [the company.] An agreement contains terms and conditions under which [the company] may obtain

> and commercialize technology invented or developed by employees, students or visitors of the University. [The company] has first right to intellectual property which the University wishes to commercialize.
>
> The University Council has adopted guidelines for University employees, students and visitors for dealing with the University's intellectual property so that the benefits to all parties can be optimized through the University's relationship with [the company.] The guidelines aim to provide equitable returns to the creators of intellectual property, both as an incentive and reward. This policy statement sets out the understanding reached between the University and [the company] on the disbursement of proceeds from commercial development.

The language here is redolent of the commercial firm. One notes such words and phrases as jointly incorporated company, develop commercially, joint venture agreement, property, commercialize, optimizing benefits, equitable returns, incentive and reward, disbursement of proceeds and commercial development. What is particularly significant is that the scholars of the university are referred to as 'employees, students and visitors'. This is to say that the paid academics, or professional intellectuals, are no longer to be thought of as being in a collegial relation to the administrative officers of the University, but rather as those who sell their labour – to whom?

To 'the university.' But who is the university? Since, given these commercial developments, the university can no longer be thought of (even ideally) as a diversity of scholars engaged in a common pursuit, one is forced to conclude that the employers of intellectuals are not the people or the nation, but the state itself: the university becomes the research and development department of an economic enterprise called 'the national interest'. The relationship between administrators and scholars is reconstituted as a relationship between managers and employees, and the common pursuit of scholars becomes focused on the creation of (commercially viable) intellectual property. The document goes on to detail the university council's directive

> to maximize the benefit of [the University's] intellectual and physical resources and more particularly to exploit to the full mutually beneficial interactions with Australian commerce, industry and government.

Academics are reminded that

> Under common law and in its contract of employment the University is the owner of the intellectual property developed in the field of a staff member's duties.

A later clarification by the Vice-Chancellor (one of a powerful group often referred to in significantly commercial terms as the chief executive officer or CEO) covers 'the difficult issue' of assigning copyright to publishers:

> Such assignment would obviously make it difficult for the University to benefit in any commercial way from that intellectual property [i.e. publications] should it wish to do so in the future. It would be prudent, therefore, for University staff to consider the consequences for the University before making such assignment.

Such prudence includes a direction to academic staff to approach the commercial company for

> an evaluation of both the potential market value of intellectual property and possible strategies for its further development, including co-ordination with academic priorities such as publication.

It is clear that contemporary universities have a number of equally important 'priorities' to consider and that the academic pursuits of the university – research, teaching and the dissemination of knowledge – form only one part of many such priorities. The bureaucratizing of higher education and commoditization of knowledge has advanced to the extent that Szelenyi and Martin's 'knowledge class' (Gouldner's 'cultural bourgeoisie'), that is, the owners and the controllers of intellectual production, seem close to achieving the structural position in Australian society which they formerly lacked. The intellectual interests of the whole, to use Mannheim's phrase, become coterminous with those of the state, and the intellectuals become organic ruling class members. But not yet, it should be noted, the dominant fraction of that class, for they remain in the situation of subalterns and agents of the capitalist state, supporting, ideologizing and legitimating its hegemony, but not in control of it.

The National Interest and Invisible Ideology

In a social formation characterized by the constantly reiterated need for consensus and accord 'in the national interest' – actually, the economic interest of the State – education is increasingly moulded to the service of that interest. The technocratic imperative elevates job-training, 'skills formation' and the generation of 'a productive culture' as the highest educational goals, while the advancement of learning and disinterested scholarship become relegated to the ranks of the self-indulgent luxuries of individuals, or the leisure class. These are luxuries which, it is claimed, 'the nation' cannot afford.

What I want to argue here is that, while the Australian state cannot indeed 'afford', for ideological reasons, to support and encourage informed debate about and critique of its policies and practices, it is essential that the people do so engage for the protection of their liberties and for the advancement of 'the public culture.' An analysis of the hegemonic discourse of the state provides an avenue to understanding some of the ways in which competing discourses have been subverted with increasing effectiveness over the last two decades.

The 1980s in Australia witnessed the parallel development of two seemingly contradictory movements: the deregulation of collective economic affairs, and the closer regulation of personal and private lives. Such a contradiction is only apparent; in fact, each movement is predicated upon and supports the other, and both spring from the elimination of the distance between Self and Other, generative of what Lefort [1986] calls a new, and invisible, ideology. Governmental deregulation touches upon a wide range of everyday activities which affect the lives of all citizens. Banking, the mass media and foreign ownership of nationally important economic assets have been opened up to 'the free play of the market'. At the same time, privatization and 'freedom of choice' have become benchmarks of quality in fields as diverse as health, education and the welfare of the elderly or infirm, the latter legitimized in terms of returning old, handicapped or disabled people to the family and the 'community' (often called 'mainstreaming') in preference to incarceration in specially designed, equipped and staffed institutions.

Yet the regulation of personal affairs has gone on apace.[4] There has been increased though much contested acceptance of state control of the body and physical reality, particularly in relation to the tragedy of AIDS, the degradation of the natural environment, health and safety regulations in the workplace, and the physical fitness of the general populace, as evidenced by 'community announcements' concerning heart disease, breast cancer, tobacco smoking, diet and exercise in the mass media. Social relations too have become more closely regulated, especially those which bear on gender relations, questions of race and ethnicity and child-rearing practices, all of which require an army of experts and bureaucrats engaged in the work of control and oversight.

These regulatory and deregulatory practices – centralization and bureaucratization on the one hand, privatization and freedom of choice on the other – come together in the state's education policies. The 'unified national system' of universities was the result of the Commonwealth government's moves in the 1980s to abolish the binary system of higher education which separated universities as centres of scholarship and research from colleges of advanced education as centres for vocational training in fields such as teaching and nursing. It is testimony to the power of an invisible ideology which becomes evermore dominant. What Lefort calls 'a new logic of dissimulation' is brought into play, a logic whereby 'public accountability' becomes state financial accounting. The so-called 'mission statements' required of universities are transmuted into productivity deals; knowledge and learning are confused with data and information and their 'processing'; and ideas circulate only in the conditions of the marketplace, to be exchanged for profit as the intellectual property of institutions.

The restructuring of higher education over the last decade has been premised, in Australia as elsewhere, on the attainment of greater economic payoffs for both individuals and collectivities from private and public investment in education. Two basic strategies may be discerned in the process of manufacturing popular consent to, and support for, the restructuring process: the 'accountability' of higher education to 'the taxpayer' (and a concomitant 'user pays' motif) and the correlation of higher education with successful economic competition. In a country like Australia, starting with a tiny proportion of university graduates, both strategies had enormous popular (and populist) appeal. It was made clear in the press and in the electronic media that graduates individually had greater access to employment, and well remunerated employment at that. It was also clear, from surveys and analyses of rather less interest to the general public, that there was a marked statistical correlation between the proportions of graduates in a country and that country's economic status and influence on the global stage.

But there is a contradiction here, and it is one that highlights the ambivalence of egalitarian individualism. The claim is made in parliaments, budget analyses, government reports and the mass media that the nation 'needs' more highly educated people in order to boost industrial and commercial productivity and ensure a recovery in its financial fortunes [see, for example, Finn, 1991; Carmichael, 1992]. On the other hand, the claim is made even more successfully that the only real beneficiaries of higher education are the graduates themselves. This country has long suffered a dearth of support for learning by business and industry and a paucity of disinterested philanthropic foundations. While the members of such groups, often addressed by governments as 'the community', are reluctant to invest in education on any but an individual basis, and while the state so drastically reduces its support for (but not its interest in or control over) education, individual students are being forced to pay for what is seen as both a privilege *and* a right. Indeed, there is much vociferous popular objection to the refusal to 'permit' potential (Australian) students to buy university places to which overseas students are assumed to have easy access.

The National Report on Australia's Higher Education Sector [Commonwealth of Australia, 1993] characterizes the development of the higher education system in the 1980s as 'a transition from an elite to a mass system. . .accompanied by a greater convergence of general and vocational education' [ibid.: 24]. As such, it was designed to woo popular support. The twin aims of participation and equity in post-compulsory education promulgated in 1983, and of efficiency and effectiveness in 1986, came together in the Minister for Employment, Education and Training's 1987 paper, *The Challenge for Higher Education for Australia*, as aims to

> (a) increase youth participation [in higher education] through steady and sustained growth;
> (b) improve the opportunities for participation. . .by disadvantaged groups [Aboriginal and Torres Strait Islanders, immigrants, low income groups, women and people with disabilities]; and
> (c) make higher education more responsive to the needs of industry [Commonwealth of Australia, 1987].

It has been the addition of this third objective which has most crucially affected higher education policies and practices since 1987.

The reductions in government funding of higher education have shifted funding responsibilities to students (especially foreign students – usually referred to as 'international' students – who pay 'full fees' and are seen, and often exploited, as a source of revenue for universities) and to individual academic staff, as consultants or as members of teams seeking to generate 'intellectual property' [see Slaughter and Leslie, 1995]. Among other results of this financial shift, common throughout the English-speaking world, have been a more clear-cut division between teaching and research in the universities and an enormous growth in what are usually referred to as 'senior administrative' posts. A perusal of university positions advertised in May/June and October/November 1990 gives some insight into the ways in which universities have expanded their offerings to attract a broader spectrum of students and have at the same time shifted away from the traditional ideals of a liberal education and the advancement of knowledge to 'servicing' labour-market demands for 'professional training'.

Table 1 Distribution of advertized posts in higher education, 1990

Field	%May/June	%Oct/Nov	% of total
Business	23.3	13.4	18.4
Administration and Management	15.0	19.8	17.4
Health	16.6	17.8	17.2
Technology	16.9	15.4	16.5
Science and Maths	8.5	19.1	13.8
Communications	10.5	10.4	10.5
Social Science	6.3	5.0	5.7
Other	2.9	1.2	2.1

[*Source*: The Australian Higher Education Supplement]

The categories I have used above are essentially arbitrary, employed to simplify a mass of complex data. Some posts were re-advertisements, some were advertised in more than one category and some specified a vague number of posts. The constituents of the categories included those with the largest numbers of teaching and/or research posts in the following fields:

Business: accountancy and finance, management, marketing;

Administration and management: university administration and support services; educational administration, social administration, human resource management, urban planning;

Health: medicine, medical research, nursing;

Technology: computing, computer education, engineering, design, information technology.

Science and mathematics: science and science education, mathematics and applied mathematics, agriculture and environmental science.

Communications: visual arts, music, education, languages.

The fields of commerce, science, administration, education, engineering and technology, nursing and health, and medicine and paramedicine produced a total of 75 percent of the advertised fields at this time. With the exception of science (and, for other reasons, administrative support), all are deeply embroiled in the training of practitioners rather than the education of scholars. In the sciences and in other heavily emphasized fields, many research positions are funded by interested enterprises beyond the academy, often in conjunction with specially designated industry scholarships, more highly paid than other postgraduate awards provided by the Commonwealth government.

Since 1990, these trends, established during a time of restructuring and amalgamation of institutions, have hardened into priorities. Applicants for university teaching posts at even fairly junior levels are required to have 'the ability to attract external research funding', to have industry experience or contacts, 'a proven record of administrative experience', and to be engaged in making 'contributions' to the wider community. At senior levels, administrative experience is frequently seen to be of equivalent value to research and publication. Indeed, one university held out for some time against a universal trend by reserving the title of Reader for those with research qualifications and the title of Associate Professor (at the same salary level) for those whose administrative contributions to the university could be seen to stand in lieu of academic achievement.[5]

With increasing financial pressure on the universities, the advertising of academic posts has slowed dramatically. The fields which now receive most attention are more than ever concerned with the management of commerce and industry and the administration of the institution's business, with a national average ratio of non-academic staff to academic of 1.2 [Department of Employment, Education and Training, Higher Education Division, 1994].

Table 2 Distribution of advertised posts in higher education, May 1995

Field	Number
Business (accounting, marketing, management, commerce)	24
Administration and academic support (librarians, counsellors)	12
Health and medicine	11
Engineering, industrial design	11
Science (including environmental studies, ecofeminism)	10+
Anthropology, cultural studies, Aboriginal studies	7
Humanities (languages, philosophy, communications)	6
Education (including human movement studies)	6
Social sciences (psychology, political science, social work)	6
Other (applied linguistics, leisure, textiles, computing)	4

[*Source*: The Australian, The Sydney Morning Herald]

The corporatizing and globalizing of intellectual production and the marketing approach taken to intellectual consumption within the universities is the result of a state-driven conflation of education and training. Like the secondary schools, universities are required by both the state and individual clients to provide a range of services which far exceeds their strictly educational brief, endeavouring to balance calls for access and equity for previously disadvantaged groups[6] with demands for efficiency and effectiveness in serving the state. Thus the Department of Employment, Education and Training, the significantly renamed Commonwealth Department of Education (in the late 1980s, now the Department of Employment, Education, Training and Youth Affairs) seeks to place students in fields which will train useful employees, while at the same time assisting students to obtain useful qualifications through a variety of policies and support services. This is a difficult task, as the two demands often cancel each other out.

Thus in terms of the Department's institutional 'performance' criteria,

> Often the value given to an institution's performance depends upon your reason for looking at the measure. For instance, if you are looking for efficiency you might view a high student-to-staff ratio positively. Alternatively if you are a student, it is likely you would view a low ratio positively.
>
> From a public finance perspective, the cost-effectiveness of institutions can be observed with reference to input costs, output efficiency and graduate outcomes. Quality [!] considerations also need to be factored in. Focusing on the teaching function it is evident that. . .the more cost-efficient institutions have higher than national average shares of part-time and/or external enrolments. Most of these have higher than average shares of non-school leaver commencers. Generally, those universities with upwards of 7.5 percent of enrolments in research degrees and those with medical schools have high input unit costs.
>
> Interestingly, in the context of discussion about educational value added, the universities with higher than national average equity group shares of enrolments are more input-cost efficient; the universities enrolling larger shares of students from more advantaged backgrounds, including high scoring school leavers, appear comparatively less efficient. They typically have a higher mix of enrolments by fields and levels of study.
>
> [. . .] Positive graduate outcomes, the sum of employment outcomes and continuing study, vary from a low of 57.8 percent at Ballarat University College to a high of 87.3 percent at the University of Queensland. The variability of outcomes partly reflects different regional labour market conditions and the missions of institutions in respect of postgraduate offerings. [Department of Employment, Education and Training, Higher Education Division, 1994: 7]

These figures seem to suggest very strongly that those institutions with an eye to access and equity will enrol a large proportion of students in undergraduate training courses (teaching; nursing) and humanities courses with 'low input costs.' Postgraduate students and medical students are drawn disproportionately from what the Department coyly refers to as 'more advantaged' backgrounds.

The Department is also much concerned to demonstrate its concern for gender equity in particular. Its document, *Diversity and Performance of Australian Universities* [1994], lists the percentage of female academic staff (national average 32.6) and of female academics above senior lecturer (national average 15.4). The national average percentage of female students is 53.4, of Aboriginal or Torres Strait Islander students 1.0, of students with rural or remote home addresses 21.1 and of students from non-English speaking backgrounds 13.0.

The Education and/or Training of the 'New Class'

It is in the schools and universities of late twentieth-century Australia that the ideologies and practices of egalitarian individualism are played out. It is in these institutions of education *and training* that an everyday 'real-world' devotion to technocratic pragmatism is converted into the high status and highly specialized study of technique and finds the credentials and the rewards of professional expertise. The attempt to combine demands for access and equity with the state's requirements for (economic) efficiency and effectiveness has produced not only the changing habitus of academic cultures in which managerialism dominates the structures *and contents* of 'the education industry', as it is regularly called.[7] It has also, in the higher education (or 'tertiary') sector, resulted in the pitting of departments, faculties and whole universities against each other in a commercially driven effort to attract students, research monies and public recognition.

The properly egalitarian push to open up higher education to the members of social groups hitherto unable to gain access to its perceived commercial benefits has, not surprisingly, drowned out the voices of critics, who are charged with elitism and who demur that higher education ought to involve the expansion of humane learning, the challenge of discovery, analysis and synthesis, and the advancement of knowledge. That students are required to pay fees for their degrees gives added impetus to the pragmatic line and is promoted as a triumph of egalitarian practice:

> [The Prime Minister], who described Australia's education and training system as the nation's 'great comparative advantage,' spelled out the achievements of the Higher Education Contribution Scheme. [. . .] HECS, he said, had allowed the system to grow at an 'extraordinary'

> rate since 1989. HECS revenue had been one of the major reasons behind the pace of expansion in higher education, with HECS underwriting about half of the $3 billion increase in total outlays on higher education since 1990. 'This means that 50 percent of the new places are here because of HECS revenue; up to 100,000 of today's students more than likely would have been doing something else.'
>
> From 1988 to 1993 the number of higher education students from the poorest of backgrounds had grown by around 30 percent.
>
> [. . .] 'The Government will not compromise access to post-compulsory education. . .. There is no such thing as 'free' education – somebody has to pay', Mr Keating said. 'In systems with no charges, those somebodies are all taxpayers. A "free" higher education system is one paid for by the taxes of all, the majority of whom haven't had the privilege of a university education'. [*The Australian* Higher Education Supplement, 17/5/95: 23]

All these efforts to grant the *right* of every adult to the erstwhile 'privilege' of higher education, and to demystify the nature of that education have had other unlooked-for consequences for the universities. The bureaucratization and increasing professionalization of university governance has opened up a rift between the administrative and research and teaching functions of the academy, with the result that the administrative arm is now commonly referred to, and refers to itself, as management. Industry-style hierarchies and hiring practices (non-tenurable posts, part-time and casual work) are rapidly replacing what were already fairly moribund understandings of collegiality. The proliferation of specialized courses to cater to public demand for 'vocational' training is nowhere more obvious than in what Bloom [1987: 371] called 'the great disaster' of degrees in business administration, wherein the study of economics is subordinated to the study of money, a 'perfect coincidence between science and cupidity'. It has crystallized old demands for personal relevance, which once included, at least in some of the humanities and social sciences, ideals focused on learning about contemporary social, political and cultural questions, with an eye to changing and improving the contexts and practices of everyday social life. This idealism has generally been leached out of undergraduate thinking, under public and private pressure to gain a financial payoff from investments in higher education.

Unlike North American universities, Australian academies do not even pay lipservice to the idea of a liberal education for those seeking the qualifications to enter the high status, highly paid professions of law, medicine, business and so on. It is not for the technical intelligentsia to waste time and money on unproductive and profitless arts or science degrees, and objections (by students and many staff) to required 'broadening' courses in these faculties are vociferous. Furthermore, most students enrolled in professional courses have not generally been the recipients of a liberal secondary education either, in that the grades required for highly competitive entry are best obtained through a concentration on school science and mathematics offerings, areas in which technique and skill are seen to be more important than knowledge and critical reflection.

With the 'professionalizing' of less prestigious occupations, this specializing in *technique* and the parallel emphasizing of 'skills formation' has also become more true of the training of teachers, nurses, social workers and journalists. No longer does their 'professional preparation' involve more than a smattering of courses in fields outside their specialist 'vocational' interests. Like Bloom's pre-business economics majors, they not only do not take 'an interest in sociology, anthropology or political science but [they are] also persuaded that what [they] are learning can handle all that belongs to those studies' [1987: 370–1].

There are, of course, still to be found islands of dissent from the conversion of humane learning and the civilizing project of the universities to the self- and 'nation'-serving mission of current education and training priorities. But like courses of study within the universities, these small departments are often fragmented, and individuals are isolated from the mainstream of academic life, even while that mainstream battles to rid itself of the pejorative appellation 'academic' in an effort to become more relevant and attractive to a broader range of students. Thus the triumph of pragmatic anti-intellectualism,[8] inseparable from the state's political and economic project of access, equity, efficiency and effectiveness, is fundamental in the rise of the technical intelligentsia to symbolic power and dominance in contemporary civil society.

Notes

1. Cf. Peter Berger's [1966] distinction between puppets and puppeteers, or Moerman's contrast between Garfinkel's [1967] cultural dopes and his own [1968] cultural sharpies.
2. In Australia, the harassment of the journalist Wilfred Burchett in the late 1960s provides a famous example. Having reported the Korean engagement from the perspective of the North Koreans – the 'enemy' – Burchett eventually had his Australian passport revoked and was forced to live in exile. Other investigative journalists have suffered at the hands of media moguls and government regulators, as well as from the attentions of those whose activities they have investigated. The Sydney-based journalist Bob Bottom's exposés of organised crime are a case in point. The governmental surveillance of and aggression towards protestors against Australian participation in the war in Vietnam in the 1970s provided numerous students and teachers with their first taste of the state's hostility to informed dissent.
3. Donzelot's influential work *The Policing of Families* [1980] and others building on his work [e.g. Reiger 1985] suggest that a modernizing or even post-modernizing of Engels' conceptualization has continued to press for a deconstruction of what Donzelot calls 'government through the family.'
4. The introduction of a tax file number, which every adult citizen, whether taxpayer or not, is required to have, was promoted as a control mechanism to mitigate tax fraud and the abuse of welfare benefits. Electoral enrolment forms point out that the information contained in them is available 'under very strict guidelines' to 21 other government bodies, including the police. Suspicion of the very notion of identification papers remains strong amongst Australians.
5. Status-conscious academic staff often prefer the designation Associate Professor, because 'it sounds better' and because they may be addressed and referred to as 'Professor' in a system which still largely reserves that designation for the most senior members of the *academic* hierarchy.
6. 'Disadvantaged' students include Aboriginal and Torres Strait Island people, women, 'mature age' students (non-school leavers), students from non-English speaking backgrounds, geographically isolated students and students from low income groups. Many such students are enrolled as external or part-time students, and some have special entry dispensations which seek to overcome their lack of matriculation qualifications.
7. The professional association, the union of academic staff originally known as The Federation of Australian University Staff Associations,

was combined with the Union of Australian College Academics as a result of the installation of the Unified National System. The new union is called the National Tertiary Education Industry Union and includes members of the universities' general and professional staffs.

8. Of course, those who plan to be school teachers are still required to have some basic knowledge (two years in most cases) of the content of what are known as their 'teaching subjects'. Increasingly, undergraduate courses in subjects like history, science or English are being tailored to attract such students.

CHAPTER SEVEN

The Dream of Community: Bread, Circuses and Ideology

> Conloqui et conridere et vicissim benevole
> obsequi simul legere libros dulci loquos
> simul nugari et simul honestari.
>
> Conversations and jokes together, mutual
> rendering of good services, the reading
> together of sweetly phrased books, the
> sharing of nonsense and mutual attentions.
>
> St Augustine, *Confessions*.

I have argued that the search for a clear-cut distinction between high and popular cultures (or elite and mass cultures) is a sterile enterprise and that such distinctions, of great political import in egalitarian societies which are also class societies, spring from a fundamentally inegalitarian impulse. For high and/or elite cultures are so only by virtue of their being constructed as generally inaccessible to the majority of the population. This is a majority which has been denied the opportunity to accumulate that cultural capital necessary for participation in what have been created as rarefied realms of discourse by cultural guardians who would 'protect' those realms from the invasions of barbarians. The self-serving and self-enhancing understanding that high culture is only to be engaged in by those of a superior sensibility and refinement, and superior moral worth, acts not only to legitimize but also to produce structures of intellectual power and ideological domination in class society.

It will be clear that this view is opposed to an old-fashioned Marxian notion of base and superstructure. Here, I follow Raymond Williams' argument that 'we have to recognize the alternative meanings and values, the alternative opinions and attitudes, even some alternative senses of the world, which can be accommodated and tolerated within a particular effective and dominant culture' [1965: 10]. The more alternative meanings and values can be incorporated into the public culture, the more powerful the hegemony exercised by ruling groups. Moreover, the selection by the domain of 'high' culture of certain streams of thought and action common throughout the population at the expense of others parallels the selection processes of the various elite fractions of the dominant class. The tastes, sensibilities, manners and morals of the cultural bourgeoisie thereby become indicators of 'intrinsic' worth, defined and selected from the *habitus* of those whose own power and influence are grounded in quite other (real or imagined) domains – financial, social, political or educational.

It cannot be stressed too much that the constitutive elements of 'high' culture are first selected and abstracted from the whole field of cultural practices and only subsequently elevated to elite status through being made relatively unavailable to the masses of the cultural formation from whence they sprang. I therefore now want to turn to an examination of some areas of public culture which might come under the rubric of what is generally defined as 'popular' or 'mass' culture, in other words, discursive practices which are widely available to the whole population and engaged in by many. This is not to say, of course, that class, or gender, or ethnicity, or the repressive and ideological apparatuses of the state are not deeply implicated in these practices; only that, in their guise as the everyday leisure activities of all the people in one form or another, these practices have the capacity to act as platforms for the articulation, manipulation, justification and even, on occasion, resolution of social cleavages and social differentiation.

The 'Problem' of Leisure

The field of academic activity commonly known as 'leisure studies' rose to prominence over the decade of the 1980s on the back of economic recession. Until then the study of leisure, the utilization of non-work 'free' time, was considered a minority interest of market research, journalism and youth culture. As such, it was conceived of as a relatively unproblematic field of human activity, though always with the proviso in class society that those with time and money to spare – Veblen's 'leisure class' – would have a greater range of choice in their leisure pursuits than those with limited funds and limited access to facilities.

During the 1980s, with increasing rates of youth unemployment and of unemployment generally, the 'constructive use of leisure time' (always a concern of the repressive state apparatuses) became a more widely used catchcry. Once the state had been forced to concede that rising youth unemployment could not be laid at the door of poor educational preparation for the labour market, the problem of the enforced leisure of the young unemployed came to be couched in different terms. On the one hand they were exhorted to use this 'free' time to gain skills which might be of value in getting employment, and on the other to engage in voluntary work which might give them the self-respect denied them by the brute fact of unemployment. Those who were not queueing for the dole were also encouraged to 'upgrade' their skills, usually by obtaining further qualifications, and in many industries 'productivity deals' – increased output for the same costs – were struck to justify meagre wage rises.

Australians have always equated leisure with holiday time and time off work. Despite academic arguments [see, for example, Parker, 1971] about where to draw the line between work and leisure in some occupations (university teaching, professional sports, the arts), agreement is widespread that leisure involves voluntarism. From lying in the sun to orchestral performance to playing a strenuous sport, leisure means choice: doing what you want when you want to do it. But during the 1980s, leisure became more blatantly commoditized than it had ever been, the element of choice was steadily eroded and a number of new industries came to maturity. These included the whole government-sponsored area of recreation and tourism, the cargo cult of third-world economies, and within it the 'hospitality industry' (catering, hotel management, bar-tending, waiting, chamber-maiding, tour-guiding, airline-ticketing, and so on) and 'the leisure industry'. Leisure thus becomes something that has to be laboured over, in two ways. In the first place, the leisure of others becomes a major source of casual employment and income for increasing numbers of young people; secondly, those who manage to maintain themselves in employment are encouraged to use their free time in ways deemed socially responsible by the guardians, both official and self-appointed, of public morality. In other words, as leisure becomes further moralized and more strictly regulated, it also becomes more highly commoditized.

Case 8. Disciplining the Individual, Purifying Society

Perhaps the best example of the strategy of the cleansing and fortifying of society through the strengthening and disciplining of individuals (a readily acceptable notion in egalitarian individualism) is the national campaign begun in the mid-1980s called 'Life. Be In It.' The star of the campaign's television promotion was a cartoon character named, not coincidentally, Norm.[1] Norm is the archetypal beer-swilling Australian sloth, the 'Ocker' against whom, in the intellectual field, high cultural guardians have long inveighed. He is everything that the symbolic type of the energetic bushranger or sunburnt stockman is not. But he is the statistical Norm. Claiming to be a keen sportsman, he lounges all day in front of the television set, following the exploits of footballers and tennis players and athletes, and downing an incessant supply of canned beer or 'tinnies'. His heroes are cricketers and golfers of international repute, but his own physical exercise amounts to plying the remote control button of his television set and bending his elbow. Easy-going, rollicking and perversely likeable, Norm cannot imagine why anyone would exhort him to try to see his toes, which are invisible because of his overhanging paunch, and he is faintly puzzled by the lack of response from his friends whom he invites around to 'crack a few tinnies' with him. They are all out participating in the very sports he is watching.

Norm has a sister, Libby. She is trim and fit, dressed in tennis gear, leotard or fencing garb, incessantly endeavouring to rally her brother from his armchair desuetude. Eventually, she does so – Norm gets up to change television channels – and soon he is enjoying the fresh air and exercise of walking the dog and adding his voice to Libby's in the campaign to 'be in it'. Meanwhile, the Commonwealth Department of Tourism, Recreation and Sport changes the television campaign to one in which all sorts of activities, from archery to frisbee-tossing, kite-flying to walking in the park are lauded as steps on the road to fitness and 'getting more out of life.'

At the same time, the mass media ran, and continues to run, 'public service announcements' and paid advertisements on behalf of quasi-government departments and others, urging more exercise and greater dietary restraint upon the overweight and generally unhealthy population. Dietitians and nutritionists invade the cookery programmes, extolling freedom from fats and salts – to the chagrin of the pastoral industry, until 'lean beef' was promoted as a source of iron, and milk and other dairy products as being relatively low in fat and high in calcium. Cardiologists and cancer specialists add their expertise to the statisticians' analyses of the cost to taxpayers of hospitals filled with unnecessarily ill people and the numbers of days lost to production through alcoholism, drug abuse, unsafe sexual practices and respiratory diseases.

Campaigns for national fitness have a long history in Australia.[2] They resonate with patriotic fervour and the physicalist connotations of natural difference, as well as with darker understandings of intolerance and racism. They have long drawn strength from Arnoldian notions of muscular Christianity, masculinity and classical ideals of *mens sana in corpore sano*, though usually in the belief that the sound mind will 'naturally' follow from the sound body. This is a belief consistent with an Australian understanding of society as constituted in individuals, from which follows the ideal of a strong, pure and 'fit' society made up of similarly fit individuals. Furthermore, fitness campaigns answer to the needs of a capitalist economy for the reproduction and the re-creation of a sturdy labour force. In the field of physical fitness, then, people and state are as one, if not always for the same reasons.

And here the state has its trump card, for the most common definition of leisure activities in Australia centres upon sports. Physical education has for many years held an important place in the compulsory curriculum of all schools, both public and private, in stark contrast to subjects like music, art, or drama. Competitive games and athletic contests are vehicles for the articulation and celebration of both individualism and natural equality, as well as for the generation of an *esprit de corps*.[3] Trainee teachers, when quizzed about the extracurriculum (or, more fashionably and significantly, the co-curriculum) in schools, will readily list competitive team sports like cricket, football (of various codes), netball and hockey. When pressed, some will add chess, debating, or the choir or band, but these are clearly considered peripheral, especially when they are thought to be elitist or lacking in machismo, or when they do not form part of a competitive league [see Coleman, 1976; J. Kapferer, 1978]. 'Education for leisure,' a subject which has been in vogue in the schools since the early 1970s, is virtually synonymous, in the minds of teachers, pupils and the public at large, with physical education. This is despite the efforts of government departments and other agencies of the state to promote other leisure activities as having 'a powerful and essential contribution to make towards personal fulfilment and a creative life' [Commonwealth of Australia, 1980: 1]. The 1980 document *Educating for Leisure*, published by what was at that time The Office of Youth Affairs in the Department of Employment and Youth Affairs, (a precursor, with the Department of Education, of the Department of Employment, Education and Training), promulgated the view that 'the concept of leisure' was more complex than those definitions which involved relaxation, entertainment and personal development. The document, while acknowledging the element of choice, nevertheless advanced a line which can only be seen as statist:

> The concept of leisure must include personal freedom of choice on how the time available is spent. It must involve *enjoyment* and *self-fulfilment* and this would appear to require the exercise of creative capacities. It will most likely involve the enlargement of *knowledge and skills* and thus the development of *self-esteem*. It can involve, on the one hand, *participation in social groups* and on the other intense contemplative thought, which may for some only occur while alone.
>
> Yet many of these elements also apply to aspects of both education and work. Moreover the ability to make *good use* of leisure might be expected to transfer equally well to education and work. Thus the distinctions that are made in regard to education, work and leisure cannot always be sustained. All three seem to involve '*constructive* living', one of the goals which a sound education should seek. [Commonwealth of Australia, 1980: 3; I have emphasized terms still favoured fifteen years later by education policymakers]

Nonetheless, there are many other forms of leisure (or extra-curricular) activity which remain outside the ambit of state control. (This is not to say, of course, that they may not be subject to commercial pressures or harassment by experts or law enforcers, only that they are not (yet) officially regulated.) School children over the age of about twelve [see W.F. Connell et al., 1975] still prefer the unstructured (and unconstructive?) collective pleasures of hanging around with friends, talking, window-shopping and listening to popular music. Almost every high school can boast a pop group staffed by (most usually) boys, who receive much encouragement from their peers but little from their teachers, except in those cases where the school has entered statewide competitions known as Rock Eisteddfods. Young adults flock to those activities and venues where meeting and courting are central concerns: pubs, clubs, concerts and discos. The most favoured of all adult leisure pursuits is gardening, again an activity which is widely and cheaply accessible and not bound by the rules and regulations of public space or official sporting codes and competitive engagement.

Cultural Heritage and Ethnic Identity

The regulating, commoditizing and moralizing of leisure and recreation serve to control and channel the non-working (or non-labouring – not the same thing) hours of the adult population. The ideals of physicalism, competition and national consensus achieve hegemony in their endorsement, through the schools and mass media, of widespread cultural discourses of egalitarianism and individualism, finding their apotheosis in sporting contests. But some of these discourses can slip through the net of ideological incorporation, particularly in a nation which boasts of its 'multiculturalism' (a term coined to designate the policies and, perhaps, the practices of inter-ethnic toleration, particularly in relation to that proportion of the population which is not of 'Anglo' descent).

Multiculturalism, though self-consciously aware and appreciative of ethnic difference, which is after all its *raison d'être*, is in general held to be blind to class, gender or age differences and conflicts. The prime organizing category of multiculturalism is ethnicity, even when the members of other dissenting social groups draw attention to, for example, 'the ethnic working class' or 'ethnic women' and so forth, and politicians woo 'the ethnic vote.' The very term 'ethnic', used to designate all Australians of Non-English-Speaking Background (sometimes referred to as NESBians) or descent, suggests a commonality of culture which lumps all such persons together in a monolithic bloc, denying all difference and negating all claims to inclusion within the common ways of life thought to be properly 'Australian.' Too often, as Hughes points out for the United States, multiculturalism exists in a profound 'ignorance of other cultures. . .. In fact, it means separatism' [1994: 88].

So non-Anglo (or Aboriginal) customary law, religious practice, the authority of elders and divided loyalties may and do clash with the laws of the Australian state and the customs of its dominant ethnic group. The state's commitment to the preservation of numerous ethnic 'heritages' in the name of consensual social harmony is often sorely tested, or perhaps its multicultural hypocrisy is exposed, as in those situations where, for example, Serbs and Croats in 1991 both demanded that the Australian government recognize the sovereignty of one over the other in Yugoslavia, and three years later (Macedonian) Greeks and 'Slav Macedonians' clashed in Victoria over ownership of the designation 'Macedonian.' Another example is the careful negotiations with school authorities about how many and which 'community languages' (including English as a Second Language) are to be taught and examined in the schools. Not to be troublesome, ethnicity (language use, religious observance, rites of passage and family ties) then comes to be seen as a private affair, or, in public, as requiring relegation to the unproblematic areas of cuisine, of song and dance and 'national' (i.e. traditional) dress.

Hence, the institution of the folk festival, which is essentially a celebration of the mythologized past of a particular ethnic group or folk, itself mythologized as a secure and stable entity bound together by ancient ties of blood and history which override any internal inequalities of class, status or party. The festival harks back to a golden age of the face-to-face village community and thus articulates a dream of community and solidarity *vis-à-vis* other ethnic communities. At the same time, it can be used to make statements about ethnicity to both insiders and outsiders, to make some money (the members of minority ethnic groups being central to the restaurant and cafe industry in even small towns) or raise funds for some worthy 'ethnic' cause, all in the course of providing a day's or weekend's entertainment – performance, contests of strength, beauty, skill and dexterity, eating and drinking, singing and dancing – in some public place open to all.

For the members of the dominant ethnic group, these events are little more than the occasion of a family outing, the chance to try out some unfamiliar cuisine or to join in a traditional dance, the noisier and more exuberant the better. The event is fully reported in the local press, together with photos of, preferably, several children of clearly different ethnic identities and surnames (Georgiou, Smith, Nguyen and Dykstra, say) enjoying some spaghetti or noodles from the same plate: the press invariably depicts such a scene as a triumph of multiculturalism.

The cultural heritage of the white, English-speaking, Australian-born majority population (generally if inaccurately referred to as 'Anglo') is taken for granted. It forms the paramount reality of everyday life, and therein lies its power. It forms the core of the school curriculum in language and literature studies, history, music and art and is the foundation of dominant behavioural codes – definitions of 'appropriate' body language and eye contact, politeness, respect, 'good manners' – which are prescribed for everyday interaction in the schools, streets, offices and factories of the nation.

It must be stressed that I refer here to *dominant* codes, not majority practice. In its very domination, the Anglo ascendancy strives to encompass all others within its domain. But in doing so, social-structural divisions and cultural differences which are ignored or glossed over at subordinated levels of ethnicity – class and gender, but also wealth, status, power and influence – resurface in the conscious action of members of the dominant ethnic group. Within the encompassing and incorporating Anglo category, such structural fissures and social inequalities continue to exist (however successfully downplayed by, for and within subordinate groups) and to be meaningful to social actors.

For the issue of ethnicity is grounded in the problems of individual and group identity thrown up by the lived experience of late-capitalist social formations. The quest for a distinctive ethnic or national identity is characteristic of ethnic groups or nations which can be conceived of as subordinate to other ethnic or national groups, particularly at times of political and economic uncertainty and instability or a perceived threat to taken-for-granted social arrangements. This search for a national(ist) identity which foregrounds the 'multicultural' nature of Australian society and seeks to define Australianness in multiculturalist terms achieved renewed urgency and a sharper focus throughout the Bicentennial celebrations of 1988.

1988 saw ideological state apparatuses at full stretch in attempting to incorporate the ethnic identities of all citizens within the totalizing framework of a dominant Australian identity. These efforts, often apparently highly successful, were nonetheless continually frustrated by the opposition of Aboriginal Australians, whose collective spokespersons have long resisted the 'ethnic' label. While I return to a more detailed discussion of this resistance in Chapter 11, it is important to note here that the comparatively recent mythologizing of Aboriginal identity in Australia resonates with the struggles of minority indigenous peoples everywhere, as well as with others suffering from race hatred and intolerance in the contemporary world. It also finds resonance in the cultural productions and discursive practices of other oppressed and dominated groups within Australian society, particularly women and workers, and draws added strength from the militancy of these groups.

In establishing or constructing a common folk identity, an identity which defines 'the people', it is necessary to differentiate 'the people' from members of other communities – to elaborate an ideal of what is distinctive about being, for example, Polish, Italian, Irish, Lebanese or Cambodian – and to suppress old internal conflicts and differentiations. At the level of the nation, however, where the state would utilize faith in a common identity against other nation states (in wartime, or economic competition, for example) 'the people' may weld themselves together by means of *opposition* to the state.[4] Globalization, some writers suggest [Hannerz, 1987], may be multiculturalism writ large; it is no doubt the goal of transnational corporations to have the members of all nations consider themselves to be harmonious global consumers in a gigantic world marketplace.

Such a thwarting of the dominant ideology of national solidarity is, of course, ceaselessly opposed by the state itself with all the repressive and ideological weaponry at its disposal. Thus while the state may lend its support (through schooling, the mass media, the ecumenical churches and multiculturalist policies) to popular traditions which may be ranged against each other and/or incorporated with relative ease into a capitalist, liberal, democratic scheme, the adversarial undercurrent of other traditions – of the working class, of the women's movement, of Aboriginal activism – requires greater circumspection.

Folk Festivals and Music-Making

Identity, whether individual or collective, is powerfully expressed through music-making. Hymns, anthems and popular songs bestow heightened meaning and greater intensity upon the everyday expression of the hopes and fears, the ecstasies and despairs of a world in which consonance and harmony often seem only fleetingly attainable. The addition of music to poetic forms and structures redoubles the impact of poetic language and convention; Culler [1975: 164] paraphrases Genette: 'The essence of poetry lies not in verbal artifice itself. . .but more simply and profoundly in the type of reading (*attitude de lecture*) which the poem imposes on its readers'. That is to say, our expectations of 'poetry' are aroused by the poetic form itself, by what Genette calls 'that *margin of silence* which isolates it in the middle of ordinary speech (but not as a deviation)' [cited in Culler, ibid.: 164]. How much more is this the case for song, wherein ordinary speech itself becomes part of the 'margin of silence', and for social groups thought to have their own 'voices' silenced by a dominant cultural communication code?

The most ubiquitous forms of popular music are, of course, those which follow the conventions of commercially powerful 'pop'. In general, pop music is characterized by simplicity of tune, lyric and rhythm. It is transnational in its mass appeal to the emotions and visceral responses of young listeners deeply concerned with their interpersonal and intersexual relations; it is emotion commoditized in a global market. As such, it forms part of what Horkheimer and Adorno [1972] called 'the culture industry', a major export commodity of the United States. The speakers (singers) of languages other than English are pressed to perform and even compose in English to assure themselves of a niche in the global pop music trade.[5] Perhaps the best-known example of this phenomenon has been the Swedish singing group ABBA, who produced a raft of transnational hits in the 1970s, but local performance all over the world still depends heavily upon the reproduction (covering) of English-language, usually North American, pop songs. Such performance even extends to the reproduction of American accents amongst other English speakers (tune = toon = tyune; new = noo = nyew; past = passt = parsst etc.) with sometimes unwittingly comic results (ass and arse, for example.) Similarly, the vocabularies of song-writers are more likely to conform to the conventions of black American speech, given that the dance styles of black Americans inspire global emulation through the medium of the videos without which pop songs can no longer expect to achieve widespread exposure.

The more specifically folk traditions of the United States have also, if to a lesser extent, affected popular cultural practice in other countries, particularly in the most highly industrialized and technologized nations. The reduced significance of the feast of Sinterklaas and the augmented significance of Kerstmas as the occasion of gift exchange, mid-winter revelry and public holiday in the Netherlands is a case in point, as is the worldwide institutionalization and commercialization of Mothers' Day and St. Valentine's Day. In Britain and Japan, there exist clubs celebrating the mythology of the American West, particularly that of Cowboys and Indians. Members, male and female, dress in buckskins or at least denims, boots and spurs, check shirts and bandannas, and stetsons. The songs they sing are about horses and cowpokes and riding the range and, less incongruously, about the eternal laments of unrequited, starcrossed or faithless love.

The American country-and-western tradition has always found a ready home in Australia, where three of the country's most revered *habitant* or consciously nativist songwriters and performers have actually been called Tex (Morton), Slim (Dusty) and Duke (Tritton). Country music, distinguished from contemporary pop by its attention to song rather than dance, its sentimentality and its (increasingly strained) loyalty to non-electronic instruments and to old-fashioned vocal and rhythmic styles, has, over the last few decades, also entered the arena of the culture industry. The Country Music Festival in Tamworth, New South Wales, attracts thousands of fans over the week before the Australia Day weekend in January, and its proceedings, particularly the awards for 'best song' and 'best vocalist,' attract much attention from the national mass media. Accommodation in the town is booked out from one year to the next, and local businesses do a roaring trade in, among other things, souvenir western outfits which are indistinguishable from those sported by Gene Autry or Roy Rogers and his sweetheart Dale Evans in 1940s westerns.

The urbanized and increasingly technologized discourse of country music focuses upon rural mythological themes (common to the United States, Australia and other countries of the New World) of pioneering and settlement and life on the land and co-opts these themes, softening their hard edges and blurring with sentimentality an often tragic and brutal past. History becomes little more than ossified legend, with only the most tenuous relation to or significance for the current struggles of a shrinking rural population, or indeed of urban workers and the urban poor.

The incorporation of country music into the popular music industry contrasts with the marginalizing of both traditional and contemporary 'folk' music. Folk music is distinguishable from the bulk of country and pop music by its more outspokenly political message and its stubborn attachment to forms of music-making and song-writing now thought to be naive and outdated – the round and part-song, the ballad and repetitive chorus, accompanied by accordion, fiddle, guitar, banjo or even lute and dulcimer and, in Australia, the occasional didgeridoo.

There are little folk-music clubs and societies scattered all around the country, based in city pubs and small town halls, with monthly meetings and socializing, and there is an annual national folk festival, staged over the Easter weekend. Unlike the Tamworth event, however, its venue is not fixed and it is largely ignored by all but local press and radio stations, particularly when it is held in small country towns where accommodation is limited and public transport unreliable. Organization is in the hands of local enthusiasts, with support from the office bearers, staff and trustees of the Australian Folk Trust headquartered in Canberra; sponsorship does not come from large transnational recording companies, but rather from local small businesses and a few specialist music interests.

However, it is important to note that the state, through the Performing Arts Board and the Community Cultural Development Committee of the Australia Council (the principal 'cultural' apparatus of the Australian State), plays a major role in funding, signalling its interest in the worthiness of the event in the arena of 'community' (usually translated as 'minority ethnic group') cultural development, and ensuring a certain amount of control over it. In 1990, the twenty-fourth Australian National Folk Festival was held in the village of Kuranda, a half-hour drive up the mountains from Cairns in Far North Queensland. An examination of some aspects of this event may help illustrate and clarify some of the points I have been making.

Case 9. Folk in the Rain Forest

The Venue

In 1989, the twenty-third annual Australian Folk Festival was staged in Maleny, a small town inland from Caloundra on the 'Sunshine Coast' of Queensland. This was the second year running it had been held in Queensland, occasioning some grumbling from participants and visitors from South Australia and Western Australia, but they were somewhat mollified by the announcement that the following year the festival would be held in South Australia, at Flinders University. In the early years of the festival, interest had generally been confined to students and academics, and university campuses were the obvious venue. But as the wife of one of the leading folk musicians pointed out, 'ordinary people like truckies [truck-drivers]' would be uncomfortable attending an event at a university, and there are many suitable small towns in South Australia (Angaston, Mt. Gambier, Callington) which have folk clubs, and others (Goolwa, Kangaroo Island, Kapunda) already hold annual festivals on a small scale. There was fairly general agreement among the 'old hands' that the festival's appeal to a broader audience might be jeopardized by the unfamiliarity of a university campus when compared with a country showground with camping facilities, or a primary school. At any rate, the Kuranda State School seemed to be a popular choice, with a day-care centre across the road as well as a camping ground. It might be surmised that the combination of tourist resort and scenic railway, a reputation for conservationist activism and 'counter-cultural' lifestyles and the atmosphere of carefree youth (marquee on the school oval, duckboards over the mud, a plethora of dogs, babies and small children, breakfast provided by the Mothers' Club in the lunch shed and adults perched on children's chairs and desks) all produced Kuranda as a town characterized by gentleness and good humour, and the festival as nostalgically reminiscent of childhood.

The Events

There was a wide range of events on offer, revolving around:

Singing in 'The Big Top' (marquee) and in an open-air amphitheatre: bands with nativist titles like 'Mantaka,' 'Snake Gully

Ensemble,' 'Mixed Relations,' 'Mangrove Jack,' 'The Mills Sisters' from Thursday Island; and solo performers, some very well-known beyond, though nationally identified with, the folk-music field: Eric Bogle, Kevin Carmody, Ted Egan, Margaret RoadKnight, Judy Small.

Lectures on history, many under the aegis of James Cook University's history department (the conflict between Aboriginal and European cultures; life on the north Queensland goldfields; growing up in Broken Hill; oral traditions; collecting and preserving folk history; the influence of the workplace on folk songs; pioneering in the northern rainforest; a female perspective on the colonial north); and *the environment* (Cape York; Fraser Island; the Barrier Reef; the Tully Millstream). Also environmental awareness sessions, with students from the Yunga Burra Rainforest Research Unit presenting games for adults and children; 'Song for Australia' detailing 'some of the negative as well as positive aspects of our impact on the Australian land, water and air'; 'Caring for our Earth': slides, songs and music on conservationist themes.

Dancing: demonstrations and workshops on Australian bush dancing, clog dancing, Greek social dancing, Scottish and English country dance, Irish set dance, square dancing, 'International folk dancing with Vera Myronenko'. Professional dance troupes: Aboriginal and Islander Dance Troupe; Sunuil Tituil (dancers from Torres Strait); Tjapukai Dance Theatre (based in Kuranda). Dance bands included the self-consciously *habitant* Wobbly Wombats and Guava Jam Bush Band.

Numerous other events, including: Poetry; Musical instruments: jam sessions and/or instruction with dulcimers, penny whistle, percussion, Celtic harp, 5-string banjo; yarning (story telling); crafts (pottery-glazing); play-reading.

Children's folk festival

Annual general meeting of the Australian Folk Trust: The Declan Affley Awards for songwriting.

Themes of the Folk

Unlike either professional pop music concerts or amateur gigs, and unlike the country music festival, the Kuranda festival had a gently didactic air about it, devoid of the frenetic hype of other large-scale musical events. Participants, performers and spectators all seemed to expect and to be expected to learn something of their shared cultural heritage – the playing of Celtic instruments, the meanings of Aboriginal dance, the yarning tradition of bush balladeers – and the ways in which it might be protected and preserved. Many of the organizers and performers, both local and national, work or have worked as teachers, and many have a background in the 'alternative' rural lifestyles and libertarian socialist politics of the 1960s and 1970s. These factors no doubt contributed to the atmosphere of courteous egalitarianism and good-humoured 'mucking in' (occasioned by the sometimes chaotic arrangements) which were everywhere evident.

The mythologizing of The Bush as vital to the construction of a distinctively Australian identity provided the dominant theme of the festival. Under this umbrella, three inter-related sub-themes are discernible:

Ethnicity and Aboriginality. Celtic roots took pride of place, not only in dancing and instrumentation, but also in the tradition, still current, though deprecated by purists, of setting local lyrics to old Scots, Welsh and particularly Irish tunes. Aboriginal performers provided what were for many the highlights of the festival. Shows by the professional Tjapukai Dance Theatre were consistently sold out, and the Aboriginal singer-songwriter Kevin Carmody, accompanied by fiddles and a didgeridoo, along with the famed Eric Bogle, a Scots immigrant, attracted the largest and most committed audiences.

The history and traditions of rural Australia provided the subject matter of the lectures and tall-story telling, as well as the songs which still celebrate the virtues of the rural workers of the nineteenth century and their descendants – shearers, drovers, diggers, bullock-drivers. The language used by performers and in the official programme is redolent of an earlier, less sophisticated era. Hyperbole is everywhere – all singers and poets are the best – in North Queensland, or in the West, or in the entire country.

Performers are described as 'Kuranda's own', 'our own legend from Sydney', 'a trio of the West's finest', 'world class', 'spectacular' or 'brilliant.' The names of bands ('Sultans of Swag', 'Kangaroo Moon', 'Boola Trio', 'Leaping Lizards', 'Mangrove Jack') and the titles of presentations ('Bushies of Yesteryear', 'While the Billy Boils', 'Bowyangs and Bassinets', 'There's Something in Me Genes', 'Under the Mango Tree', 'Afternoon Tea Party', 'Walkabout Australia') all evoke times and places which are celebrated as distinctively Australian in their dry humour and earthy simplicity. Much of this usage, especially in the flourishing of outmoded expressions like 'no gammon' (no kidding) or 'cobber' (mate, friend), is self-consciously liberal, populist and 'folksy,' and most notable in

The politics of labour, gender and environment. Many of the songs, lectures and yarns were deeply concerned with past and present oppressions, injustices and barbarities perpetrated by the state upon ordinary people and upon the land itself. The rehabilitation of women, Aborigines and workers in historiography was a major theme, but it was overshadowed by the (perhaps less sectional) emphasis upon environmental degradation and contemporary movements to conserve and reclaim the natural heritage of the country and the cultural heritage of its people. The finalists for the Declan Affley Songwriting Award included songs about water pollution, the asbestos workers of Wittenoom, the farmer as conservationist, Raymond Ap (Indonesian freedom fighter) and the massacre of students at Tienanmen Square. It is in this political theme that the essentially moderate and liberal tone of the politics of the folk movement is clarified and expanded to embrace the folk, the ordinary people of other nations. The militant, confrontational action of women, Aborigines and conservationists in other contexts becomes softened in the communal warmth and friendliness of the folk festival.

Business Festivals and Money-Making

The incorporation of the protest songs of 'the people', more advanced in country music but increasingly discernible in folk music, into the state's wider project of 'national' consensus is testimony to the capacity of the dominant culture to accommodate alternative meanings and values. The personal, individual problems of women or Aborigines and the concerns of conservationists, gathered up and focused in popular song, become collectivized and nationalized as ultimately actually definitional of Australianness. The women's movement, the Aboriginal Land Rights Movement and the conservationist tradition become sanitized and respectable, the stuff of government inquiries and legislation. A truce is called between people and state, folk singers and performers are lionized and become the comperes of radio and television programmes, and children in school learn the old protest songs as if they were nursery rhymes. Perhaps this is to overstate the case, but I think not. The way in which activities conceived of as owing nothing to the state or to business interests can become a part of the state's own ruling agenda seems to me to indicate the effectiveness of ideological incorporation in the establishment and reinforcement of hegemony. However, if the home-made bread and circuses of popular music can be ideologized and incorporated in this way, it is also possible for the people to subvert the commercialized fiestas of the state to their own individual purposes. I turn now to a brief examination of two urban festivals, highly commercial events celebrating technology and mythologizing spectatorship, which exhibit this subversive potential.

Case 10. The Melbourne Cup and the Adelaide Grand Prix

Every year since 1861, at 3.30 p.m. on the first Tuesday in November, Australians everywhere, on farms and worksites, in shops and offices and factories, even in hospitals and schools, have suspended their labours to follow a three-minute horse race in Melbourne, Victoria. Even weighty affairs of state are susceptible to disruption:

> More than one protest against the announcement of the Cup result was dismissed yesterday.
>
> Acting Senate President Mal Colston surmounted an Opposition protest on the matter.
>
> He announced the Cup winner in an aside during the debate on alleged comments by Queensland ALP Senator Bryant Burns on the Tienanmen Square massacre.

> Liberal Senator Bronwyn Bishop complained. [*Telegraph Mirror*, 6/11/91: 5]

Interest is intense, for horse-racing is not only freely admitted to be the sport of kings and a favoured pastime of tycoons and magnates, it is also the sport of the common people. Every Saturday, punters take to the city's racecourses for an afternoon's entertainment, and many more place bets with the State run Totalisator Board, the TAB. As *The Sydney Morning Herald* points out, on the day of the big race it has long been 'the dream of breeders and bettors, bankers and beggars, to own, train, ride or even simply to back the winner of the nation's greatest sporting event' [5/11/91: 1w]. Thousands more – 'plebs and patricians' as the *Herald* put it on November 4 – flock to the Flemington Racecourse to place a bet and parade their egalitarianism.

For days before the race, tonnes of newsprint are expended on form guides, homely tales and pictures of horses and jockeys and trainers, forms to be cut out to provide sweep tickets for informal betting, predictions and tips from racing commentators, sports writers, bar-tenders and any number of 'celebrities', be they socialites, politicians, television stars or cricketers.

The Melbourne Cup is the distillation of a wide range of popular cultural preoccupations and discourses, thus providing itself a 'form guide' to the people's interpretations of the society in which they live and the myths they create about it. Egalitarian individualism reigns over all: anyone, rich or poor, in the members' stand, on the flat or at the local TAB (the State-controlled off-course betting agency, once an illegal activity) in Bourke or Broome, can place a bet, large or small; and most, even puritans, do so, for the Cup lends an aura of respectability, tradition and excitement to an otherwise dubious activity – gambling, and dependence on luck. Fate, of course, is a great equalizer, and the competition between horses and their riders can be seen as an expression of natural excellence and talent. Horses are believed to exhibit admirable human traits like bravery and courage. The 1991 winner, Let's Elope, is eulogized in the following terms:

> She is somehow both flashy and demure, a filly of hot ice and cold iron.
>
> Even in the afterglow of winning the Melbourne Cup. . .Let's Elope stalked the saddling enclosure at Flemington, a picture of seething intensity.

> She has the head of a duchess, the bum of a ballet dancer, and walks like a woman with business on her mind. . .. There was a fury about her unexpended energy. . .. In their own way, all great females are mysterious. [*Sydney Morning Herald*, 6/11/91: 58]

The *Herald*'s 1991 Cup Day 'Wrap-Around' supplement featured a lengthy article on the way in which technological advances have had little effect on improving thoroughbred racehorses. It quotes the *Scientific American* of May 1991:

> Contrary to what one would expect from the efforts to breed and train winners, the racing performance of the thoroughbred is not uniformly improving. . .compared with other domestic species, horses, and thoroughbreds in particular, are practically untouched by science. [5/11/91: 2w]

Nonetheless, advances in veterinary science, in diet and nutrition, and even in the design of horseshoes are agreed to have been instrumental in the production of winners.

Racing, and the Melbourne Cup in particular, is about money. As such, it has always attracted, and displayed, elements of larrikinism and criminality, gleefully reported in the mass media and often sympathetically endorsed by punters around the country. Tales of ring-ins (substitutions) and nobbling (doping) are legion, and the 1991 Cup added its share of drama to them with a rare complaint about interference in the course of the race and the subsequent suspension of three jockeys. As one of the most widely televised events in the country, the Cup is also big business. In 1985, Carlton and United Brewery, manufacturers of Fosters beer, took over its sponsorship, but it is noticeable that press reports and general conversation still fail to give the race its official title, 'The Fosters Melbourne Cup', preferring, at any time of the year, simply 'The Cup' (cf. Paterson's line in 'The Man from Snowy River': 'There was Harrison, who made his pile when Pardon won the cup').

The Melbourne Cup is not only the occasion of 'the nation's greatest sporting event' (and as such, the delight of 'Norm' and all others who prefer spectatorship to participation), it is also the nation's premier venue for the subversion of tradition and the deflation of hierarchy. Modelled upon the great European racing carnivals, especially the English Ascot and Derby, the Melbourne Cup, with its elegantly dressed women and formally attired men, its exclusive members' enclosures and traditionally garbed stewards, continually threatens to overturn the seriousness of money-making and the social pretensions of the dominant fractions of the ruling class. Playfulness is evident in the outfits of young racegoers, who, for example, combine top hats and tails with colourful shorts, or those who win the 'Crazy Hat Awards' and upstage the winners of 'Best-Dressed Awards' with their cheeky irreverence. Many, of course, do not even observe the social conventions of dressing up for a day at the races and consume pies and beer with at least as much gusto as those who sip champagne and nibble on chicken in the members' stands and car parks. Class, status, creed, ethnicity and gender are all apparently ignored in the anticipation of backing a winner and clearing one's way out of debt or doldrums with a flutter on the horses.

The atmosphere of the (Fosters) Australian Grand Prix Formula One World Championship motor race, staged from 1985 to 95 in Adelaide early in November, is altogether different. While it is one of the few Formula One races where betting is permissible, this is not the primary interest of racegoers. Formula One racing is a multinational, multi-million dollar enterprise, publicized as a team sport but in reality a fast-moving test laboratory for engines, fuels and automobile parts. The glamour and excitement of Grand Prix motor racing lie in its high-speed, high-tech, ultra-modern image, and its attraction for sponsors and promoters is grounded in its advertising potential:

> Carlton and United Breweries spend an estimated $5 million on sponsorship for the Foster's Australian Grand Prix. . .. Sources put the sponsorship deal at more than $3 million, with CUB spending another $1.5 million on entertaining.
>
> CUB's sponsorship entitles the company to naming rights, signage around the circuit and entertainment facilities at the track.
>
> And then there is the international advertising to an estimated 7 million television viewers.
>
> Mr Ormonde [general manager of group public affairs for CUB] said the sponsorship was 'value for money' because of the international coverage, and had helped Foster's beer become a big seller here and overseas. [*The Advertiser* 2/11/91: 48]

Further, the city fathers of Adelaide and the state government of South Australia view the event as a great tourist attraction, enticing motor-racing enthusiasts and members of the global leisure class to an unfamiliar part of the world:

> It was estimated 5000 international and 40,000 national visitors would again be in Adelaide for the event.
>
> 'And there's the added spin-off', Mr Schaeffer [marketing manager of the Adelaide Convention and Tourism Authority] said. 'As well as the three or four days they are here for the racing, many of them take a few days holidaying somewhere in the State.' [*Advertiser* 26/10/91: 6][6]

Unlike a horse race, an entire motor race cannot be observed from a single vantage point on the circuit. The cheapest tickets, for four day 'General Admission', cost $75, a Gold Pass sold for $230 and seats in the chicane stand for $370. Also, numerous business corporations entertain clients, major shareholders and senior management in corporate boxes. For such large financial layouts, the race promoters and the city itself need to offer more than a glimpse of advertisement-bedecked cars flashing by. The Adelaide Grand Prix is surrounded by numerous events and entertainments for locals and visitors whose interest in motor-racing is limited, events which are conceived of as adding further excitement to a city usually better known for its sedate style, but one which for some years adopted the Grand Prix slogan 'Adelaide Alive'.

Thus the Grand Prix period offers a two-day street party in the centre of the shopping district; go-kart racing; a touring car rally, 'now in its fourth year [which] has become the traditional lead up event to the Grand Prix' [*GP News* No. 4, 1991]; aerobatic displays; truck-racing and 'family entertainment', including buskers, face-painting, stilt-walking, magicians and puppeteers, and 'A giant Starvision video screen. . .located on the oval in the General Admission area where patrons will be able to see all the race action, as well as entertainment features, sports clips and music videos. . .. The highlight of entertainment of course will be the Paul Simon concert after the big race on Sunday, November 3' [ibid.].

But 'the social event of the year' (according to the *City Messenger*, 30/10/91: 7) is the Grand Prix Ball at the Adelaide Convention Centre, sponsored by the department store Myers and with tickets costing $325 each, for which 'guests will get a three-course meal, Moet champagne, Andrew Garrett wines and Fosters beer'. Similarly, Myers' rival David Jones sponsors an International

Ladies' Day on the racecourse members' lawns, where, for $75, 'women sporting the latest fashions will be sipping champagne, indulging in fine food and watching parades of high fashion' [ibid.]. Further glamour accrues to the event with young women, 'Fosters Girls' or 'Sony Girls' or 'Yamaha Girls', playing the role of ushers and with the Celebrity Challenge race (sponsored by car-makers BMW) featuring television 'personalities', sports people, pop musicians and, highlight of the 1991 event, an internationally renowned model, Elle Macpherson, who, though predictably reported as 'driving like Elle', finished a careful last.

Meanwhile, for the lesser social lights, there is a Not The Grand Prix Ball at the Old Lion Hotel, for which tickets cost $16.

The Dream of Community and the Ideology of the Capitalist State

Formula One motor racing is a business, not a sport. As such, its appeal lies in the vicarious excitement generated by risk and danger and the seductive 'new class' sophistications of high technology and great wealth. It is not an activity in which followers can engage cheaply or regularly, and despite strenuous efforts by the mass media it cannot be turned into a people's party. Unlike folk singers or racehorses, motor cars do not exhibit personality or character, they do not express a mythic naturalness. Racing drivers may be lionized in an effort to evoke ideals of natural talent honed to perfection, but their dependence upon manufacturers, engineers, pit crews, team managers and corporate employers only emphasizes the inegalitarianism and machine-like character of a spectator sport as spectacle, one dominated by and serving the interests of corporate profit and corporate ideology.

The breathless commercialism of 'Adelaide Alive,' 'Thunder Down Under' and 'Roar Energy' – all popular Grand Prix slogans – produces a frenetic party atmosphere, with noise and petrol fumes and the kind of riotous public inebriation which is otherwise severely deprecated in Adelaide. It is a long way from the tropical mud and humidity of the rain forest, or the greensward elegance of The Cup. Far from being narrowed, the gap between rich and poor, between celebrities and nonentities, is accentuated and hierarchy proclaimed and extolled. Fellow feeling is precluded by the absence of any sentiments or symbols of identity and shared history. National fitness now appears, in its post-modern guise, as ruthlessly competitive technological excellence, and the physical fitness of ordinary Australians becomes irrelevant. There is no *Geschlecht* here, and no desire for it either.

The old-fashioned, chaotic playfulness of the Kuranda State School and the traditionalist excitement of the Flemington Racecourse present a telling contrast to the nervy, hard-edged tension of the streets of Adelaide during the Grand Prix. The tension, artificially created in and for the event itself, is social and financial, only tenuously related to the competition on the racetrack but deeply connected to the social, economic and political divisions and contests of everyday life in capitalist society. Here, the popular dream of community is shattered by the government and business-sponsored screech of tyres, the thunder of engines and the tearing of metal.

Notes

1. Australians, in true egalitarian style, like to shorten people's names or give them nicknames. But not only does Norman become Norm, he also represents the statistical norm, that is, Everyman.
2. For many years the National Fitness Camps provided state-organized camps for rural school children particularly to engage in sports and other outdoor activities for which their local schools and districts had few facilities. The camps were provided by state National Fitness Councils under the umbrella of the Commonwealth government's National Fitness Campaign, inaugurated in 1939 as a response to the general lack of physical fitness observed in military recruits. [I am indebted to R.J. Paddick of Flinders University for this information.] A corollary development was that of the Children's Playground Movement, for which the National Fitness Officer in 1943 claimed great social benefit:

> The proper use of leisure time is important for adults; the proper use by the child of its leisure time periods is even more important, as habits are formed at this age. . .. [W]ith the congregation of big populations in cities where small houses and flats are becoming more common, and there is little space available in back yards for children to play, the urgent need of playgrounds and playing fields is obvious. . .. We do not want to see develop in Australia conditions

which are not uncommon in American and European cities – small lanes and streets stopped to traffic for certain hours in the day in order to provide safe playing areas for children. The alternative is the children's playground [Apps, 1943: 11; see also Hamilton-Smith and Robertson, 1977].

3. Cheerleaders and 'spirit girls' were, until the 1980s, largely absent from the Australian high school experience. While professional sports, especially football and basketball, have adopted the trappings of cheerleading, the influence of the women's movement has tended to keep these activities outside the schools. 'Team spirit' is most commonly displayed, by supporters of the team in question, through the flourishing of scarves, banners, rosettes and other items of clothing in the colours of the team, whether that be at school, district, state or national levels. In schools, such identification with players is encouraged as being supportive of the school itself and becomes transmuted into 'school spirit.'
4. Such resistance has a long history: slave and peasant uprisings, the Jarrow Hunger Marches, the *maquis*, general strikes, anti-war moratoria and other popular protests bear witness to the abilities of the people to resist, however fleetingly, the depredations of their rulers. The distinction between people and state, an important one for my purposes in this volume, is by no means new [see e.g. Clastres, 1977; B. Kapferer, 1988] but is one that has particular force in Australian everyday life.
5. The advent of 'World Music' as a distinctive genre is generally most celebrated within limited circles of *cognoscenti*, well-travelled, socially 'aware' and often musically trained. World Music rarely makes an impact upon the sales ratings charts of 'mainstream' pop and is widely considered, in Australia at least, to fall more easily within the purview of 'high' cultural work.
6. The attraction to South Australia of large numbers of free-spending tourists, much extolled by local chambers of commerce and other business interests, received a mortal blow from the announcement early in 1994 that the state of Victoria would take over the staging of the Grand Prix in 1996. Newspapers and talkback radio were inundated with accusations of unneighbourly behaviour, and the (vain) fury of the city fathers was awful to behold.

CHAPTER EIGHT

Presenting the Nation to the People: Commodity and Community

Grass is across the waggon-tracks,
and plough strikes bone beneath the grass,
and vineyards cover all the slopes
where the dead teams were used to pass.

O vine, grow close upon that bone
and hold it with your rooted hand.
The prophet Moses feeds the grape,
and fruitful is the Promised Land.

Judith Wright, *Bullocky* [1971 [1946]: 17]

While the discursive practices of both the Australian people and the Australian state may be, and indeed continually are, counterposed, aligned and realigned in a democratic and often acrimonious dialogue between the two, it is rare to find a discourse in which virtually all the nation engages, and engages harmoniously. Despite the rhetoric and mythologies which surround them, folk festivals, horse races and car-racing ultimately address a finite and specialized community of interest. Events which invoke and orchestrate the nationalist sentiments of an entire people in support of a state – war, religious fervour, international sporting contests – are infrequent and difficult to control. When, however, the ongoing project of the state is one of capital accumulation and global economic competition, the attachment of the hearts and minds of citizens to an abstract and distant goal – and one seemingly irrelevant to the everyday concerns of ordinary working people – presents a more difficult ideological problem.

All the apparatuses of the state, ideological and repressive, are brought to bear on this problem. Educational policy, 'cultural' policy, welfare provision, law and order, the mass media, the political process and human relations themselves are ceaselessly directed and redirected by the agents of the state in line with the economic and political aims of ruling groups, groups seldom even agreed among themselves. The economic goals of the state are promoted, though with varying success, as the personal and individual goals of all citizens, of both community and society, of the nation-in-concert.

In an earlier age, the church, the extended family and/or the local community could utilize the shared knowledge of people and custom generated in daily face-to-face interaction to ensure a degree of social order and ideological control. A carefully, often oppressively nurtured understanding of belonging, co-operation, social duty and contribution to the common weal could be turned to the advantage of the whole community and made the object of congratulation, even reverence, and emulation. In mass society, the occasion and opportunity for the creation and structuration of such a sense of community has to be provided by mass apparatuses. And because to be effective these occasions need to be regular and universally available, they must be organized and co-ordinated and must have a wide appeal to the interests and ambitions of ordinary people across the country.

One such occasion, organized across the land by independent bodies known as the (sometimes Royal) Agricultural Society, the Horticultural Society or the Exhibition Society, is the Show. The Show is an occasion for blurring the difference between town and country, for negating their oppositions and celebrating an ideal of the formalized and officially defined nation *as* community, as the 'natural' construction of a people whose differences are less important than their similarities.

The Show

Once a year, all over the country, Australians flock to the Show. Country towns have their one-, two- or three-day festivals, while the state capitals stage events lasting a week or more. In Sydney, it is the Royal Easter Show; in Brisbane, The Exhibition; in Adelaide, in the spring, it is the Royal Adelaide Show. Young and old, rich and poor, rural and urban dwellers pass through the gates of showgrounds to gaze at prize-winning farm animals, performances and displays, to feast on meat pies, hot dogs and fairy floss (spun sugar, cotton candy), to hear bands and listen to the shrieks of riders on gut-wrenching machines like the Mad Mouse, the Gravitron, the Hurricane or the Loop-the-Loop.

The Show is an assault on all the senses, but the sense that is primarily engaged is that of sight. The principal activity of the Show is to bring into full public view the products of a capitalist society with the object of selling them, and selling itself to itself. In so doing, it plays a part in legitimizing and celebrating the very social, political and economic order which generates it, and in an important sense is generated and sustained by it. For the Show refracts a particular and very powerful understanding of Australian society as imbued with the pioneering spirit of the (originally rural) 'battler' – long mythologized as self-sufficient, independent and truly productive, however buffeted by bad seasons, ill luck, changing financial policies and other economic vicissitudes beyond the control of ordinary workers and their dependents. The Show is a reminder of past struggles and triumphs, interwoven with carefully tended beliefs about the continuing and mutually interdependent progress and prosperity of individuals and of the country as a whole, intermittent as such progress and prosperity may appear to be. It is, as its vernacular title implies, a display, a show-case of hard-won achievement; it provides both performers and spectators, congratulation and inspiration. It lauds competition as the spur to success and rewards winners with trophies, ribbons and cash prizes, while encouraging the runners-up and also-rans with a profusion of certificates of commendation. It is also a festive occasion of holiday and respite from the labour which produces it and is its reason for being.

Four major aspects of the Show – pleasure, trade, competition and community – constitute the event as a secular carnival. My analysis here is grounded in participant observation of the sesquicentennial Royal Adelaide Show in 1989 and the 1991 rural Show at Nimmitabel in New South Wales. As such, it does not pretend to present a definitive portrait of the multifarious activities of this widespread event. What I hope to do, rather, is to look beyond the sound and light, the noise and colour of promotion and entertainment to the significance of the Show as a bearer of some of the focal cultural meanings of contemporary Australian society.

The Show has its origins in the fairs and market days of

mediaeval and early industrial Europe and Britain. But the activities of the fair – the exchange of goods and produce, the relaying of news, propaganda and advertising, entertainment and amusement, competition and display – are now all inflected through a mode of production and a state-subsidized organization which allow scant participation on the part of ordinary people. The vast majority of showgoers, especially in the cities, are spectators and consumers, not actors and producers. Unlike the Carnival in Latin America, embedded in a past dominated by Catholicism and slavery [see, for example, Juneja, 1988], the Show in Australia is a secular celebration, sturdily rooted in Protestantism and Anglo-Celtic exploitative settlement. Successive generations of immigrants and shifting hierarchies of economic and moral value have built upon these foundations, diversifying and enriching the experience and impact of the Show, but its stated purposes remain didactic, and, as always, it lauds the work ethic and private enterprise.

Unlike, too, the great expositions and world fairs [see, for example, Rydell, 1984] the Show is less concerned with establishing a national image and ideology on a world stage. Rydell cites Wilbur O. Atwater of the U.S. Agriculture Department in 1923:

> The exposition should not be merely a show, a fair or a colossal shop, but also and pre-eminently an exposition of the principles which underlie our national and individual welfare, of our *material, intellectual and moral status,* of the elements of our weakness and of our strength, of the progress we have made, the plane on which we live and the ways in which we shall rise higher. [1984: 7, my emphasis]

The Show in Australia has always lacked the conscious comparative focus of American world fairs and other international expositions: it has few exotic exhibits from foreign lands, nor does it have the 'ethnological villages' or the triumphant displays of national technological inventiveness and progress so characteristic of late nineteenth- and early twentieth-century expositions. The Show has never laid claim to exhibiting 'principles underlying . . . [Australian] intellectual and moral status', and the emphasis on science, religion, arts and architecture which Rydell discerns is missing. Localism, even parochialism, is a more salient feature of all Australian shows, including the big-city ones, which still retain crucial elements of their past as agricultural fairs in their emphasis on agricultural, pastoral and horticultural production and on the cottage crafts of an earlier era. Furthermore, the Show is directed to a local community rather than a global society. Its self-regard has little to do with asserting national status and nationalist superiority and much to do with the assertion of what sometimes seems to be a rather naive faith in the productive skills and abilities of the Australian people.

This assertion is channelled through the provision of a venue and organization which claims a community of interest, on the part of producers and consumers alike, in commercial production of all types. Even the smallest rural shows exhibit the non-commercial results of 'the productive use of leisure time' in their displays of amateur photography, cake-decorating, lace-making, rose- or gladiolus-growing, doll-dressing and so on. That many showgoers are unaware of, or totally uninterested in, the function of the Show as a vehicle for advertisement, encouragement and recognition of such productivity *and its ordering* does not detract from the didactic effect of the Show as a whole. Those who attend, as many do, 'merely a show, a fair or a colossal shop' nonetheless retain an impression of the size, the sights and sounds and smells of a many-faceted industriousness and the satisfaction and pride of production this entails.

Like the Grand Prix or the Melbourne Cup, the Show is instrumental in constructing and organizing a mythology of community solidarity within a framework of holiday, amusement and entertainment, and executing it through a complex structure of bureaucracy and status relations. In this mythology, everyone, from primary school children to old age pensioners, is conceived of as having the capacity and moral duty to contribute to local and ultimately national prosperity.

The South Australian Agricultural Society, established towards the end of 1839, a bare three years after the proclamation of the colony, held its first show in a hotel yard in December 1840. The promoters of the event constituted 'one of the most numerous and respectable meetings ever assembled in the colony', representing commercial interests, pastoralists and the colonial government, their aim being 'the encouragement and improvement of all descriptions of agriculture, rearing of stock, &c.' [cited in Kerr and Kerr, 1983: 1].

This 'encouragement and improvement' must be seen in the context of a newly established colony which was not only concerned with sustaining itself, but already had plans for export and trade with other colonies and the mother country. The encouragement and improvement of (agricultural and pastoral) production rested crucially upon the development of supportive attitudes and values throughout the population towards the creation of surplus value, hard work and what is now called 'productivity'. The 'respectable' colonists were deeply concerned, particularly with regard to schooling, to inculcate a moral economy which condemned laziness and selfishness, lauded individual enterprise and achievement and strongly believed that 'God helps those who help themselves' while 'Satan finds mischief for idle hands to do' [see, for example, Nimon, 1987].

The didactic and promotional purposes of the Show remain central to it, though they are less concerned with primary production than they were when, it was said, Australia rode on the sheep's back. Today, agriculture is studied in universities: the Commonwealth Scientific and Industrial Research Organisation (the CSIRO), the state and federal Departments of Agriculture and Primary Industry, manufacturers and distributors of farm machinery and university extra-mural departments all arrange field days to instruct and inform farmers and pastoralists. The mechanization of agriculture has largely rendered sheaf-tossing, ploughing or pruning competitions little more than a display of archaic skills. Shearing and woodchopping competitions which, with their big prize-money, attract interstate and even overseas competitors, have become sporting contests rather than a demonstration of techniques or tools crucial to efficient primary production.

Both agricultural exports and the prestige of agriculture itself as central to Australians' image of themselves as autonomous battlers, against capricious monetary policies and the depredations of nature alike, have declined. Instead, there have been increases in the bureaucratic planning and surveillance of agriculture, and a heightened emphasis on the national importance of tertiary (service) industries with, for example, tourism replacing agriculture as the country's largest earner of foreign currency. These altered economic and cultural circumstances generate a changing perspective upon mythologically characteristic Australian understandings of independence and interdependence as expressed in the imagery of the rural battler. The farmer, indeed, is now more frequently depicted in cartoons and editorials as a reactionary and complaining parasite, palm ever-extended for a government handout, than as a proudly independent rock upon whom the nation's prosperity rests – that is, when individual farmers have managed to avoid the consolidation and 'rationalization' of rural properties into large agribusiness estates. The 'farmer's wife' (now more often than not a partner in a pastoral company, or indeed a farmer herself) is less often presented as a sturdy bulwark and support than as a deeply conservative upholder of a simplistic moralism. The timber-getter, in the face of conservationist pressure, is depicted as a chainsaw-wielding thuggish boor. It is now the free-ranging entrepreneur, the financier, hotelier or restaurateur, the professional sportsperson or entertainer who is more likely to take centre stage as symbolizing the skills and aptitudes required for individual – and perhaps, by an optimistic extension, also national – economic well-being.

Nonetheless, farming and pastoralism remain vitally important to the national economy, and although they engage fewer and fewer workers in their operations, they can be seen as less egocentric and more puritanically respectable than those occupations which entail either monetary speculation or blatantly ruthless competition. The modern Show is able to accommodate both, and willingly does so. The events in the show-ring are balanced by numerous other happenings outside the central arena, events which include, for example, contests between adolescent musical groups with noted radio or television 'personalities' compering, well-known gourmets tasting and judging the foods and wines which have been entered in competition, and designers judging fashion shows.

Today, the Show has become a grand spectacle, a part of 'the laudatory monologue which the present order maintains about itself' [Debord, 1970: 24]. It is, as Debord suggests, an essentially unilateral communication, and its message is consumption: consumption of food and drink, of sensation, of commodities, and above all of myth and ideology, consumption, moreover, which can be couched in terms of a national or at least community duty.

The Show mediates production and consumption, and also fractions of capital, momentarily unifying them and applauding their achievements. In the words of the director of the Royal Adelaide Show, it 'brings the country to the city', thus defining a community of interest between the landowners, the industrialists and the consumers of their products. The resurgent nationalism of the past two decades has, as one of its major tenets, a celebration of the rural, of the land itself and of its productive but morally and fiscally responsible exploitation. At the Show, city people can see and hear, smell and touch what is everywhere propounded as their national heritage, the sunburnt lucky country whose major earners of foreign currency are the land and its products: tourism and primary industry. In small country towns like Nimmitabel in New South Wales, the Show provides an occasion for the mixing of the local pastoralists, labourers and shopkeepers as if they were all equal members of the same productive community. Here (and the occasion is rare enough), they are on terms of first-name familiarity with the techniques and skills of each other's working lives, confidently informed in their own judgements of the lightest Victoria sponge cake or the grand champion Merino ram.

At the Show, a mythologized rural past is juxtaposed and intertwined with a technological urban present, and both are projected on to the screen of an optimistic global future. The messages of adversity overcome through collaborative action, of common goals and community solidarity, are relayed through a parade of the fruits of the labour of individuals – on farms, in factories, in bureaucratic board rooms and CSIRO laboratories, in kitchens, school rooms and studios. The Show is presented as a co-operative endeavour on the part of all the 'ordinary' people (and in egalitarian individualism, everyone is 'ordinary') of the nation. That social distinctions are maintained, through, for example, the Members' Bar and Members' Stands at the big-city showgrounds, is of little consequence, if it is noticed at all. There are many other bars and grandstands at the grounds, so that as Hobbes would have it, all are satisfied with their own share. At small rural shows there is only one bar and one tea-room in which all mingle, but this does not suggest to any of the participants that everyday social distinctions will not be re-asserted once they have left the showgrounds behind.

The Image of the City State

The Royal Adelaide Show may be conceptualized as a miniature city state of the capitalist world. Adelaide itself, being the residence of around 75 percent of the population of South Australia, is often referred to in this way, and in this it is an extreme example of the oft-noted tendency of Australian settlement to be concentrated in coastal cities and of the centralization of economic and political power in state capitals.

As well as being the display case of South Australian production, the Show is also the exhibition centre for hegemonic understandings of community and society, the rights and duties of citizenship and the mutual interdependence and responsibilities of all in advancing the welfare of what the state's frequent official promotions refer to as 'a Great State, Mate', 'SA Great' and 'Our State.' The proprietorial, egalitarian tone of these slogans, often uttered on television by people whom we take to be, given the production sets of the advertisements, bus drivers, welders, housewives, telephonists or school teachers, emphasizes the stake that ordinary working people have in the prosperity of South Australia. The message is clear that if 'we' all work just a little bit harder, South Australia (which, given its lack of diversity in industrial and manufacturing output and its small local markets, often bears the brunt of nationwide economic recession and unemployment) will be an even greater state in which to live.

Bounded, in Adelaide, by livestock stalls, parklands and arterial roads, the showground miniaturizes the social and commercial life of the state. Almost all of human life may be observed or hinted at in the activities and pursuits of the showgoers. Commerce and industry are here, farming and folk culture, education, leisure and recreation, even a certain understated Disney-like fantasy world. Also strongly manifested are pride in material production, in competition and performance in a range of individual and collective income-producing operations or archaic skills.

The repressive state apparatuses, the police and army, are present and represented as friendly and protective. Their information stands are staffed by men and women in distinctive uniforms, their promotional literature holds out the promise of satisfying careers, in doing something for yourself and something for society at the same time. Their displays of equipment (finger-printing, lie-detecting, field-communications) are demonstrated by young police officers or soldiers and allow 'hands-on' experience of their workings. Displays of weaponry are backed by promotional films focusing on the Army Reserve, though the line is drawn at the actual handling of lethal (and enormously expensive) weapons and armoury by an interested public.

The message of these exhibits is twofold: the police and military perform a service of immense importance to the well-being of the community, and they therefore require the moral and financial support of an informed and committed citizenry. They keep the peace, find lost children and are the guardians of sovereignty. The role of the police and armed forces is presented as protecting honest citizens against, usually and thankfully, an imagined threat to national security and/or personal safety. (Their use by the State in, for example, riot and crowd control or strike-breaking is never mentioned, nor are the frequent commissions investigating police corruption. And of course they would not be, for these are issues which divide the community and point up relations of class conflict, allowing a glimpse of the iron hand of violence and repression in the velvet glove of the protective welfare state.) At the Show, the often historical depiction of the malefactions and capture of dangerous criminals, or drug-busting adventures, or of operations against terrorists or hypothetical invaders provides for a mildly exciting prickle of fear and, in consequence, grateful recognition of the national and local value of the forces of law and order and the vigilant defence of the nation.

The ideological state apparatuses – education, the mass media, families, churches and cultural institutions, as well as charities and voluntary associations, are also hard at work. All, in their different ways, are engaged in a celebration of themselves as pillars of a warm-hearted community. Some, like the churches, and voluntary associations like the Country Women's Association, the Young Farmers' Association or the Returned Services League, focus their activities upon serving visitors to the Show, providing rest places, tea rooms and meeting venues. No other South Australian crowd offers the concentration of small children and disabled people that the Show provides, nor are facilities for the entertainment of children, baby-feeding, child-minding or wheelchairs so readily accessible elsewhere, despite continuous desperate calls for further state funding of childcare places, sheltered workshops or special teachers in the schools.

The Show is publicized as a 'family affair', with entrance fees for families being discounted, and schoolchildren may be granted a holiday for the occasion. Many exhibits, particulary in the 'junior' categories of the arts and handicrafts sections, are the works of school students, undertaken for credit in, for example, hand-writing, carpentry, dressmaking or photography classes. Similarly, many of the competitive ring events feature hotly contested junior categories, especially in horse-riding. Children and young people are prominent in caring for show animals, grooming and feeding them, mucking out stalls and leading beasts around the show ring.

One of the most popular displays, sponsored by a bank, is the 'farmyard nursery', where small children from the suburbs view the antics of, and may even be permitted to handle, chickens, ducklings, piglets, puppies, lambs and calves.

Beyond the showground in Adelaide lie the central business district and the residential suburbs, and beyond these, the open countryside. At showtime, the city engulfs the country, inverting the normal spatial order of the Australian landscape. The workaday economic order seems to be inverted too, for although many people are employed at the Show, its atmosphere is one of relaxation and leisure. Everyday disciplines are slackened, as children are indulged and expensive junk foods are heedlessly ingested by young and old. The country people do their business (often the culmination of a year's labour) and then set off to see the sights, go shopping 'in town' and catch up with friends and acquaintances at bars, tea rooms or the various stockbreeding societies' annual dinners. City people too take a day off work or school, peruse the horticultural and handicraft exhibits, buy plants or gadgets and go courting among the sideshows. And yet, the perceived inversion of the everyday order of things is illusory. It is part of the magic and excitement of the Show and the pleasure of show-going, but the realities of trade and commerce, of advertising and promotion not only of goods and services for sale but also of a world view and a way of life, lie very near the surface of the spectacle.

The Spatial Organization of The Show and its Project

The terrain of the Adelaide Show provides a schematic representation of the meeting of rural and urban interests so greatly extolled by the Show's organizers and the mass media. Broadly speaking, the southern end of the showground in Adelaide is devoted to agricultural production, while the northern end, nearer the city, is the site of consumption and commerce. The overtly primary activities of the Show – contest and display – are centrally located in the main arena and the judging rings and pavilions surrounding it. Also centrally located, in permanent buildings, are the administrative and business activities of the Show: the major banks, the offices of the big stock and station agents and the stockbreeding societies, and the vine-covered offices of the Show administration itself.

Wrapped up in and surrounded by the seeming disorder of the

amusements and the nostalgia of country fairs, both of which are important in generating the holiday atmosphere of the Show, the bureaucratic-administrative supports of the Show and of the commercial interests which dominate it are sited in a position of command and authority. They are by no means hidden from view, even if most showgoers have little interest in them; they are permanently and securely located, easily found [see Figure 1] and easily accessible.

At the Show, people engage in a wide range of everyday activities in a confined space. They obtain cash (D4) or boiling water (D5), go to the toilet (B7, D8, C6, D4), receive first aid (E4), find lost children (D5), leave messages (D4), post mail (D8), borrow wheelchairs or hire strollers (D2). There are food stalls everywhere, offering a variety of fast foods – fairy floss and toffee apples, Dutch pancakes, Lebanese kebabs and Vietnamese spring rolls – and there are cafeterias, tea rooms and a licensed restaurant. Most importantly for the commercial success of the Show, one may place orders for the purchase of all manner of consumer goods being demonstrated: sewing machines, glassware, gardening equipment, farm machinery, encyclopaedias or sporting goods at stands in the avenues, pavilions and halls which contain the commercial exhibits.

The pavilions and halls also house the exhibits of 23 voluntary associations, including the Royal Society for the Prevention of Cruelty to Animals (RSPCA), the Australian Retired Persons' Association (ARPA), World Vision, the Christadelphians and the Blind Welfare Gift Shop. Ten quasi-government instrumentalities are represented here, including the Australian Meat and Lifestock Corporation, the South Australian Avocado Growers' Association and the Barley Board; there are also nine animal breeding societies (e.g. Charollais, Murray Grey, South Devon) and nineteen government departments, including the Bureau of Meteorology, the Commonwealth Employment Service and the Drug and Alcohol Services Council. At all the stands and displays, one may receive free advice on such matters as energy conservation, cholesterol control or mass tree-planting. The major political parties are conspicuous, as are the major banks. It is the boast of the Show that it contains 'something for everyone', and this would appear to be the case, at least as far as commodity relations are concerned.

For the majority of city showgoers, the Show is a pleasurable leisure activity. The judging of farm animals and farm produce,

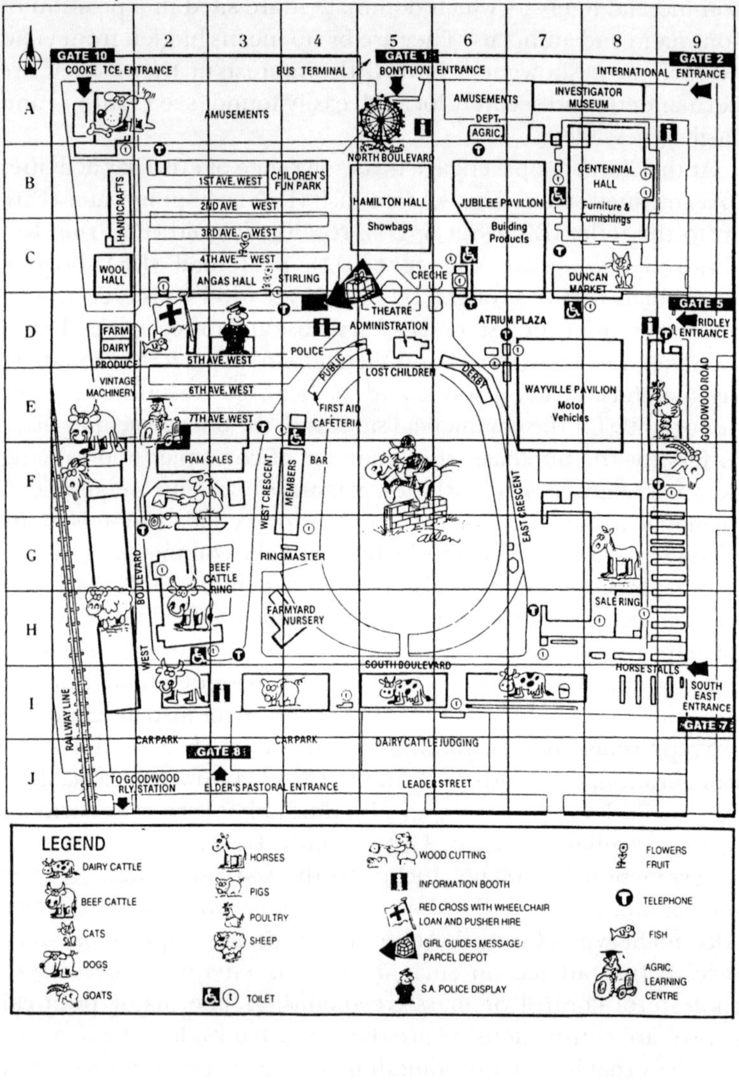

Figure 1 Royal Adelaide Show 1992
(*Source*: Show Guide)

of poultry, pigeons, goats and horses, fruit, vegetables and dairy products, is not their central concern. What is of interest is the display of activities in which they may themselves engage: floriculture, handicrafts, cars and caravans, furniture and home decoration, and the Wool Parades (a fashion parade of woollen garments.) Many of the competitors in these activities are themselves city people, and not infrequently they may also be professionally involved in horticulture, cake-decorating or dress design. But still, most showgoers are there as observers, not participants. They are there to 'give the kids some fun' or to have a family outing, to pick up some tips on gardening or do-it-yourself home improvements, or for adolescents to engineer 'chance' meetings with like-minded others. But, unlike country showgoers, they are not likely to be personally familiar with handicrafts prizewinners or the owners of champion dogs or cats or budgerigars, let alone the owners of draught horses or bulls. Nor are they as likely to have developed their own expertise or even competence in the animal husbandry or arts and crafts paraded before them.

This distancing from the mythologized *raison d'être* of the Show is reduced through the practice of encouraging first-hand experience of at least some of its activities. The farmyard nursery and farm-machinery displays allow city showgoers to touch and feel the warmth and vulnerability of small animals or to operate the gears and levers of tractors, balers and reapers. Through such play, the urban fantasy of rural self-sufficiency, tranquillity and independence from government interference is permitted to override everyday understandings of the accumulating debts, bureaucratic bungling, land-degradation and often grinding toil of life on the land. The conservative 'traditional values' of a rural past are invoked and reasserted, however fleetingly, through the Show's generation of fellow feeling between farmers and city-dwellers, producers and consumers.

The joyrides and sideshows in particular also allow for some display of skill and dexterity, for example in the shooting galleries (where an outdated survival skill is rewarded by kewpie dolls and plaster animals) and the eternally popular 'Dodg'em Cars' (where the driving 'skills' of boys and young men/girls and young women combine with aggressive fearlessness and daring to impress youthful rivals and potential girl/boy friends). The more dizzying or perilous joy rides also allow for much impression-management and an excuse for ostensibly shy maidens to clutch at brave escorts. In these activities, the Show provides a legitimate venue for quite different kinds of display and advertisement, fantasy and desire, from those normally associated with it.

Commodity Education in Late Capitalist Society

Above all else, the Show is a carnival of commodities and commodity relations. It mediates production and consumption, valorizing both while it directs and cajoles producers to increase their output and consumers to increase their intake.

Case 11. The Showbag

Fifty years ago, children attending the Show could obtain, at little or no cost, a range of small articles to be collected in a 'sample bag'. Such samples might include a paint card from the manufacturers of house paints; a hank of unprocessed wool and a tiny swatch of blanket material from wool manufacturers like Laconia or Onkaparinga; a sliver of processed cheese from a local or national dairy; a minuscule packet of peanuts from Kingaroy, or a packet of seeds from Yates' nurseries; a remnant of untanned hide and one of leather from a shoemaking company; a little notebook from a papermaker; or an illustrated pamphlet on soil or water conservation, on the state forestry commission, railways or ambulance service. School teachers encouraged their pupils to make a wide selection of such articles, which could then be used in social studies 'projects' (generally a scrapbook with samples, labels, advertisements and photographs or drawings strung together by handwritten commentary drawn from textbooks and encyclopaedias) on such topics as agriculture, industry, transport, communications, trade and commerce in the local region, the state or the country as a whole.

Much enjoyment accrued to the collectors of sample bags, with envious comparison and dogged haggling over 'swaps'. The sample bag, along with the sideshows (Jimmy Sharman's boxing tent, shooting galleries, coconut shies, two-headed creatures) and (in the days before the invention of the Salk vaccine) the frequently forbidden consumption of fairy floss and toffee apples, was one of the highlights of the Show. That the sample bags were primarily a vehicle of training in brand awareness and civic duty occurred to and troubled no one, least of all their collectors. Even if it had occurred to them, the burghers of the 1940s and 1950s, like the school teachers, would have considered this a perfectly proper outcome and a large return upon a small investment.

The sample bag is no longer available at the Show. What there is instead is the showbag. Showbags are pre-packed and sold at different prices, depending upon their size and elaborateness, at a number of stalls around the city shows. They contain a selection of well-known sweets, potato crisps and chocolate bars and one or two items such as Batman masks or frisbees, yo-yos, spinning tops, pencils or other small 'novelty toys' with Coca Cola or Pepsi Cola, State Bank (now defunct) or Hindmarsh Building Society insignia, inflatable cushions, more complex toy cars – sporting the brand names of the cigarette-manufacturing sponsors of car races – or helicopters and aeroplanes with commercial, police or Royal Australian Air Force markings. However thinly disguised in the past, the didactic and civic-awareness aspects of the sample bag have now disappeared, and the consumer-education element has been replaced by a straightforward understanding of 'you get what you (or your parents) pay for'. This is not to say that the buyers of showbags may not be subjected to homilies about 'value for money', and indeed it is true that a more highly structured, critical and reflective consumer education is offered in today's schools. But what the purchase of showbags does point to is the increased distance that now exists between production and consumption and the further commodification of social relations in late capitalist society. And this is so despite all the ideological efforts of the Show to remind us of the solid community spirit of a mythologized rural past and to re-insert such a spirit into a commoditized urban present.

Case 12. The Woodchop

Perennially popular at all Shows, large and small, rural and urban, is an event known to showgoers as the Woodchop, and to Show organisers as Wood-Cutting (Axe) [see Figure 1]. The felling of trees and the sawing and milling of timber are potent symbols of a pioneering past, of clearing the land, building homes and fashioning a new civilization out of virgin forests. More than this, the act of timber-getting, without the aid of chainsaws and bulldozers, symbolizes not only the *machismo*, the strength, toughness and physical dauntlessness of the ideal-typical Australian male, it is also evocative of an ancient skill, cognate with hunting 'for the pot' (rather than 'for sport') or the construction of settled homesteads and villages, environmentally responsible and thus equally acceptable to those who otherwise oppose the mechanized operations of the contemporary timber industry.

The Woodchop provides a simple and telling image of humanity's conquest of nature with the aid of its distinctive technology. The long-handled axe, in use as a domestic tool for centuries, is by no means the most expressive symbol of either machine-driven mass production or high-tech electronic industry, but in its familiarity and homeliness it is a highly effective statement of the ability of *Homo faber* to subdue and control the elements and to turn natural resources to advantage. The axe, wielded by a single human hand, is indicative of independent and personal direction in the making of a way of life, self-sufficient and self-reliant, in a manner almost but not quite impossible to imagine in an age of high-technology mass production.

> Axe-fall, echo and axe-fall. Noonday silence.
> Though I go to the cities, turning my back on these hills,
> for the talk and dazzle of cities, for the sake of belonging
> for months and years at a time to the twentieth century,
>
> The city will never quite hold me. . ..
>
> Les Murray, *Noonday Axeman* [1991 [1965]: 5]

Furthermore, and most obviously, the competition between the speed, strength and dexterity of teams and individuals provides for an exciting spectator sport, with brawny competitors correctly attired in workers' singlets and white trousers and shady lawns for observers to loll in comfort. Events include 'standing block' and 'underhand handicaps' and 'championships', 'tree-felling', 'double-handed sawing', relays and team events. Prize money exceeds $40,000. The Showguide entices competitors and spectators thus:

> The unique Aussie sport of Woodcutting is on again this year. The Royal Adelaide Show can boast the first purpose-built log storage area, complete with sprinkler system that will keep the logs at just the right moisture content for competition. . ..

> But this traditional Iron Man's sport with its 149 years of Royal Show history is in for a few surprises this year. Fourteen women have entered the fray, including an entrant in the open competition. Move over lads, these women will provide some tough competition. . ..
>
> Father's Day will see Dads and sons team up in a combination relay, providing a chance for showgoers to see the 'chips off the old blocks' in action. . ..
>
> For those 'Norms' who Woodcut from the spectators' area year after year, here is a chance to ''ave a go.' The National Bank is sponsoring lunchtime coaching clinics. Under the expert eye of Tasmania's Paul Hogan and World Champions David Foster and Daryl Haydn, many a potential champ may be discovered. It could be you!!! [Royal Adelaide Show, 1988: 26]

The Woodchop is a metonym of the Show. Couched in history and tradition, like British sheepdog trials or North American rodeos, it is a discourse of human power and independence, individualism and 'natural' equality. It bespeaks and ideologizes the control of nature in the production and reproduction of a style of life which is presented as distinctively Australian – tough, straightforward, unsentimental, even harsh. It refers to egalitarian relations of production and to an archaic working environment now lost to an urbanized and industrialized labour force – lost, but still dreamt of. Both the Woodchop and the Show identify, celebrate and continually mythologize a culture and an ideology which keep alive the ideals of community and equality.

The 'laudatory monologue' that the state presents to the people through the discourse and spectacle of the Show dramatizes and insists upon the role of ordinary men and women in the creation and furtherance of the well-being of the nation – themselves, their forebears and their successors. That the discourse *is* a monologue is only thinly disguised by the opportunities the Show provides for participation and personal experience. The organization of the Show, its administration and ordering of physical sensation, its control of crowds and of the definition of legitimate enjoyment, all remain firmly in the hands of those who have always dominated the social formation which is eulogized by the Show: the urban and rural ruling class and their subalterns.

CHAPTER NINE

The Architecture of Identity: Parliament House and the Stockman's Hall of Fame

Australia's recorded history is short: less than one hundred years (since 1901) as an independent nation state, and just over two hundred years (since the First Fleet arrived in New South Wales in 1788) as a collection of British colonies. The indigenous Aborigines, however, refer to forty thousand years of continuous habitation, to which much archaeological evidence attests; and all later immigrant groups – English, Irish, Scots, Greek, Italian, Serb, Croat, Polish, Lebanese, Chinese, Cambodian – participate to varying degrees in the long histories of the lands from whence their forebears, or they themselves, migrated.

Geologically too, Australia is an extremely ancient phenomenon, its volcanoes long extinct, its mountains rounded and flattened by millennia of winds and rains, its soils leached and eroded. The native flora and fauna provide numerous examples of life forms conceptualized elsewhere as prehistoric: monotremes, for example, and cycads. Like Petra, Australia is 'half as old as time', or even older. The Aboriginal concept of the Dreamtime, dimly understood by the great majority of Australians, combines with a much later romantic literary tradition to see Australia as a 'timeless' land [see, for example, Dark, 1963]. It is this ideal of timelessness, of natural continuity, of oneness between the land and its people, which structures an understanding of history which is at once deeply rooted in the primordial and incessantly applied to everyday life by contemporary mythology. Between the primaeval Dreamtime and the recent history of the last two hundred years stretches a vast uncharted territory of time and space, sparsely illuminated by archaeological and geological discoveries which only enhance the understanding of Australian history as an uneasy blend of Stone-Age autochthony and brash immaturity.

More than most other Western industrial nations, Australia has a history which appears, quite blatantly, to be always in the process of creation. This is not, of course, to suggest that the history of any country is not a constant creation and recreation of past events considered significant by one or another interested party. Rather, it is to make the point that 'new' nations – most particularly ex-colonies of European imperialist adventures – are engaged in a highly self-conscious process of what used to be called in Africa in the 1960s 'nation-building' [see, for example, Cowan et al., 1965]. The welding together of disparate peoples, often traditional enemies, into a modern nation state requires, according to the ideology of nation-building, the formation of political and social institutions which conform to some universal 'standard'. Such standards are imposed, often through military force and state terrorism, by the superpowers of the day. In the twentieth century, these great powers have included Britain, Germany, the United States, Russia (in the guise of the USSR) and Japan.

As a British colony and a member of the 'old' British Commonwealth (the erstwhile British Empire), Australia has participated in the Westminster parliamentary tradition and the British political structure to a marked degree, although always in the position of a (sometimes unruly) junior partner. As befits such a relationship, Australia's sons and daughters have fought and died for Britain at Bloemfontein and Pozières, at Tobruk and on the Burma Railway, and most famously in Palestine and the Dardanelles. Australian legal and governmental institutions are British: the Magna Carta is prominently displayed in Parliament House in Canberra, a gift from the British government in 1988. It was only in 1986, after negotiations begun in 1972–5, that the British Privy Council ceased to be the final court of appeal for Australians convicted of serious crimes and was replaced by the Australian High Court; and in 1975 the Governor General, as representative of the Queen, could still formally and definitively dismiss an elected government from office, and did so.

Since 1945, the balance of foreign power and influence in Australia has shifted in favour of the United States. American influence in popular culture has been ubiquitous, most obviously in the mass media, despite attempts by the state to legislate for a mandatory 'Australian content' in film and television production and programming.[1] The themes of commercially successful Australian films like *Breaker Morant* or *Gallipoli* have generally been recognizably Australian in, as White [1983: 120] points out, their emphasis on 'men, mateship and militarism', despite increasing numbers of films with a more universal appeal. Actors and technicians have also generally been Australian citizens, even if their box-office attractiveness has been augmented by American stars and American voice coaches. But these observations are essentially epiphenomenal. White comes closer to unlocking the problem of what, all over the world, has been called 'Americanization', and what the political left in Australia used sternly to call 'US cultural imperialism', and later more frivolously termed 'Coca-Colonization', in concluding that 'the Americanization process becomes far more formidable when the fundamental concepts of a society's national identity are remodelled in the American image' [1983: 120–1].

As White himself suggests, such imagery includes an anti-British republicanism which is actually not discernible in the histories of the Boer War and the Great War. But White's view of 'culture,' as his earlier work [1981] makes clear, is largely confined to the complex of art, literature and music. Thus it remains unclear about what these 'fundamental concepts of national identity' might actually be. Given this view, he can readily assume that political institutions like democracy are virtually indistinguishable in their American or Australian manifestations. Yet the role of trade unions in the twentieth century in industrial relations, the development of social welfare legislation and wage negotiations provides a telling example of the different understandings of the relation between capital and labour, or bosses and workers, in the two countries. Similarly, the contrast between American-style participatory democracy and Australian-style representative democracy is not drawn. The institution of the electoral college in the United States, for instance, as compared with that of the pre-selection of candidates for office by constituency party members and the power of the parliamentary party organization, makes for wide variations in everyday understandings of the political process and of the roles and statuses of politicians and voters. In the same vein, although members of the Australian Shooters' Party, a gun lobby, have taken to invoking their 'constitutional right to bear arms', the *Australian* constitution enshrines no such right. Freedom of the press, too, is very differently interpreted by American and Australian legal and customary practice: the institution of *sub judice* as protection of the rights of the accused on trial in Australia is opposed on the grounds of freedom of expression by the American mass media.

The ending of the Cold War in 1990, the formation of the Commonwealth of Independent States from the ruins of the USSR, the economic resurgence of Europe and the emergence of East Asia as a powerful economic force have given a new impetus to the long-simmering thesis of globalization. In some respects, this is the thesis of Coca-Colonization in post-modern dress. The whole world can now be conceptualized as a gigantic source of raw materials, a vast reservoir of labour, a huge market for the consumption of 'value-added' goods and services: a quarry, reservoir and market which cross national boundaries and owe allegiance to no one and nothing other than 'the market' itself. That this is too simple, static and broad a characterization is illustrated, for example, by the festering balance-of-trade problems between the United States and Japan, the clumsy attempts by many nations, including Australia, to imitate the educational and industrial-relations practices of the Japanese, or the chasms of understanding which separate countries like Pakistan and India, or Iran and Iraq, and even more perilously, Muslim and non-Muslim societies. Nonetheless this characterization suggests a logical progression from the nationalism of local economies to the multi- or transnationalism of the great business corporations and their powerful home bases. The globalization of trade is assumed to go hand in hand with the globalization of cultural practices.

Such is the equation of Democracy with the Free Market Economy, an equation assiduously promulgated by the President of the United States and his staff and seemingly unquestioned by the new Russian President and his staff on the occasion of the re-emergence of Russia as a single sovereign nation in 1991. In its conformity to an American-imposed standard of democracy, Russia was made welcome in what the then American President Bush called 'the new world order'.

The Uses of History

Nation-building in the 1990s requires, then, both the construction of political and social institutions, including systems of trade and commerce, which conform to the most powerful global definitions, and the creation of ideologies which support and legitimize those same institutions. Thus histories and moralities are rethought, rewritten and differentially evaluated.

This is by no means a simple task. The re-jigging of economic and financial institutions is perhaps the least difficult aspect of the construction and reconstruction of national identity in that it calls to the most basic human needs for sustenance and shelter, translated into national needs for self-sufficiency and self-respect. But ideological reconstruction is an altogether more complex operation, as those who seek 'the end of ideology' are constantly reminded [cf. Bell, 1960]. The definition and protection of such broadly and variously understood elements of political democracy as 'human rights', 'civil liberties' or 'individual freedoms' requires a concerted effort on the part of ideological state apparatuses everywhere.[2] This is especially the case when such rights and freedoms are seen to be incompatible with the operation of a free-market economy, or simply beyond the financial means of any one nation or transnational corporation to produce and maintain. Witness, for example, the problems attendant upon the banning of nuclear testing, the control of pollution and greenhouse gas emissions, the disposal of toxic wastes, the preservation of the environment; or the guarantee of freedom from hunger or preventable disease, or the universal availability of health care, adequate housing and education.

The human impulse to totalize, to make coherent a world that appears to be in a constant state of fracturing and splintering, finds expression in the myths, ideologies and discursive practices of community. But for the modern nation state this strategy, however necessary, is insufficient. The power relations of individual states and their political and economic interrelations with other states in a global formation entail the operation of many-tentacled bureaucracies and commercial-industrial conglomerates and financial institutions, whose officials are not elected and are quite unknown to the millions affected by their decisions. In countries like Australia, where transnational conglomerates can close down entire manufacturing plants without any reference to local governments or economic policies and where the decisions of foreign trading blocs imperil the livelihoods of thousands of workers, the only possible response of ordinary people is one of impotent and short-lived rage. The moral high ground of free trade is constantly eroded by reference to the cut-throat 'realities' of global economic competition, in which, as politicians constantly declaim, Australia must compete or perish, just as not so long ago Australians were encouraged to populate (by means of immigration or rising birthrates) or perish.

The building and maintenance of a national(ist) identity is seriously threatened by the demolition machinery powered by global capitalism and the nationalism of other, more powerful states. The destruction of 'old' traditions and ways of life, however derivative they may be, and the erection of shiny new imported structures in their place may be productive of both optimism and pessimism about the future of the nation – often simultaneously. But it is a prime interest of the state to utilize all the means at its disposal – political, economic, ideological and above all 'cultural' – to foster the optimistic and minimize the pessimistic reaction. And furthermore, it must do so on a *national* scale: anything less risks the resurfacing of the sectional gloom and despair that presages the fall of governments, or even the fury that portends revolution.

The fundamental source of the building materials of national identity is history, a history, moreover, that is one of many possible histories, one that is constantly being created, thought, rethought, emphasized and glossed. This is so not only for the foundations upon which people construct their present and their future, but also for *the design and planning of* that present and future. For as Nietzsche observed in 1874 (1983: 67),

> History pertains to the living [being] in three respects. . .as a being who acts and strives, as a being who preserves and reveres, as a being who suffers and seeks deliverance. This threefold relationship corresponds to three species of history – in so far as it is permissible to distinguish between a *monumental*, an *antiquarian* and a *critical* species of history.

Permissible or not, this threefold distinction provides an illuminating heuristic device for the analysis of nationalist discourse. *Of course*, as Nietzsche was himself at pains to make clear, an undue stress upon one aspect of history at the expense of the others is 'unhealthy' for the life of the nation and its culture; and *of course* each aspect has advantages and disadvantages which are peculiar to it. In this way, although it may inspire and encourage a people, an age or a culture to honour and to high achievement, the monumentalist conception of history, the history of great deeds and great personages runs the danger of separating cause and effect to the extent that phenomena are treated as 'effects in themselves' [ibid.: 70]. The antiquarian conception, in its care and reverence for the past, has the potential to restrict the field of vision, so that 'it cannot relate what it sees to anything else and it therefore accords everything it sees equal importance and therefore to each individual thing too great importance' [ibid.: 74]. The problem with the critical or what Deleuze [1986: 149] prefers to call the ethical conception of history is of a different order. The judgement and condemnation of the past, or of institutions and practices rooted in the past, which is the same thing, risks the condemnation and destruction of the present:

> [M]en and ages which serve life by judging and destroying a past are always dangerous and endangered men and ages. For since we are the outcome of earlier generations, we are also the outcome of their aberrations, passions and errors, and indeed of their crimes; it is not possible wholly to free oneself from this chain. [Nietzsche, 1983: 76]

Nonetheless, as Nietzsche implies, the possibility of overcoming 'our inherited and hereditary nature' is ever present, and from this we may conclude that it is the ethical sense of history which has the potential to temper the risks and pitfalls of too great an emphasis upon the monumental and/or antiquarian perspectives. I examine below two examples of monumental and antiquarian history and suggest that it is the differing interpretations of these works which creates the space for a critical history to mediate them.

Parliament House: The Intersection of Nation and State

> Let us now praise famous men, and our fathers that begat us. [*Ecclesiasticus*, xliv: 1]

In May 1988, in the midst of year-long celebrations of the bicentenary of European settlement in Australia, Her Majesty Queen Elizabeth II officially opened Australia's new Parliament House in Canberra, the nation's capital. It was sixty-one years to the day since the first ('provisional') Federal Parliament House had been opened in Canberra in 1927, which was in turn twenty-six years to the day that the first Australian Parliament had been opened at its 'temporary' site in Melbourne in 1901.

It was not until 1909 that Canberra was formally selected as the site for the new nation's capital. In 1911, a competition was launched for the design of the new city, and in 1912 the first prize in this contest was awarded to an American, Walter Burley Griffin, out of 137 entries from all over the world, 'despite a boycott by British architects who objected to the form of adjudication in which the final decision was to be left to the Minister for Home Affairs (whom the Institute claimed lacked the professional qualifications to make a competent judgement)' [A. Fitzgerald, 1983: 23].

The design competition has become a time-honoured device in Australia in making decisions of public moment. It satisfies egalitarian understandings of openness and fairness and individualist understandings of skill and talent, while at the same time leaving final decisions to bureaucratic 'experts' who are expected to have a care (on behalf of taxpayers) for the financial implications of their decisions. Qualifications in architecture or design are taken for granted in the entrants; questions of cost and timing are the concern of the people, through their elected representatives and the work of public service bureaucracies. The aesthetic is balanced with the prudential, the ideal with the practicable, the intellectual with the pragmatic.[3] In this way, the design competition can be, and often is, characterized as democracy in action. Momentous choices are seen to be made by the people, rather than by a professional elite – one highly qualified, no doubt, but lacking in common sense and, more significantly, 'the common touch'.[4]

To this day, many Australians express dissatisfaction with Canberra's remoteness from the world of industry and commerce, a city for bureaucrats and diplomats, without a soul [see, for example, Quarry, 1983; cf. Holston, 1989]. Many more maintain the now traditional populist complaint of wastage, of money spent on monuments instead of causes considered more worthy in parts of the country considered more needy. National pride is still, with one exception, tempered by public prudence.

That exception is the Australian War Memorial, opened in Canberra in 1941, though a commemoration stone was laid in 1929, in belated memory of those who fell in the Great War. The War Memorial is, as Bruce Kapferer [1988: 122] notes, 'the central symbol of the Australian nation'; it valorizes and sacralizes the mythic qualities of the Anzac soldiers and their exploits at Gallipoli in 1915 – their purity, youth, courage and egalitarianism, and the birth of a new order through their sacrifice at the hands of distant Old World bureaucrats and mindless military authorities [cf. ibid.: 135]. Despite the War Memorial's emphasis upon, as White [1981: 82] would have it, 'men, mateship and militarism', it has retained its pre-eminence as a national symbol. As a monument of the people, it echoes on a grand scale the little monuments which adorn small towns throughout the country and which are dedicated to the memory of the fallen in the Boer War, the Great War and the Second World War, as well as in Korea and Vietnam. Its message, as is theirs, is one of tragedy, suffering and loss, a tragedy shared by the whole nation, as constant rearrangements of the War Memorial displays (more serious attention to the role of women and the importance of the home front, for example), and slight alterations to the Anzac Day ceremonies attest.[5]

Across the waters of Lake Burley Griffin, the War Memorial and Parliament House face each other in a permanent symbolizing of people against the state. The sacred, cathedral-like structure of the War Memorial, domed, built in the shape of a cross, and with its stained-glass windows facing the east, can be juxtaposed with the vaulting secular magnificence of the new Parliament House. The contrast is not a simple one of church and state, though there are clearly discernible elements of this opposition; rather, it expresses a constant tension in Australian nationalist thinking, a tension which places the 'natural' Australian people in opposition to 'artificially' created social and political structures and authorities. These authorities, by their very artificiality, cannot automatically command the allegiance of autonomous individual citizens conceptualized as sacred in their very individuality and as *naturally* autonomous.

Parliament House is not only the site of national power but above all, a discourse of power and hegemony. It presents an embarrassment of symbols, from the selection and preparation of the building site, through the carefully documented and justified choice of building materials, to the calculated visual impact of its giant flagpole. It is monumental in conception and execution, and in its piling up of what might be called semiological units it constitutes a semiotician's paradise [see, for example, Indyk, 1988]. At the same time, in its semiotic richness, Parliament House runs the risk of confusion or misinterpretation on the part of those who would read it. Guided tours, which have the uncomfortable authoritarian atmosphere of a school excursion and a plethora of official guidebooks, from cheap pamphlets to glossy 'coffee table' tomes, make every effort to ensure that visitors get their symbols right.

Case 13. Guide to Parliament House[6]

'The winning entry in the 1979 Parliament House competition was by American architects Mitchell/Giurgola and their partner, Australian architect Richard Thorp' [p.26]. Another design competition, another American winner! This time, there were '329 entries from around the world' (p.4) with no boycotts, and the blow to Australian architectural pride was softened by the fact that Richard Thorp, although domiciled in the United States, had graduated from Melbourne University.

> '[The design] was described by the assessors as "an outstandingly successful design in every respect, brilliantly blending together the requirements of architectural quality, sensitivity, symbolic identity, functional efficiency, building feasibility and relative economy which the new Parliament House must satisfy".' (p.26)

Three criteria for the aesthetes and nationalists, three for the bureaucrats and taxpayers. In sum, these criteria reflect an altogether grander approach than that of the Federal Capital Advisory Committee of 1921, which envisaged the first stages of Canberra's development as having 'simple, pleasing and unpretentious buildings – mostly single storey – planned nevertheless, to afford adequate comfort and reasonable convenience' [cited in Fitzgerald, 1983: 28]. They also reflect a greater sensitivity to the views of a more highly educated and critical tax-paying public, members of which can nevertheless be heard to mutter, on first viewing the buildings, imprecations concerning the luxurious working conditions of politicians: 'Geez, you can see where all the money went'. Such criticism is tempered by others who point out the 'necessity' for a building which befits the status of the national parliament in a country like Australia: 'You get what you pay for'. And, of course, the Parliament House buildings represent much more than an ordinary building job: 'The architects, consultants, contractors and suppliers, and their workforce of *more than 10,000 committed individuals* created a building of exceptional quality and character' (p.26, my emphasis).

In effect, each individual contributor to the building and its furnishings freely and willingly put his or her individual heart and soul into the construction of what the design judges saw as 'a building that will become, as it deserves, a national symbol' [cited p.4], though they are unclear as to exactly what it is that is being symbolized. And perhaps this does not matter, in that the wealth of symbols could allow egalitarian individualists to decide for themselves. But this hardly seems likely, given the didactic tone of the guidebooks and the strict controls exercised by the guides themselves. Parliament is also, in theory at least, the final authority for the public service, the authoritarian and unwieldy bureaucracy which colours Australian thinking about 'the Government' or 'the system'.

As the proud pointer to '10,000 individuals' suggests, size is considered an important selling point for an Australian public concerned about value for money in a project which cost over $1,000 million, 'inflation accounting for about 45 percent of the total' [p.25]. 'With 4,500 rooms, public galleries seating 1,000, parking for 2,000 vehicles, and a kitchen capable of producing 8,000 meals per day, the new building has a gross floor area of more than 250,000m^2 . . . Some 3,500 people work in Parliament House, and around 2,000,000 visitors attend annually' [p.4]. Technological modernity is important too, particularly in creating a serious and businesslike working atmosphere:

> The sound and vision system in the Parliament House incorporates technology capable of meeting virtually any broadcasting requirement. A multi-channel radio and cable television system monitors activities. . .. A public address and emergency warning network is broadcast through 12,000 speakers and local announcements can be made in 58 specific locations [. . .] There are 2,500 clocks and another 500 separate sets of division lights. [p.20] These are in addition to speakers in every room of the building, 'no matter how small' [p.20], so that parliamentarians can hear division bells wherever they may be.

The design scale, splendour and symbolic resonances of Parliament House leave no room for doubt that this is the home of the

Australian State. 'The flag mast, already an established national symbol of the Parliament, the nation and the people of Australia weighs 220 tonnes and is one of the largest stainless steel structures in the world' [p.6]; the great flag (12.8 metres by 6.4 metres), floodlit by night, is reflected in a pool at the centre of the Members' Hall, and four different interpretations of the Australian coat of arms are placed over the main entrance doors.

What is needed is a more warm and intimate scale, to make Parliament House equally credible as the home of the Australian people and nation. A start is made on the colour schemes of the working centre of Parliament: 'The traditional Westminster colours are red for the Senate [the Upper House] and green for the House of Representatives. In the Parliament House the colours reflect the Australian environment with leaf-green eucalyptus shades for the House and the ochre-red of the soils of north and central Australia for the Senate' (p.13). Depictions of landscapes and of native flora and fauna appear regularly in a wide variety of artistic media (paintings, ceramics, tapestries, marquetry, sculptures) and the primordial landscape is continually stressed, most particularly with reference to the way the building is located, 'nestling' [p.6] into the curves of Capital Hill, appearing to grow out of the earth itself. The interiors of the building are 'bathed' [p.10] and 'flooded' [p.11] with natural light, which 'filters' [pp.8, 26] through windows, skylights and glassed walkways:

> The Foyer is a welcoming space reminiscent of the outdoors where natural light filters from windows and skylights over the stairs through a forest of columns clad in grey-green Cipollino marble. [p.8] Australian timbers are featured extensively throughout the building and contribute to the warm and inviting atmosphere. [p.11] While the chambers are spacious there is a sense of intimacy within the horseshoe shaped seating which is conducive to debate. [p.12][7]

The works of well-known Australian artists like Arthur Boyd and Sidney Nolan are mixed with the productions of nameless craftspeople like the Victorian Tapestry Workshop and the Embroiderers' Guilds of Australia. The dignity of high culture mingles with the vitality of popular crafts as a unified expression of the spirit of the nation. The special Art Program, culminating in some seventy commissioned works and three thousand purchased pieces, was 'designed to *add meaning* to individual spaces within the building, and to evoke a theme of the Australian land and its people' [p.24, my emphasis]. The collection of artworks also 'completes the building as an expression of the nation' [p.22].

Ideologically, all the people of Australia must be represented, electorally *and* metaphorically, in the Parliament House: 'This is a building built by and for Australians using the skills of individuals and companies from every State and Territory. Reflecting the ethnic diversity of the country, the work force. . .was drawn from more than 30 cultural backgrounds' [p.8]. And to close the mythic semiotic circle of people, state and nation, of nature and original purity, individualism and egalitarianism:

> Australia's Aboriginal Heritage is evoked in the Forecourt at the front of the building by a mosaic of 100,000 pieces of granite from a painting by Papunya artist Michael Tjakamarra Nelson. [p.6] The theme of the mosaic is a gathering of large groups of tribes of the kangaroo, wallaby and goanna ancestors, congregated to enact important ceremonial obligations [p.28], [and] is an explicit reference to the long history of Aboriginal culture in Australia pre-dating European exploration. [p.9]

The intertwined discourses of history and power presented by the Australian Parliament House focus at a single point the *unity* of the Australian people and the Australian state. But despite the determined efforts of publicists and other mythologizers to, as it were, 'humanize' and popularize the 'meeting place of our nation', its grandeur and opulence finally defeat such attempts. Far from the great conurbations, from the country towns and open spaces of the outback, the monumentalizing of Australian identity (and the sanitizing of urban strife and rural depression in parliamentary debates conducted in the smooth orderliness of the national capital) are overwhelmed by their own monumentalism. Canberra remains, in the minds of ordinary Australians who live and work elsewhere, a town for bureaucrats and politicians bent on their own self-aggrandisement. Parliament House only serves to underline this apprehension.

Monumental history is oriented to encompassment, to the universal. It 'favours the analogies or parallels between one civilization and another: the great moments of humanity, however distant they are, are supposed to communicate via the peaks' [Deleuze, 1986: 149]. As monumental history, the War Memorial, with its stained-glass windows, its banners and statues and dioramas does very well. But its monumentalism is tempered by its inclusion of aspects of the homely, the mundane and the antiquarian: souvenirs (sacralized, but not monumentalized, as 'relics') of battlefields; depictions and artefacts of everyday life on farms and factories engaged in wartime production, with coupons and ration cards, tractors and production lines 'manned' by women; or the letters and diaries of enlisted men whose names are long forgotten by all but their families and descendants.[8]

No such domestication of the monumental graces Parliament House. It is an effect in itself, and as such it suggests that so too are parliamentary democracy, national identity and the unity of nation and state.

Not so the Australian Stockman's Hall of Fame and Outback Heritage Centre, opened, not coincidentally, by Her Majesty Queen Elizabeth II in April 1988 in Longreach, Queensland. Here the antiquarian aspect of history is to be found in full outback flower. It is not the universalist peak moments of history that are recorded and memorialized here, but rather the particular understandings of the everyday life of the nameless and 'unsung heroes' – as the souvenir edition of the Hall of Fame's guidebook *Outback* (hereafter referred to as ASHOF 1990) has it and the displays themselves reiterate. These are the 'heroes' who pioneered and settled the land and provided the template for the construction of the symbolic type of the rural Australian worker.

The Stockman's Hall of Fame: Land, People and Heritage

> And some there be, which have no memorial. [*Ecclesiasticus*, xliv: 9]

All over Australia, and often in the most inauspicious locations, the cultural explorer comes across signposts to 'National Monuments' which turn out to be some natural feature of the landscape. They may be marked by a cairn of stones recording its discovery by early surveyors or botanists, or by a government-erected sign announcing that one is in a National Park administered by a government department known as The Parks and Wildlife Service, prohibiting the lighting of fires, fishing, swimming, the use of off-road vehicles, shooting and littering.

There is likely to be a smaller accompanying sign erected by a voluntary association, admonishing visitors to Keep Australia Beautiful.

The designation of frequently undistinguished topographical features as National Monuments is indicative of the close association Australians understand to exist between land and history.[9] The sacred Aboriginal Dreamtime tie between land and people is admitted by most contemporary white Australians to be of a different order from that born of mere patriotism or love of country. These days, indeed, much of the ideology and mythology of the Dreamtime has been incorporated into political practice and bureaucratic policy concerning particularly land ownership and/ or custodianship and the study of ecology and conservationist politics in general, as well as being exploited as a major tourist attraction. As the now defunct Australian Airlines 1989–90 brochure, *The Centre*, puts it:

> The red heart of Australia pulsates with a life all its own. It is a harsh land, born out of a turbulent natural history, a rich heritage spanning the ages. Uluru, the Olgas, desert and bush. Steeped in Aboriginal legend and the mysteries of the Dreamtime, its haunting, mythical character is only part of its fascination. Ancient, enduring, resilient, with a vigorous, uncompromising and awe-inspiring majesty, this is outback Australia at its best. Treat it with respect,[10] and enjoy an uncommon beauty. [p.2] Where all else is flat, Ayers Rock looms gigantic, dominating the landscape and more striking for the contrast it affords. Golden tussocked plains surround the Rock which projects 348 metres skyward and, together with the Olgas, makes up part of an immense buried mountain range. This is the spiritual realm of the Yankunjatjara and Pitanjatjara tribes which find sanctity in the inviolable permanence and infinite secrets of the moody monolith. Folklore and legend cast the Rock deep into the Dreamtime consciousness of the Aboriginal people and shroud it in a mysticism that is an integral part of the lure of the whole region. [p.5]

Uluru has everything to qualify it as a mythic shrine and a national monument. It is the 'heart' of the country, 'pulsating' (earlier guidebooks used to refer, less enticingly, to the Centre as 'the dead heart'), 'with a life all its own'. It is ancient and natural, constituting a 'heritage' which is 'born out of a turbulent natural history. . .spanning the ages.' The Centre is legendary, mysterious, haunting, mythical; there is a suggestion of transferred epithet from the land to the people: 'ancient, enduring, resilient, vigorous, uncompromising'. Uluru is big: gigantic, immense, permanent, infinite. It *is*, in mythological terms, the land and people of Australia.

Australia's monumental history focuses upon these ancient natural monuments. Lacking Roman ruins, jungle temples, mediaeval manor houses or Gothic cathedrals, it is the land itself which offers the rare experience of sublimity to its pragmatic and egalitarian people. The inspiration to honour and glory lies not in the great deeds of kings and warriors, statesmen and ecclesiastics, artists and poets, nor does it lie in their memorials; rather, in Australia it resides in the land which both tests and sustains the everyday valour of its sons and daughters.

At the same time, official histories of exploration and settlement, family tales of pioneering ancestors and a plethora of local histories and folk museums which have sprung up over the last thirty years in small towns around the country all conduce to the mythologizing of land-and-people-as-one in Australian cultural practice, drummed into generations of schoolchildren by reciting Dorothea Mackellar's *My Country*, the final verse of which is reproduced below:

> An opal-hearted country,
> A wilful, lavish land -
> All you who have not loved her,
> You will not understand -
> Though Earth holds many splendours,
> Wherever I may die,
> I know to what brown country
> My homing thoughts will fly.
>
> Mackaness and Mackaness [1934: 143–5]

The family tales and folk museums present the antiquarian aspect of history in exemplary fashion. They *are* antiquarian history. Where detail is missing or accounts sketchy, every tiny particularity which can be established becomes significant. These may be found in an attic or outbuilding, or more commonly in recent years in an old cottage set aside for the specific purpose of being the repository of local history, often voluntarily staffed and funded by public subscription. Here, domestic utensils like flatirons and washboards and agrarian implements – harrows, ploughshares, branding irons – jostle for display space with ancient worn photographs, letters and newspapers and children's toys. Many of these items are in a decrepit state, cracked, broken, rusted or with moving parts missing altogether. Most were constructed from cheap materials, and few were lovingly crafted. (Silverware, crystal, fine china and furniture remain tended carefully as private heirlooms or in the city galleries or auction houses.) As antiques, the contents of local history museums are without value; as antiquities, however, they are beyond price.

Whole 'pioneer villages' have been recreated (Sovereign Hill, Old Tailem Bend, Old Sydney Town) to enable modern tourists and parties of schoolchildren to 'step back into the past' and 'relive the experience' of their forebears. At Sovereign Hill one may pan for gold; at Tailem Bend one may sit in the one-teacher schoolhouse at a wrought-iron and timber desk with old initials carved in its surface. One may have one's photograph taken posing as a member of a Victorian family group, complete with long skirt and bonnet or fake handlebar moustache and sepia toning. One may watch a farrier at work, or a shearer, or purchase the products of leather workers or silversmiths. Refreshments include 'authentic' billy tea and damper (though Hungry Jack's and Macdonalds, the transnational fast food chains, are sited close by and likely to engage in a brisker trade).

Many visitors to the folk museums and replica pioneer villages can themselves remember from their childhood the use of implements considered by their children or grandchildren to be laughably old-fashioned, but by the museum curators as having immense 'historic' value. I note these reactions because they highlight the brevity of Australia's experience as a producer of 'history' and because they point to the importance of age as being, *in itself,* crucial to the understanding of, and reverence for, a past which is both personal and shared with other 'ordinary folk' like oneself. Thus the folk museum memorializes, in Gray's words,

> Some village Hampden that with dauntless breast
> The little tyrant of his fields withstood
>
> [*Elegy Written in a Country Churchyard*]

And it can be nothing other than elegiac and antiquarian in its orientation. As such, it serves the purpose of the maintenance of tradition and the attachment of a people to their place in time, drawing sustenance from the past, preserving it and passing it on from one generation to the next. But also, as Nietzsche predicted, it cannot distinguish the wood for the trees: in its preservation of and reverence for the artefacts of bygone years and for the values and structures which produced them, antiquarian history feeds the conservative and the reactionary. It cannot generate a new history.

However, museums like the Stockman's Hall of Fame and Outback Heritage Centre can. In its displays, its historiography, in the activities it promotes, it does utilise and popularise an antiquarian perspective on history. But in its conception, in its outback setting and in the design of its buildings, it speaks to what might be called the Australian monumental. In this way, the Stockman's Hall of Fame has the potential to combine the best, or the worst, of both historical worlds.

Case 14. Annotated History of the Stockman's Hall of Fame[11]

1974: 'concept mooted by outback artist Hugh Sawrey; meeting held in Boonah, Queensland, and company name registered'. 1974 saw rural Australia coming to terms with and beginning to recover from a deep economic recession, in which one of the salient factors was considered to be betrayal by Britain. In 1972, the 'mother country', in connection with its entry into the European Economic Community, had abruptly ended Commonwealth preferences in trade in primary products, a practice which countries like Australia had become dangerously dependent on. For decades, Australia had, in a popular metaphor, 'ridden on the sheep's back', and despite the warnings of observers like Donald Horne in his semi-ironically titled *The Lucky Country* [1964], the rural economy had become complacent over the post-war years of the long boom. An important aspect of the recovery from the shock of Britain's perfidy was an increased emphasis upon a nationalism which stressed economic independence, and, making a virtue of necessity, a slow turning towards the markets of the Asian-Pacific region. At the same time, the new so-called entrepreneurial spirit which was taking hold in Western industrial economies and having an impact in the cities was coming to be applied in the bush as well. Family farms became partnerships and trusts in a flurry of tax avoidance, negative gearing and investment strategies. It is significant that in this climate, the people who conceived and planned the Stockman's Hall of Fame constituted themselves as a private company, with at the time no state assistance.

> 1975–7: 'progress continued through volunteers. Company constitution put together and list of convenors growing. 28 June, 1977: company incorporated and registered in all Australian States. 6 August, 1977: submissions called for the siting of the Hall of Fame. 1977–8: over forty submissions received and assessed, criteria being authenticity, viability, accessibility, availability of water, local support and adequate land available. Likely sites visited and inspected. 13 October, 1978: Longreach, Queensland, selected.'

The story of the selection of Longreach is a fascinating one, in both the somewhat sanitized official version, reproduced below, and the unofficial version, obtained through interviews. It is important to remember that Australia was going through a process of economic and cultural re-orientation, much of which focused upon the ways in which the country could be conceived of as different from, and at least equal (if not superior) to, other 'developed' nations. A vital element of this reconceptualization concerned new ways of exploiting the land which had for so long been central to Australia's economic well-being. In a climate of 'service industries' and 'value-added' productivity, tourism became a major plank of local, regional and national economic planning. Hence the rising interest in local history and the establishment of tourist 'attractions' in locations far removed from the sun, surf, camping and caravanning of the country's traditional holiday resorts. The first (May 1980) issue of the Stockman's Hall of Fame newspaper, under the page 6 headline 'Why Longreach?' had this to say:

> '"Why Longreach?" is the question directors have been confronted with since the site location was decided in 1978.
>
> Spare a thought for the directors each time the question is raised. They've lost track of the number of times they've answered it.
>
> As the project is national, many sites were considered and inspected. Among those nominated were Alice Springs, Dubbo, Tamworth,

> Canberra, Sydney, Toowoomba, Rockhampton, Albury-Wodonga, Longreach, Warwick and Cloncurry.
>
> The thought was always foremost in directors' minds that the project should take roots in the wide brown land where pioneer history had been made.
>
> They wanted no city or seaside site to parade the legend, nor any town that did not bespeak dirt-brown authenticity.
>
> The final decision in a national ballot was between Cloncurry, Longreach and Rockhampton.
>
> Rockhampton, the cattle nerve-centre of Australia, is on the coast and was deemed to have not enough of the inland spirit; Cloncurry in the north-west of Queensland was considered too remote. . ..
>
> There was plenty to recommend [Longreach]. It was the place where Qantas, one of Australia's great pioneering outfits, first made its mark. It was in the territory where Banjo Paterson wrote "Waltzing Matilda", a little bit of something from the bush that has stuck like glue ever since.[12]
>
> It was in the heart of the Mitchell grasslands where the sheep country merged with the cattle country, which was an important consideration. Not all of our outback pioneers were cattle men. Sheep breeders featured prominently among them. Although tourism was never the major consideration, accessibility was a prime thought.
>
> Longreach fitted most of the requirements. It was central and accessible. The major highway linking Sydney, Melbourne and Brisbane with Darwin and Alice Springs passes through Longreach.
>
> Indeed there are only 80 kilometres of gravel in an otherwise all-bitumen road from Melbourne to Darwin. Southern tourists travelling this way en route to the Northern Territory and Ayers Rock number hundreds of thousands each year.
>
> It is the land of the gem stone and the min min light;[13] of the red sandhills, the great inland lakes and the vast flood plains magically carpeted with wild flowers after the rain. It is now only beginning to be opened up with bitumen roads running out from Longreach to link with beef roads through Windorah to Betoota, Birdsville and Bedourie.'

The style and content of this piece, with its Mackellar-esque allusions (wide brown land, gem stones, red sandhills and magic carpets of wildflowers) and its 'dirt-brown', pragmatic concerns for accessibility, bitumen roads and popular nationalist ideas about outback toughness, is neatly fitted to the process of mythologization. At the same time, it glosses over the cunning, trickery and jockeying for influence that accompanied the directors' selection of Longreach as the site for the Hall of Fame.

I have no evidence for the assertion made to me at the Ringers' Muster (Drovers' Reunion) at Longreach in 1990 that the choice of Longreach was pre-empted by the donation of suitable land, and (despite conflicting dates) by R.M. Williams' unilateral decision to commence the building of a stone cottage which eventually became the gate-house of the Hall of Fame. But I have no evidence to the contrary either, and it is significant that such a story circulates at all.

> January 1979: 'head office opened in Toowoomba to begin active development of the company. 21 August, 1979: tax-deductible status of organization granted.' January 1980: 'Australia-wide submissions called for architectural design via two-stage design competition co-ordinated by the Royal Australian Institute of Architects. Competition sponsored by Consolidated Press and Queensland Government. May 1980: first edition of newspaper Stockman's Hall of Fame published by the Hall of Fame, printed by News Limited.' December 1980: 'architect Feiko Bouman of Sydney named as winner of design competition.'

This time, the design competition was not an international one (though it has been suggested that the original idea of the Hall of Fame was inspired by The Cowboy Hall of Fame in the United States). Furthermore, the co-ordination and judging of the contest was in the hands of the profession, not a group of bureaucratic assessors. During the period 1979–80, the Hall of Fame came to take on a more businesslike aura, with sponsors and patrons being recruited around the country. Ken Cowley of News Limited was a founder board member, and its newspaper has been published over the years by News Limited's owner, Rupert Murdoch (now an American citizen), a longtime patron. Consolidated Press is owned by another Australian media magnate, Kerry Packer. That the other sponsor of the design competition was the Queensland government is indicative of the way in which, by the early 1980s, private enterprise and government economic policy were coming closer together.

> 1981: 'R.M. Williams [cattleman and "bushman's outfitter"] set up camp on site in Longreach to construct, from stone, the Bruce Yeates Memorial Administration Centre.' 1982: 'Queensland Department of Works assists by re-assessing costings of winning design and in 1983 by preparing a "pre-design report" outlining exact requirements of the

> Centre, with advice from galleries, libraries and museums. 17 May, 1982: Queensland government announces special grant of $500,000 towards project. July 1982: formal submission made to Australian Bicentennial Authority for funding as a National/State Commemorative Bicentennial Project. 1984: Groundwork is laid for Corporate Fund Raising Campaign to commence upon the announcement of funding by the ABA. 28 September, 1984: ABA announces funding of capital cost of building ($6 million at July 1982 costs).'

While the Hall of Fame professes to memorialize the 'unsung heroes (men and women)' of the bush, it did in fact, almost from its inception, engage in courtship of the rich and influential. An honour board near the front entrance of the Hall bears the names of major sponsors, ordinary sponsors and benefactors, the classification depending upon the size of sums donated. Major sponsors include Australian government bodies and the Longreach Shire Council. Ordinary sponsors include mining and pastoral companies, shipping companies and the XXXX (Four-Ex) Brewery. One individual is listed, the millionaire Warren Anderson, whose (outback) address is given as Tipperary Station. Benefactors include other wealthy individuals, some of whom have since fallen from grace through corruption and scandal – Dick Smith (electronics), L.R. Connell (financier), Sir James Walker (pastoralist), A.C.A. Thiess (construction) and Lord McAlpine (landowner), as well as corporate bodies like banks and transport companies. The Corporate Fund Raising Campaign was clearly successful. To this day, the Hall, which charges an entrance fee of (in 1990) $12.00, justifies its doing so on the grounds that it is totally dependent upon the money it raises itself and is thereby independent of both government funding and government interference. Nonetheless, it no doubt gave a great boost to the Hall's image and prospects to have its official opening televised as part of the Bicentennial celebrations: 29 April, 1988: *Official Opening by Her Majesty The Queen.*

Unlike Parliament House in Canberra, the Australian Stockman's Hall of Fame and Outback Heritage Centre has, in its layout and design, little of the monumental in its construction. Where Parliament House is fitted into the side of a hill, surrounded on all sides by the leafy green orderliness of the capital city, the Hall of Fame crouches over the hot dry earth of the outback, with the red plains stretching away to the west.[14] According to *Outback*, its overall design recalls 'familiar features of the Australian landscape – corrugated roofs, water tanks, silos, wool sheds and shady verandahs' [ASHOF, 1990: 54]. Towering above the hall, and separate from it, looms an immense 'Southern Cross' windmill stark against the sky, a telling contrast to the flagmast of Parliament House. The former signals the homely use-value of a pragmatic technology; the latter is a free-floating signifier.

The materials of the actual building of the Hall of Fame are uncompromisingly authentic: sandstone and corrugated iron. There are no apologetic caveats of the Parliament House kind: 'About 90 percent of the materials and products in the building are Australian. . .. The materials in the Foyer. . .were combined with selected imported marble when Australian marble was not available' [AGPS, 1989: 8].

Canberra is urban, metropolitan even, glass, steel, concrete, wealth and power. Longreach is the rural hinterland, weatherboard, stone, barbed wire and corrugated iron. What is venerated in Longreach is not the splendour of the state but the courage and fortitude of the pioneers, the Australian people. That many of the Australian people have been ignored in the Hall of Fame is a critique which has not been lost on its organizers. The 'unsung heroes' who are its theme are almost invariably men, and white men at that. The Aborigines and women who do feature are mostly nameless, unlike the proud listings and photographs of numerous stockmen, drovers, explorers and pastoralists who 'opened up' the west. These include men like Nathaniel (Nat) Buchanan, who in the 1860s 'established no empire to be remembered by. However, the *instinctive bushcraft* and feats of droving of this remarkable explorer and overlander are legendary' [display caption, my emphasis]. Or the twentieth-century drover Matt Savage, about whom songs are sung and 'whose *instinctive* skills always led him to the waterholes and the bush tucker (food) necessary for survival' [display caption, my emphasis]. There is no mention here of the help and succour afforded to overlanders and drovers by local Aborigines and 'drover's boys' – frequently young Aboriginal women.

The prospectus which solicited donations for The Tribute to Australia's Pioneer Women, an extension to the Outback Heritage Centre honouring 'the achievements of pioneer women in the heart of the land they loved', referred to these women as 'The Hearts

That Made A Nation,' a phrase drawn from George Essex Evans' sentimental Victorian *The Women of the West.*:

> Well have we held our fathers' creed. No call has passed us by.
> We faced and fought the wilderness, we sent our sons to die.
> And we have hearts to do and dare, and yet, o'er all the rest,
> The hearts that made the Nation were the Women of the West.

The prospectus suggested that 'If men pioneered the inland, women civilized it. . .', and that 'our forebears – of all colours, races and creeds – were all pioneers in their own way. The bush started where the cities ran into scrub'.

These slogans, and the emphases and lacunae in the Hall of Fame displays, speak volumes of the dark side of an Australian egalitarianism which can discover equality only in identity. The assumptions which underlie much of Australian racism and sexism can be traced directly to a kind of racial and sexual apartheid which, in its egalitarian mode, is premised on the understanding of 'separate *but* equal.' The separation of male and female, white and black, is mapped on to a fundamental distinction in Australian egalitarianism between culture and nature, mind and body [cf. Rorty, 1979]. It is, however, an unusual distinction in the ways in which females and blacks are seen, as in many other contemporary and historical social formations, in contradictory, or confused, perspectives. On the one hand, women (and Aboriginal people) are conceived of as embodying the natural (and dangerous), men the cultural and creative. Women are body, men are mind. *But at the same time* women are cast in the role of instruments of civilization and moral regeneration, as national reproducers [cf. Chatterjee, 1989]. In recent years in Australia, Aboriginal people have also adopted, or had imposed upon them, the same burden of maintaining moral rectitude as keepers of the conscience of an oppressive – but doggedly egalitarian! – white majority.

Notes

1. Australia, of course, is hardly alone in this attempt to protect its cultural borders. Moreover, the onset of global television coverage, pay and cable television, the Internet and an increasing monopoly of media ownership have created further alarm in the 1990s, resulting most particularly in this country in legislative attempts to control 'cross-media ownership.' This is most tellingly demonstrated in those cases where the ownership or control of the large daily newspapers can be thought of as being preyed upon by citizens of other, more culturally powerful nations.
2. This is becoming even more troublesome a question in international relations, as the often strained relationship between the Australian government and its near northern neighbours, principally Malaysia and Indonesia but also Burma and Cambodia, makes painfully clear.
3. That this is a task fraught with peril is illustrated by the stormy course of Griffin's employment as Federal Capital Director of Design and Construction from 1914 to 1920, a period in which his plans and designs were constantly thwarted by the Ministry of Works. The new Minister for Home Affairs in 1914, a former Adelaide wharf labourer known as William 'The Wombat' Archibald, described Griffin as a 'Yankee bounder' who wasted his time 'with grand theorizing, moonshine and dreaming' [cited in Fitzgerald, 1983: 26].
4. That architects themselves see the design competition in quite another light is illustrated by Magali Sarfatti Larson's [1994] characterization of them as 'discursive events'. Larson cites Robert Gutman: 'the basic intention of the design competition method. . .is to bring architectural markets closer to the condition that economic theory calls "perfect competition"' [1994: 470].
5. To take one example, the role of women in wartime, and by extension their role in the birth of nationhood and national identity, has, since the protests of the 1970s by groups like Women Against Rape in War, become progressively integrated with that of men in a more obvious way than was ever considered feasible or appropriate in an earlier era. The wreaths laid by women at Anzac Day services, of barbed wire and green and purple ribbons, commemorate the unknown civilian women who have suffered at the hands of armies over the centuries and have a haunting power which owes not a little to their resemblance to the Christian symbol of sacrifice, the crown of thorns. In this way, what began as an anti-war protest becomes appropriated and sacralized within and by a nationalist ceremony which re-unifies the people of the nation, suppressing, if only momentarily, their everyday secular antagonisms and stressing their egalitarian ideals.

6. Unless otherwise indicated, all quotations in this section are from *Australia's Parliament House: the Meeting Place of Our Nation*, produced by the Joint House Department, Canberra, and published by the Australian Government Publishing Service, Canberra, 1989 Commonwealth of Australia Copyright, reproduced by permission.
7. Many Australians might snigger at this characterization, given the robust and often highly inventive nature of personal interchanges in Parliamentary debates. 'Intimacy' is frequently the hallmark of invective, rather than an implication of thoughtful and reasonable discourse – not that many Australians do not admire such inventiveness, as perhaps the only acceptable façade of ratbaggery and larrikinism in high places.
8. The war in Vietnam, in what many Australians take to be its ignoble defence of the imperialist pretensions of another country and the Australian government's self-serving kow-towing to those pretensions, has had difficulty in being accepted as part of the universal 'peak experience' of the defence of homeland and human freedom. The War Memorial has rearranged many of its displays to accommodate ideas of the monumental and to subdue its antiquarian aspects in an attempt to ennoble the Vietnam venture and thus downplay popular antagonism to it. The Vietnam veterans were officially recognized by a belated 'Welcome Home' parade in October 1987 (modelled on a similar event in the United States), and the Vietnam War memorial in Canberra was dedicated in October 1992, almost exactly ten years after the Vietnam Veterans Memorial in Washington [cf. Bodnar, 1992, who has a particularly telling disquisition on the perils of design competitions for war memorials].
9. Aboriginal historiography is explicit on this point, as the case of Uluru, originally named by white explorers as Ayers Rock, attests. For Aboriginal people Uluru (like many other natural features) has a mythic and totemic significance which goes far beyond the tourist brochures' eulogies about its awe-inspiring grandeur, and strenuous efforts are made to protect its Dreamtime sanctity from the depredations of the ignorant and the uninitiated.
10. Even in the midst of superlatives, and in an advertising brochure designed to entice visitors and to 'sell' the region to customers who must always be right, an Australian company cannot resist this hortatory little warning. As with the Keep Australia Beautiful signs, the authoritarian nature of Australian bureaucratic practice is never far from the consciousness of Australians and overseas visitors alike, as I have noted elsewhere [J. Kapferer, forthcoming].
11. Except where otherwise stated, all quotations in this section have been adapted from ASHOF, 1990: 52.

12. This observation stretches the truth somewhat. QANTAS, Australia's national carrier, began life in the town of Winton, 173 km. from Longreach, as the Queensland and Northern Territory Aerial Service. 'It is perhaps a bit ironic that the 747 'Jumbo' is far too big to land on Winton's airstrip – the runway that launched its ancestors' [Cottam, 1988: 8.] But one should add that such large aircraft cannot land at Longreach either. 'Accessibility' can also be relativized and politicized. Australia's best-known bush balladeer, Andrew Barton (Banjo) Paterson, wrote the lyrics of *Waltzing Matilda* – the national song, if not the national anthem – at Dagworth Station between Kynuna and Winton in 1895.
13. Defined in homely, outback imagery by ASHOF's *Glossary of Outback Terms* as 'a strange, wandering light which appears occasionally in Western Queensland. It is a circle of brightness, about the size of a kitchen table, suspended above the ground, often around the level of a man on horseback. It moves swiftly over flat country' [1988: 11].
14. Recalling, perhaps unwittingly, the Parliament House guidebooks and brochures, the Queensland publication *Travel Action* observes: 'The hall itself seems to grow out of the ground' [1989: 30]. The concern to appear to be 'growing out of' the land speaks of the concern for natural generation that runs deep in Australian ideologies and mythologies.

CHAPTER TEN

Exploring Community, Imagining Society

And so I return to the question of human sociality: its givenness as definitional of human being; its continual creation, manifestation and, particularly now, its interpretation.

The central ground, the field upon which sociality is manifested and substantialized, contested and, however tenuously, achieved, is that of the discursive practices of everyday life within a defined social formation. Such practices, celebrated or derided as 'popular' or 'mass' understandings of being in the world, are the stuff of the universal and the commonplace: birth and death, sexuality and generation, families, friends and neighbours, accident and coincidence, fate and design, the comic and the tragic. They constitute the central subject matter of the social and human sciences: the quest for an understanding of human motivation, social action and collective experience.

As such, the investigation of sociality probes the everyday lives of all sorts and conditions of being: the dominant and subordinate, the rich and poor, the famous and the unknown. Human beings, endlessly divided and categorized, nonetheless join with others in a common endeavour to make sense of their lives, to attach meaning to human existence. In literate communities the record of their struggles is kept in prosaic letters, diaries, bookkeeping ledgers, newspaper reports, epitaphs, records and almanacs, as well as in the more self-consciously 'cultivated' productions of 'high' culture: poetry, novels, essays, learned theses, technology, science, psychiatry and philosophy, all collected together in publicly accessible libraries, galleries and museums.[1] But 'literate' communities also share with non-literate societies a panoply of communicative devices and acts – songs, music, visual and plastic arts, crafts, dance, ritual and drama. What is important in all of these is the *shared* nature of communication within human groups. It is the signs, symbols and signifiers, the speech and language (in their broadest senses) which are common to the whole group – and may indeed actually define that group – which constitute the stock of knowledge upon which that group is able to draw in order to explain, justify and imagine their world, and to persuade others of its power, beneficence, righteousness and perfectibility.

The significance of shared means of communication is so taken for granted that in many literate communities, the formal learning of the mother tongue (grammar, spelling, reading and writing) is so bound to the study of the creative literature of that tongue (poetry, prose or drama) that the two, language and literature, are assumed to be indivisible: they constitute one 'subject' – English, or Deutsch, or Nederlandse, or Svenska, for example. But the formal learning of other languages sharply separates the linguistic component from the literary, except in the advanced stages of language learning. This is so despite contemporary emphases on 'culture' in school foreign language classes, with a portion of the timetable being devoted to history, geography, family life, festivals, cuisine, customs, religion and so on.[2]

This separation of speech and literature, and the differential evaluation of the ability to encode (a bare minimum of which all are expected to acquire in school) and decode (which is left, beyond the achievement of 'basic literacy', to a highly structured 'personal' choice or an expert judgement of ability to profit from the study of literature), lies at the heart of some of the most serious cultural problems which beset contemporary communities. The distinction between high culture and popular culture stems from it; the recognition of the importance of the mother tongue in the maintenance and enhancement of ethnicity in multicultural society arises from it; the taken-for-grantedness of what constitutes cultural capital and the ability to accumulate it are inextricably bound up with it.

The sharing of a common spoken and written language is the necessary foundation for the creation and maintenance of intersubjectivity and the We-relation which is definitional of community [see Schutz, 1962]. But it is by no means a sufficient foundation, either in what might be called its own or proper arena of communicative action, or as the only possible means to the attainment of intersubjective understanding and social consensus.

The space for misunderstanding, misinterpretation and misrecognition among speakers of the 'same' language is vast.

In the first place, in the terms of Bernstein's [1959] analysis of restricted and elaborated language codes, there is a world of difference between the restricted code usage of phrases which assume a common social relation among participants towards an object of discussion, such as 'Isn't it?' or 'Don't they?', and an elaborated code usage which assumes a variable relation in need of careful clarification and qualification: 'Let us define our terms' or 'I'm not sure one can generalize so broadly'. I say a world of difference because the users of a restricted code inhabit a different symbolic world from that of the elaborated code users; they also, and not coincidentally, engage in a different – and subordinate – relation to discourses of power and influence in the everyday life of the wider social formation.[3]

If the restricted code confines its users to the familiar and the workaday, the elaborated code does little more for those who manipulate it except – and this is an important exception – that it enables (but cannot force) its users to enter upon other symbolic worlds of the abstract, the unfamiliar and the exotic through imagination. For them, language mediates a range of experience beyond their own immediate lives and concerns; by the same token, they are also in a position to act as mediators to those whose restricted language code constrains their ability (in G.H. Mead's [1934] terms) to take the role of the (unknown) Other – the receivers of the messages transmitted by the mediators, and often translated by them as well.

The mediators may thus be thought of as transmitters, or teachers, of a message which originates and is fashioned elsewhere in the social system. For there is a third symbolic world of language which achieves its power outside and beyond language, in its silences and its reading-between-the-lines. In its own way, such a code can be and often is as 'restricted' in its taken-for-grantedness as the first or as 'elaborated' in nuance and subtlety as the second. It is a code of social and symbolic power and as such constitutes both the currency of what Bourdieu [1973; 1977; Bourdieu and Passeron, 1977] calls cultural capital and the means whereby symbolic violence is perpetrated upon those who have no access to that capital.

Beyond language, beyond the sphere of spoken or written nuance and subtlety, restriction and elaboration, beyond the whole arena of linguistic communicative action spreads the ocean of non-linguistic symbolic communication, as subtle and varied, as capable of restriction and elaboration, as anything offered by the oral or literary traditions of human groups. The codes of gesture, facial expression, bodily stance and of the arts and sciences through which human beings also express themselves and their humanity are also necessary for the achievement of commonality. And at the same time, they are insufficient in themselves to create and sustain the sense of community, being as subject to misinterpretation and misunderstanding – even 'misreading' – as any verbal message.

In this case too, there are those who transmit and mediate the messages of those who hold the position of cultural producers and artificers – and those who, in turn, control their production – to those whose own productions have little cultural currency. The worlds of taste and distinction, of glamour, celebrity, fame, fashion and fortune are moulded and created by those who profit most directly from the production and sale of artefacts (including human artefacts like the 'stars' and 'personalities' of the mass media) defined by themselves as valuable. It is not the actors and singers, the painters and designers, athletes and scholars – the producers of value, the elaborated code users of the non-linguistic sphere – who have the symbolic power in any society, nor yet those who mediate these conceptions of value, the editors, retailers, advertisers and teachers. Rather, it is those who control the market for these commodities, those who buy, hire and sell them and decide their price, who define their social worth. At the same time, the owners and controllers of the means of symbolic, or cultural, production, define their own worth, and their own legitimacy, as economic, political and social dominators and rulers.

The ability to inflict symbolic (as well as actual) violence on others is limited, in democratic societies, by the recognition (however hard-fought) of the rights and duties of both individuals and groups within the overall social formation. Yet there is a potential contradiction in egalitarian societies between the freedom and integrity of the individual on the one hand and the well-being of the collectivity on the other. The resolution of this fundamental problematic of human sociality ranges from Plato's exegesis of the Guardians and Hobbes' great apologia for the state, through Mills' placement of a single condition of non-interference on individual liberty and the Benthamite justification of the greatest happiness of the greatest number, to the anarchist conception (à la Bakunin) of the individual as the embodiment of the social, a conception which, I argue, resonates deeply with much of Australian cultural and social practice.

In cultures which simultaneously place great value on the freedom and autonomy of the (adult) individual and on the equality of those individuals, the achievement of sociality, particularly within the framework of the modern state and a totalizing world system, is likely to place a correspondingly great strain upon social relations within and between communities and upon the social fabric itself. The attainment and cultivation of We-ness and identity is at once more and less difficult in societies which profess egalitarianism and individualism in equal measure, even when they fall far short of them in everyday practice. It is more difficult because of the potential for alienation, fragmentation and isolation inherent in the rampant competitive individualism of the *sauve qui peut* war of all against all. This kind of individualism endows egalitarianism with its own brand of harshness and cruelty, its deadening conformism and its moralizing rules for inclusion and exclusion concerning those who would be treated as equals. It is less difficult because the strain towards egalitarianism has the potential for including ever-widening circles of individuals within it, not only glorying, in de Foigny's phrase, in being all equal and alike, but also discerning fundamental human likeness beneath superficial (and often highly creative) individual difference.

The problems of welding together disparate communities within the bounds of contemporary mass societies, of constructing national states with distinctive identities, are compounded by the nature of the relation between the people (nation) and the state. In hierarchically organized societies [see, for example, Dumont, 1977; B. Kapferer, 1988], the power and integrity of the individual is drawn from, and vested in, the situation of that individual's encompassment within the higher order of the state. Here, society and the state precede the individual. But in non-hierarchical, egalitarian societies, individual and, subsequently, community precede society; furthermore, the state is seen as a threat to that individual's integrity rather than a guarantee of it. It is in this context that anarchism, of both an individualist libertarian kind and of a collective radical kind, flowers. Thus people and state can conceive of each other as mutually threatening to identity, autonomy and freedom to act.

In egalitarian societies, therefore, the construction and the maintenance of national identity and a We-relation *vis-à-vis* the 'They' of other societies is an ongoing task of the national state. This is because internal law and order, the peace and stability upon which the state depends for its continued existence and legitimacy, are premised upon the sense of community and of loyalty to that community *as embodied in the State*. Thus its rulers seek to control the societal institutions of government, law and the economy and are largely permitted to do so by the people. But the state must also seek to control those institutions whereby individuals and communities engage with a world of ideas which may be contrary or hostile to the welfare of the state. Here, the family, the school, the church, the mass media are vital instruments of and for state control, for it is in these institutions that individuals may learn to assert their own beliefs and values above those of the nation state. The greater the extent to which the state is able to incorporate and give direction to the popular mythologies and ideologies that circulate with greater or lesser intensity within its realm, the greater its capacity to claim unforced, democratically won loyalty and to have that claim upheld.

Presenting What Has Been: The Uses of History

The ways in which a society investigates itself are complexly interwoven with the ways in which it ideologizes itself. The questions a people asks, individually and collectively, of their social groupings and institutions begin with the practical and the mundane – how to perform certain tasks (transport, communication, the provision of food and shelter, for example) more efficiently or effectively. They continue through the weighing of risks and costs, potential benefits and deficits, the adjudication of opposing claims (the battles between developers and conservationists offer a good example), and move to (or from) and circulate within questions of morality: what ought to be, what should be, what must be.

In giving such a listing, I do not mean to suggest that one type of question precedes another. In practice, each is bound up with the others. Even the seemingly most utilitarian questions like those concerning the movement of workers from home to workplace with the maximum efficiency involve what often appear as intractable financial and moral problems of town planning. Many planned modern cities, like Canberra for example, employ rigid divisions between residential, commercial and light and heavy industrial zones. Such divisions are based upon aesthetic and safety considerations as well as economic ones, as in the placement of railway freight yards in the same area as passenger train facilities and factories and offices far from the residential suburbs where city workers live. The evolution of dormitory suburbs which are emptied of all but the unemployed and the unemployable during highly regulated 'working hours' is predicated upon the separation, consequent on industrialization, of living space from working space. But the same problems arise in older, unplanned cities - Sydney, for example - which developed haphazardly from small market towns and regional administrative centres. Here, the inner urban area of expensive real estate (known as the CBD or Central Business District) is increasingly given over to trading and commercial activities, forcing even the very wealthy into the suburbs in search of fresh air, quietness, greenery, space - and safety. Paradoxically, the journey to and from work, whether by private vehicle or public transport - train or bus - is fraught with the very perils of noise and air pollution, overcrowding, speed and delay, tension, hostility and violent aggression which the retreat to suburbia sought to avoid.

In both planned and unplanned cities, the problems of transportation are never solely matters of moving people around in effective and efficient ways. The siting of new transport corridors, airport runways, arterial roads and railway lines, the relocation of old ones and the whole management of urban traffic flows all provoke furious dispute within communities affected by proposed 'improvements'. Compulsory land purchase, compensation for dispossession, eviction, parking regulations and traffic offences, provide employment for thousands of bankers, lawyers, bureaucrats, engineers, architects, builders and police in their planning and execution. But they also provide work for hospital casualty departments, psychiatrists, social workers, financial counsellors and others who deal with the personal traumas associated with unwilling compliance with the edicts of higher authorities. The greatest happiness of the greatest number is more and more open to conflicting definitions not only of the numbers immediately or indirectly involved, but also of what their 'happiness' might or ought to be.

In examining itself and its social institutions, a people uses a stock of knowledge about the paramount reality of everyday life which, in general, is thought to be taken for granted. Human beings, for example, must work in order to survive; in capitalist societies, they must 'earn' a living; there are more and less attractive ways of doing so; some people are more capable, or more fortunate, than others; job satisfaction for most consists in more than high wages. But while there may be widespread agreement about these statements, the *meanings* of terms like work, earn, living, attractive, capable, fortunate and satisfaction are open to similarly widespread disagreement. In the interests of the communal harmony and societal consensus necessary to the continued legitimacy and socio-economic existence of the nation state, it becomes necessary for the agents of the state to control as far as possible the meanings which people attach to the important signs, terms and activities of their everyday life.

In this endeavour, the formal and informal education of young people plays a crucial role in the formation and building[4] of the kinds of knowledges, skills, attitudes and values, the ideologies which support consensus (or compliance with the ruling definitions of reality) and eradicate dissensus. For those beyond the reach of formal education, other agents and apparatuses of ideological formation and maintenance – the mass media, the family, the workplace, the church, the political party or the peer group – reinforce the work of the schools and institutions of higher learning. It is here that the uses of history become apparent.

Unlike most obviously the United States, Australian education does not demand of its young people that they make a serious or sustained study of their own history or that of others. From the perspective of ideological training, there are both advantages and disadvantages in this *laissez-faire* approach. The major advantage is that what *is* learned or picked up through, for example, commercial film and television, is of such a piecemeal and disconnected nature that it can be assumed to be unproblematic and unthreatening to views more strongly entrenched by other means. The history of Aboriginal and white relations since 1788 is rapidly glossed by reference to noble savagery and primitivism and a cursory nod in the direction of apparently isolated and aberrant instances of barbarity and atrocity. While current courses in Aboriginal Studies undertake a somewhat stronger line on racism, they are generally more concerned with language and cultural heritage than with questions which might be construed as political and therefore to be excluded from school syllabuses. The slogans which appear sporadically, pleading with teachers, special interest groups or the not-always-concordant state authorities themselves to 'keep politics out of education' are directed towards the possibility that students may actually gain access to dangerous knowledge which they are thought not, or not yet, capable of assimilating or interpreting in a 'mature' and 'responsible' manner (that is to say, a manner which upholds statist ideologies). The sloganeers rarely question the likelihood of education's own commitment to one political stance which is supportive of the social, political and economic status quo.

The process – one might almost say, the strategy – of marginalizing the study of history produces the triumphalist and celebratory tone of the monumental history which dominates Australian school studies. 'Progress' is presented as a linear development from an unenlightened past to a more enlightened present; individuals, good and evil, are depicted as having the capacity to turn and direct the course of history. These same individuals can be held up as models for ethical behaviour or as dreadful examples and object lessons of villainy, villainy which will be punished 'in the end'. Even revisionist histories, which seek to overturn and revise these triumphalist conceptions of the past and the lessons it holds for the future, largely do little more than reverse the roles of heroes and villains. The bases of judgement, though they shift, remain nonetheless within the same universe. Ned Kelly, execrated in his lifetime as a criminal and a menace to the law and order of the state, becomes transmogrified as a hero of the people opposed to the state and eventually celebrated *by the State itself* as a 'typical' Australian democrat, whose means may have been rough and ready, but whose ends were impeccably egalitarian.

As Pauline Johnson remarks in her discussion of the necessity of avoiding 'the false democracy of a radical populist alternative' in theories of aesthetics:

> In recent years, a number of leftist culture theorists have become interested in the attempt to describe 'alternative' cultural styles and in the attempt to locate a nascent resistant consciousness within a variety of popular culture practices. There is, however, an important problem with the uncritical pursuit of this enterprise. Whilst avoiding the *overt* elitism of much of the classical tradition this project can lend itself to an insidious, covert elitism which looses the far-reaching claims of a

> humanistic perspective on emancipation and is content to claim only the satisfaction of those needs realizable within the terms of the present. [1984: 148, emphasis in original]

Thus the radical populist interpretations of literature, history and the cultural practices of everyday life also run the risk of a presentist celebration of mundanity and immediate popular relevance at the expense of exploring and furthering the human potential for the sublime.

Thus too heroes like Ned Kelly or Don Bradman, sites like Eureka or Barcaldine, Suvla Bay or the Kokoda Trail, and latterly, Maralinga or Uluru, and events like horse races, football matches or surf carnivals, the heroes, places and experiences of the ordinary people and underdogs of Australian society, become co-opted and incorporated by the rulers of those people. It is the Queen (and behind her, as it were, the power and panoply of imperialism) who opens the Stockman's Hall of Fame; it is the Prime Minister (and behind him the ruthless charm of democratic election and populist appeal) who is asked for racing tips and pictured on television celebrating 'his' win.

The processes of co-optation entail a hygeinization of the circumstances of the past which gave rise to the popular mythologies and discursive practices of workers and soldiers, battlers and sportspeople – the whole anarchic race of egalitarian individualists. And many who would call themselves liberal or radical have been complicit in this process.

Both 'liberal' historians (A.G.L. Shaw, 1955; Manning Clark, 1962; 1962–87; Geoffrey Blainey, 1975) and 'critical' historians (McQueen, 1970; Reynolds, 1972; 1982; Connell and Irving, 1980; Macintyre, 1985; R. Hughes, 1987; Grimshaw et al., 1994) engage in a kind of sleight of hand which elevates those who were previously denigrated or ignored – women, Aborigines or trade union leaders on the part of the revisionist critics; the Japanese army in World War II or the role of the United States as global guardian of democracy on the part of the rationalist liberals. Both groups also decry those who were previously praised, but again their targets are different. The critics take aim at the *dramatis personae* of the 'great man' theories of monumental history: General Douglas MacArthur and Winston Churchill, of course, but also Stalin, Ho Chi Minh or Mao Zedong; the liberals seek to demolish the antiquarian fascination with the letters and diaries of ordinary folk as trivial clutter, worth little more than a footnote, dismissed as 'pop' history.

Nonetheless, all this wrangling takes place within the protected realms of academic history. And each side of the debate is influenced by the claims and arguments of the other. The apologias for one set of 'heroes' – say, early settlers and explorers who engaged in the massacre of Aborigines in an imperialist age, when actively or passively resistant native peoples were brutalized by their conquerors (military, missionary or mercantile) as a matter of course – become apologias for the new protectors of the erstwhile (and current) victims of a still brutal and racist society. Now the racism and brutality is masked by the paternalism of the welfare state and its apparatuses of control and assistance: health and welfare services, education, land rights, legal aid and so forth. That such welfare provision and even the dependency it engenders are still enormously preferable to the naked exploitation and savagery of the murderous past cannot disguise the reality of the racism which produces both the illness *and* its alleviation. Symbolic violence is still violence.

Case 15. Black Deaths in Custody

Source: Royal Commission into Aboriginal Deaths in Custody (Commissioner Elliott Johnston, QC) [1991], *National Report: Overview and Recommendations* Canberra: AGPS. Commonwealth of Australia, copyright reproduced by permission.

Between the beginning of January 1980 and the end of May 1989, in the space of almost ten years, the deaths of ninety-nine Aboriginal and Torres Strait Islander people occurred while in the custody of prison, police or juvenile detention institutions. Thirty of these deaths occurred by hanging, twelve resulted from head injuries, four from gunshot wounds, seven from 'other external trauma' and 37 from 'natural causes' [p.4].

In October 1987, a Royal Commission was established to enquire into the circumstances of these deaths, 'in response to a growing public concern that [the deaths] were too common and public explanations were too evasive to discount the possibility that foul play was a factor in many of them' [p.1]. Several independent commissioners conducted investigations in different states and territories at different times, and all became linked through a

National Commissioner, Elliott Johnson QC, who produced his report in 1991.

The Commission of Inquiry, whether Royal or Government sponsored, federal or state, is a traditional method of investigating matters causing grave concern amongst members of the public: educational or health provision, questions concerning immigration or broadcasting, the incidence of crime or corruption and so on. Commissioners, particularly those chairing the inquiry, are likely to be prominent lawyers or academics who may be thought of as unbiased and open to a range of points of view put to them (whether by invitation or demand) by members of the public, lobbies, interest groups or persons directly concerned with the issue under review. In general, Commissioners are perceived less cynically than other government officials – coroners, welfare workers or teachers, who may be implicated in the findings of an inquiry. Final reports, often amounting to multiple volumes of evidence and recommendations, are published and made available for sale, though seldom in sufficient numbers to satisfy demand. Though 'evidence' may be given in camera and 'witnesses' protected, the final report, or a summary of it, is made available upon being tabled in Parliament.

Conducted under the aegis of the state, the Commission of Inquiry may be seen to be an exemplary aspect of open government, the work of a state in tune with the people and answerable to all citizens, not only to those who are most powerful and influential in public life. In a society in which power is distributed among politicians (widely perceived as corrupt), nameless unelected bureaucrats (widely perceived as petty misanthropes, not incorruptible themselves) and the grey eminences of business and industrial enterprises who are accountable to no one other than their stockholders, the public inquiry can act as a major safety valve for the expression of anger and frustration on the part of those who have few other means of seeking redress for wrongs. It also acts as a powerful legitimation device for the current form of government, for representative parliamentary democracy, the liberal capitalist welfare state and the work of its elected representatives.

Nonetheless, the recommendations of submitted reports are subject to parliamentary, legal and bureaucratic debate and may not be acted upon for many years, if at all. This is, however, less the case for Royal Commissions, which are, perhaps for this reason, less frequently resorted to and address only the most grave matters. The establishment of a Royal Commission is an indication, though not a guarantee, to all concerned that the issue will be vigorously investigated and that its findings will be acted upon.

The agitation, by anguished Aboriginal people for an inquiry into black deaths in custody had been gathering force for a number of years before it was successful. As the National Commissioner noted:

> It is a revealing commentary on the life experience of Aboriginal people in 1987 and of their history that it would have been assumed by so many Aboriginal people that many, if not most, of the deaths would have been murder committed if not on behalf of the State at least by officers of the State. . .. [M]any non-Aboriginal people [shared the] expectation that Aboriginal people would suffer and die from the same discrimination and brutality as they experienced during life. [1991: 1]

Thus the commissioners were authorized, in expanded terms of reference, to take into account any social, cultural and legal factors which might appear to have a bearing upon the deaths.

The history of relations between Aboriginal people and the Australian State is a tale of horror and shame. Individual or collective acts of ferocious cruelty – murder, rape, torture, the forcible dispossession of land and children – committed by settlers, vagabonds, police and other government officials, such as the superintendents of reservations, have been ignored, denied or condoned by the state [see, for example, Reynolds, 1972; Macintyre, 1985]. Such actions have indeed often been committed at the behest of the state. Today the situation is only a little improved:

> Relations between Aboriginal people and non-Aboriginal people were historically influenced by racism, often of the overt, outspoken and sanctimonious kind; but more often, particularly in later times, of the quiet assumption [of superiority] that scarcely recognizes itself. [Report, p.10] Aboriginal people have a unique history of being ordered, controlled and monitored by the State. For each individual there are files maintained by the State; schools, community welfare, adoption, medical, police, prison, probation and parole and, finally, coroners' files document each life to a degree that few non-Aboriginal people's lives would be recorded. [p.4]

Indeed, few non-Aboriginal people have such unrelenting contact with officials of the state, nor do non-Aboriginal people in general suffer from such contact with such calamitous consequences. Of the ninety-nine who died in custody, 83 had been unemployed when last detained; only two had completed secondary-level schooling; 43 had been separated, as children, by the state from their natural families; 73 had been charged with an offence by the age of 19 (43 by the age of 15); most had last been taken into custody for alcohol-related reasons. 'Generally speaking, the standard of health of the ninety-nine varied from poor to very bad. . .. Their economic position was disastrous and their social position at the margin of society; they misused alcohol to a grave extent. . ..' [p.6].

Aboriginal people do not die at a greater rate than non-Aboriginal people in custody. But what the work of the Commission of Inquiry established was that the rate at which Aboriginal people came into custody was *twenty-nine times* that of non-Aboriginal people. As the report notes (p.6), too many Aboriginal people are in custody too often. The most significant contributing factor to this situation, according to the report, 'is the disadvantaged and unequal position in which Aboriginal people find themselves in the society – socially, economically and culturally' [p.15].

This conclusion leads the Commissioner to make a number of wide-ranging recommendations beyond those directly relevant to the criminal justice system. These come under the overall heading of reducing and eliminating disadvantage and empowering Aboriginal people. To this end, three basic prerequisites are listed: the desire and capacity of Aboriginal people to take control of their own lives; the moral and financial support of the wider society; and the maintenance of independence and adherence to the principles of self-determination.

The National Commissioner and his fellow commissioners found much evidence of the will to self-determination in the proliferation of strong Aboriginal organizations engaged in the performance of statutory functions (land councils, for example), the provision of services to Aboriginal people (education, health, housing), the provision of advice to governments (education), and a multiplicity of other functions. Moreover, an official policy of bipartisan support for positive discrimination and Aboriginal self-determination is espoused by all governments, which provide the funding for Aboriginal projects and organizations, as they do for other disadvantaged minorities. There is perhaps less evidence adduced for the goodwill and support of the wider community, as the careful tone of the report when dealing with non-Aboriginal attitudes suggests:

> Non-Aboriginal Australia must face the fact that for a very long time we have proceeded on the basis that Aboriginal people were inferior, were unable to make decisions affecting themselves, that we knew what was best for them, that we had to make decisions affecting them; it became second nature for us to have that attitude. It is very easy for us to adopt that attitude without even being aware that we are adopting it. . .. It is an attitude which is very deeply resented by Aboriginal people [and] would, indeed, be by us if roles were reversed. . .. [Before examining the files] I had no conception of the degree of pin-pricking domination, abuse of personal power, utter paternalism, open contempt and total indifference with which so many Aboriginal people were visited on a day to day basis [p.20].

The maintenance of the independence of Aboriginal people and their organisations requires both an abrogation of paternalism and the replacement of indifference by concerned support and non-interference on the part of non-Aboriginal Australians. To this end, the report opposes the 'mainstreaming' of current specialized services for Aboriginal people.

It is in this apparently innocuous recommendation that the Royal Commission comes up against the deep-seated values of egalitarian individualism which are fundamental to Australian social theory and practice. For what such egalitarianism demands is equality, not equity. This is what I mean by the harshness of an egalitarianism which is premised upon equality in nature: it is an ideology which leaves little room for mitigating circumstances, for cultural distinctiveness, for different ways of being in the world. It is an ideology intolerant of otherness, one which produces the bureaucrat's plea of inability to make exceptions; it encourages the reiteration of individualist maxims like 'God helps those who help themselves', and, in its capitalist manifestation, 'he who pays the piper calls the tune'. It also produces the special pleading of, or on behalf of, young people in trouble with a law that claims that ignorance is no excuse for wrongdoing: their social circumstances are the sole cause of their crime [cf. Matza, 1967].

From time to time, the members of groups classified as

disadvantaged, or more often those who speak for them, suggest, for the best of egalitarian motives, that services and special provisions for these groups be 'mainstreamed', that is, included in the overall provisions which are available as of right to every member of the population. There are risks in doing so: although financial support may turn out to be less than that earmarked for groups with special needs over and above those of 'ordinary' groups, the recognition that those with special needs are *essentially* no different from others is an outcome often considered worth that risk. Conversely, categories of people defined as different or disadvantaged according to statistical averages, or oppressed according to ethical judgements, may decide that their own ends are best served by going it alone and opting out of the mainstream. Groups as varied as ethnic or religious minorities, the mentally or physically handicapped, women, the aged, the unemployed, small business operators and Aboriginal people have argued both for and against the mainstreaming of support on these grounds.[5] Conflicting and successive government policies of protection, assimilation, integration or self-determination express the ambivalence of the 'disadvantaged' in the context of egalitarian individualism and the power of the (welfare) state in the making and unmaking of special arrangements for those whose styles of life and very existence may threaten its legitimacy.

The Commission of Inquiry is only the most conspicuous of the many ways in which a parliamentary democracy like Australia investigates itself. It is a major demonstration of democracy in action. The public inquiry takes into account the views of all parties with a clear interest in its outcomes (though it ignores those with a less obvious stake in its deliberations), and it places those views within a historical framework which acts to explain injustices and inequities requiring public redress. It also takes careful account of the social, political, legal, cultural and ethical standards upon which the social formation is believed to rest and which invest the State with its righteousness and claims to the loyalty of all its citizens.

But the public inquiry, with its high costs and the high expectation of its recommendations being enacted, is resorted to infrequently. There are many other less conspicuous but perhaps more efficacious ways in which a society investigates itself and examines its progress, ways which reach a broader range of people and satisfy a wider spectrum of both egalitarian and individualist concerns. These include public education in the social sciences, publicly funded research, public scrutiny of the policies and platforms of political parties and the regular assessment of the competence of government, industry and commerce. In all such investigations, it is the mass media that play a crucial role in organizing and collating the results of the inquiries of others and in bringing the outcomes of these inquiries into the public realm. It is the mass media too which have the resources and the ability to conduct their own interrogations of society and its institutions and of encouraging and directing open debate and discussion of controversial issues. That this capability is rarely utilized to its fullest extent, and when it is, that it requires of journalists physical and moral courage and an implacable conviction of their own rightness, speaks loudly of the contradictions of a free press in capitalist society.

For such a society, and the state whose interest it is bound to serve, must examine all the information presented to it in terms of the ideological value of that information. Which subjects are fit for debate? Which topics are better suppressed or dismissed as the complaints of cranks or lunatics? Who has a right, or a need, to know? In very many ways, the historical and contemporary situation of Aboriginal people in Australia – persecuted, patronized and protected – represents the highest stage of the welfare state in its egalitarian individualist aspect. It is the central contradiction of that state and its operations that the logic of egalitarianism can be turned into a justification of tyranny and the logic of individualism into a legitimation of ostrich-like indifference to it.

Notes

1. The more explicitly didactic and intellectual works which also form a crucial part of that literature – religion, philosophy, history, biography, politics and so forth, all the works collectively called non-fiction by librarians and reviewers and booksellers – are not generally considered as Literature with a capital L except in so far as their style and language may be considered exemplary. Such texts as *The Bible*

as Literature come to mind in this connection, or less flippantly the works of essayists commonly deemed to be 'classics' (in English, Bacon or Hazlitt, for example) or canonical social commentators like Pepys or Fuller or Cobbett.

2. This is the case in most Australian schools today, although there are variations. The state of Victoria, for example, has long separated English Language (compulsory) from English Literature (elective) in the final year of secondary schooling. The latter has enjoyed considerably higher status as a result. It should be noted too that English as a Second Language (ESL), designed to help recently arrived non-English speaking students to participate in the everyday life of the school, concentrates solely on language acquisition and has little of the conscious 'cultural dimension' of languages other than English (LOTE – a phrase calculated to ward off accusations of Anglocentricity thought to inhere in the term 'foreign') beyond that which may be picked up in the practice of the language. In some fields, indeed, teachers concentrate more heavily on culture than on language – Classical Studies, for example, which has students reading Greek and Latin literatures in translation.
3. By no means do I wish to suggest here a variation of the 'false consciousness' line, that those who lack social power or who mediate conceptions of that power are unwitting pawns in a ruling-class power play. Nor would I suggest that resistance is impossible or fruitless. Resistance to cultural domination, however inchoately understood or expressed, is a necessary condition of a creative democratic society. The danger to human community lies in the recourse to the docility and resignation of socially enforced compliance and false consensus much more than in the continued contestation of power and its legitimacy.
4. Northern European and Scandinavian languages make the connection between schooling and what is sometimes called 'character training' much more explicitly than English. The terms *utbildning* in Swedish, *vorming* in Dutch and *Bildung* in German all connote the active moulding and shaping of a human being. The Latinate *education,* on the other hand, connotes a drawing forth of something that was already present in the individual mind. Perhaps terms like 'character formation' in English smack too much of mind control for them to be so unselfconsciously used by contemporary English-speaking pedagogues.
5. There is no antonym for 'disadvantaged' in the welfare lexicon, nor in common parlance: 'advantaged' suggests a lack of fairness which is politically and rhetorically damaging, unless advantage can clearly be seen to be a matter of luck. 'Disadvantaged' is in fact a euphemism for 'oppressed' or 'persecuted' – much like Frank's [1969]

characterization of 'underdevelopment' – leaving open questions of agency and fault, and implying eventual solution by people of goodwill. Like all such euphemisms, its effectiveness is shortlived, and it requires constant re-touching. The moves from 'handicapped' to 'disabled' to 'less able' to 'challenged' are a case in point. Egalitarian discourse demands this incessant rejigging of language as attitudes and evaluations shift within the ruling group, whose definitions are always the most influential.

CHAPTER ELEVEN

Community, State, Nation Power and Praxis

In an era of a dangerous resurgence of nationalisms around the world and the reshuffling of former imagined communities into new or, more usually, *renewed* imagined communities – balkanization in post-modern dress – the survival of the nation state becomes the most urgent problem of realpolitik in the new world (dis)order. Threatened by the economic hardships attendant upon the dissolution of empire like the new nations of Africa in the 1960s, and invigorated by often hard won independence and political freedoms, the neo-nations of the late twentieth century once again face the task of nation-building.

Not only the new but also the 'old' independent states are presented with this task: how to weld a number of disparate and frequently antagonistic local communities, tribes and traditions into a broader, more encompassing and more unified nation? Divisions of caste and class, religion and language, are not abolished by redrawing borders and renaming territories. The destruction of the land and peoples of Nagorno-Karabakh in the struggle between Armenia and Azerbaijan for sovereignty and control is a case in point, as is the long-term violence of Serbo-Croatian-Bosnian animosity in the Balkan peninsula itself and the political and social problems of a re-unified Germany, not least among them the revival of Nazism.

And there's the rub. For it cannot be forgotten that National Socialism was born in, and drew its appeal from, a vicious and totalitarian *nationalism*, a nationalism which savagely perverted the human ideal of community in the construction of the *Herrenvolk* and in the destruction of all others who opposed it or were excluded from it. It was a nationalism too which exploited a cornucopia of myth, symbol and ritual - opera and folksong, history and religion, art and literature, film and architecture, physical training, medals, uniforms, flags and anthems - in its drive for populist support and nationalist fervour. Like all nationalisms, it revolved around questions of purity and defilement [cf. Douglas, 1966], inclusion and exclusion [cf. Herzfeld, 1986]. The ransacking, categorizing and statisticalizing of the nation and later other nations in the hunt for 'racial purity' as the sole criterion for national identity set a Herculean task for taxonomers [see E. Hughes, 1958], partly because racial purity becomes cultural (and political - see Handler, 1988) purity, since it cannot be observed or measured in anything like the detail demanded for the classification of such a spongy concept. The rise of the radical right and of neo-Nazi movements in Britain, Europe, the United States and Australia and of fundamentalist religious sects around the world indeed attests to the lurking success of appeals to humanity's most base and atavistic emotions in the face of both rational argument and humane compassion.

But cultural purity turns out to be no more efficient a criterion, no more easily identified and categorized, with no less fuzzy boundary markers as those applied to 'race.' It is here that the 'old' established nation states of Europe come up against the same quandaries as those newly emerging from the colonial or imperial past. Labour migration, political exile, flight from economic or political oppression have all contributed to the swelling of populations in western Europe in the same way that in earlier times they helped populate the 'new worlds' of North America and the southern hemisphere. Now, Britain, France, Germany and Spain fix quotas for the entry and labour opportunities of immigrants, engage in widespread investigations of inter-ethnic and interracial relations within their territorial borders, and promulgate policies and codes to regulate the practice of these relations in a newly urgent quest for national harmony. As with those societies which have long conceived themselves as immigrant societies, as multicultural entities, the old nations have also begun to concern themselves with local problems of equity and identity and global questions of foreign economic dominance and cultural control [see, for example, Mattelart, 1979, 1983; Crough and Wheelwright, 1982].

The 'old' nation states, once secure in their assumptions of cultural superiority, become newly threatened by the emergence of trading blocs and trade wars within which they are forced to participate as equal partners with others formerly considered inferior. Without such participation, their claims to cultural pre-eminence and to cultural control within their own borders begin to ring hollow, particularly in the ears of those beleaguered citizens who see work opportunities shrinking in the face of 'invasions' of cheap labour from beyond those borders. In a new kind of circulation of elites, one which matches the circulation of labour, long-established nation states also become sucked into a competitive brain drain. The attempt to retain control over the economic life of the nation is fundamental to the idea of economic union with nearby states: the Commonwealth of Independent States arising from the ashes of the USSR follows the pattern set down by the establishment of the European Union, the United States of America and, on a smaller but perhaps clearer scale, the Commonwealth of Australia, which abolished trade barriers between the erstwhile colonies.

But economic federation brings in its wake what was always already there: the implication of and demand for social and cultural federation. The European Union has long since dropped the word 'Economic' from its title, and member nations, though still fiercely protective of their economic rights, now wrangle about the control of cultural matters such as the pasteurising of French cheeses, the expansion of welfare provisions in Britain to meet the standards already in force in northern Europe or British agitation for the abolition of blood sports like the corrida in Spain (matched by a riposte on fox-hunting). The problematics of multiculturalism within one nation like the United States or the Commonwealth of Australia (wherein one social-economic-cultural grouping is dominant) achieve heightened force, even ferocity, when battle is joined by equally powerful national-ethnic groups across national borders, but removed from everyday contact between each other.

In this process of federalizing, the *habitus* and *doxa* of a national dominant class or an economically powerful region become sanctified, elevated, lifted out of their taken-for-granted ground. They cease to be doxic and become part of a public discourse, open to interrogation and conflicting interpretation and thus objectified as part of a national *heterodoxy*. Customs and conventions which were once specific to particular cultural groups can thus become free-floating and act as agents of cultural change and indicators of national identity. Those who would previously never have given tuppence, or a fig (to use a cross-cultural economic zeugma), for Camembert or Stilton, soccer or rugby, animal liberation or maternity leave, find themselves in vociferous support of what come, with apparent suddenness, to be thought of as venerable 'national' institutions – institutions, moreover, which cut across old divisions of class, status, party, gender, religious affiliation or even personal taste and preference, in an attempt to characterize 'national' traits and achieve national identity.

Presenting What Is: Sociology and Technologies of Power

The uses of history in the constitution and legitimation of ideologies of power, and especially of ideologies of the state-as-nation, have been documented with increasing frequency over the last decade,[1] and for a fascinatingly wide range of national territories. Many of these writers address the ways in which different historiographies, the 'voices' of observers occupying different perspectives on past events, produce conflicting versions of these events in the process of rehabilitating past heroes.[2] Many also examine the question of the re-presentation of the past in national museums and 'revisionist' histories [see, for example, McBryde [ed.], 1985; Stocking [ed.], 1985; Dominguez, 1986; Lass, 1988].

As Corrigan and Sayer remarked in launching the *Journal of Historical Sociology* in 1988, there has been 'a growing rapprochement – or at least communication – between different disciplines in the humanities and social sciences' [1988: 3]. As a credo for their new journal, they cite the increased attention paid by journals of the political left and of women's, black and Hispanic studies – 'overtly feminist, anti-racist and radical history' [ibid.: 2] – as well as older established history and sociology journals to 'Philip Abrams' statement that good sociology. . .*must* be historical, and good history, by the same token, must be sociological' [ibid.: 3]. Their emphasis on the first of these imperatives but not the second is suggestive of a widespread understanding in the social sciences and in the humanities that 'sociological' implies a concern for questions of class and status, for the study of the underdogs who have been written out of history but have provided the bulk of sociological subject-matter for so long [cf. Becker, 1970]. Social history, with its concern for the everyday life of the common people, can thus be beefed up by reference to, for example, class processes in the formation of revolution and the production of poverty and injustice. Alternatively, the importation of a little historical background material allows for a more rigorous analysis of current processes. Both approaches remain, however, centrally concerned with a linear construction and reconstruction of the historical past and the social present and with questions of cause and effect.

Sociology, if it is to be emancipatory in any sense, is at least partly concerned with the critique of history itself and of the social formations which are born, and not haphazardly, out of that history. Sociologically informed history, one might conjecture, is the equivalent of Nietzsche's 'critical' (Deleuze's 'ethical') history. Historically informed sociology requires more than the telling of a single master-narrative of past causes of current effects.

Following Deleuze, we might think of what has been called critical sociology or critical theory [see, for example, Horkheimer and Adorno, 1972] as 'ethical' sociology: that is to say, a historically informed sociology which seeks out the origins and twists and turns in the development of those social structures and social practices now considered, with the hindsight afforded by the backward glancing sociological gaze, to be worthy of condemnation. As an ethical sociology, it focuses critically on those structures and practices of the past and present which buttress and legitimize the continued oppression and manipulation of subject peoples. (Less frequently perhaps, such a sociology may provide the tools for a radical critique of, and a radical praxis in, current contexts of injustice.)

But if we can posit an ethical sociology, can we also posit a monumental or antiquarian sociology? I think it is possible to distinguish at least crude parallels: what I will call the ideological and the popular-cultural strands of sociology.

In so far as it is permissible, I will suggest here that the grand systems theories of sociology – specifically their application in the study of formal organizations, political institutions, and the arts of administration, education and suasion – serve ends similar to those pursued by monumental history. Macrosociology, so called, is a provider of those explanations of (mass) social behaviour and those solutions to social problems threatening hegemony which ruling groups depend on for the effective practice of their power. They depend upon market research, census and poll-taking, the compilation of statistics, and a cool faith in the potency of norms and averages (Mr, Mrs, or Ms Average, the man or woman in the street, the common man or woman, the Average Family) to convince waverers or the disaffected of the rightness of the (statistical) majority. All these techniques comprise the kind of sociology which enables the ideological apparatuses of the state to perform effectively. Like monumental history, macrosociology deals with effects in themselves.

Popular-cultural sociology, on the other hand, although it has its undoubted uses in the ideological realm, exchanges the telescope of the ideological for the microscope of the (inter)personal, the small-scale, the sub-cultural and the everyday. Its focus is upon ordinary people and their routine practice rather than upon social institutions. Such a sociology concerns itself with the symbolic and the interactional, with the minutiae of the social construction of everyday realities. Domestic activities (cooking, cleaning, decorating or gardening), questions of taste and distinction and leisure activities of all kinds come within the sphere of popular-cultural sociology. And herein lies the risk of such a narrowed focus: the emphasis upon taste and opinion, upon individual action or small group processes, may produce little more than an anecdotal catalogue, interesting but essentially ephemeral, in the manner of good journalism – unless it is cast, that is, like the work of Bourdieu, for example, within a wider, theoretical and constantly theorized, perspective. Otherwise, all is flux and change, accidental, aleatory, mere coincidence.

As with Nietzsche's three varieties of history, then, so with these three varieties of sociology. Each is necessary to add its weight and expertise to the service of humanity; an overbalancing upon one or the other produces the same kinds of frustration, withdrawal, complacency or fragmentation which an emancipatory sociology seeks to conquer.

In seeking to tell social life and social action 'as it is', replete with conflict, tentative consensus and compromise, while taking a critical stance towards society and its institutions, sociology must be implicated in the processes of mythologizing, demythologizing and remythologizing[3] society in general, and also in the mythological practices of specific historical social formations.

Ideological conceptions of identity are formed in both history and society. As such, they shift and waver, subject to a multiplicity of forces which both shape and are shaped by particular ideological orientations to power and power relations within contemporary social contexts. The 'multidirectionality' (to use B. Kapferer's [1992] term) of social forces at work in any one social situation forms the battleground, the contested terrain of ideological domination. That the battle is unceasing attests to the openness of the arena of contestation and the vast array of weapons which may be used by one side or the other in the struggle for ideological supremacy. The openness of the arena also underscores the impact of a post-modernist critique which denies the determinism and functionalism of those cause-and-effect macrosociologies which would bind all social life into the straitjacket of the 'normal' (in both senses of the word) and the 'model'.

The Simulacrum of the Social

The mythologies of class struggle, ethnic or gender identity, family solidarity, economic rationality or national sovereignty (to take examples at random) are realities for all those who live within them – which is to say, for all of us social beings – and can never be entirely escaped or transcended. But they can be and are constantly re-worked and re-moulded to fit and to make meaningful new situations, changed fortunes and novel circumstances.

It is primarily the work of the myth-makers and the mythologizers to make the arbitrary and the contingent seem natural and commonsensical. In this work, both history and sociology have been, and frequently still are, deeply complicit, presenting and re-presenting copies, pictures and stories about society as if they were faithful models, icons of an ideal sociality. The understanding that beneath or behind the simulation and dissimulation of myth-making lurks something 'real' and 'true' implies, as Baudrillard observes, 'a theology of truth and secrecy (to which the notion of ideology still belongs)' [1988: 170]. In this way, the pioneer village, recreated and simulated for the benefit of tourists, purports to reflect a basic reality of a bygone era; to the ideology critic, the village 'masks' and 'perverts' (the terms are Baudrillard's) that basic reality. But beyond this second 'phase of the image' lies a third, in which what is masked is the *absence* of any basic reality, and a fourth and final phase, in which the image 'bears no relation to any reality whatever: it is its own pure simulacrum' [1988: 170] and real in itself.

The idea of the true and the false, the model and the copy (whether a true copy or a false one) is integral to the project of modernity, a project which post-modernism (and deconstructionism as a pivotal moment of post-modernism) seeks to overthrow. This 'post-modern' project has much in common with that of Nietzsche, a project directed towards knocking off its axis the whole Platonic question of distinguishing essence and appearance, model and copy, and their relation to the false, dissembling copy, the simulacrum. It becomes, as Deleuze remarks, a question of overcoming dualism and replacing it with series and divergencies and convergencies, a 'continually decentred chaos' [1983: 51].[4]

But it is just such a chaos, affirmative and emancipatory, which ruling groups and fractions within any social formation cannot tolerate. It is within their power, and in their interest, to maintain a single dominant narrative, smoothing out differences and divergencies, incorporating oppositions, and where they cannot, repressing or obliterating the narratives and perspectives of others. It is such a narrative that is pursued within an official policy of 'multiculturalism' – just, compassionate, equitable – by the Australian state in its search for societal harmony and consensus, or at least for the appearance, the simulacrum (which may be all that is necessary), of such harmonious relations within the nation state.

The problems of establishing a national identity are writ large in a nation whose citizenry traces its genealogies through a variegated maze of interlocking and/or mutually hostile ethnic roots. And these problems are further compounded for a society in which the dominant ideology is that of egalitarian individualism, commending similarity and disparaging difference as natural, given and taken-for-granted. The studious disattention to social difference, especially differences in wealth, among groups of men sharing a round of drinks in the pub (see B. Kapferer, 1988: 160) or other groups dividing up a restaurant bill or engaging in voluntary community labour displays a deep-seated tendency to what Kapferer calls 'antidifferentiation' – an essential element of Australian egalitarian practice.[5] Such an attitude and practice flies in the face of those understandings and practices which are rooted in different historical pasts and oriented to different social arrangements and which accord a careful recognition to social difference and differentiation.

The clash of one such habitus (the logic of the dominant, mainstream or host culture) with another (subordinated, peripheralized or immigrant) is productive of socially threatening discord and misunderstanding. In a country like Australia, efforts to 'assimilate' immigrants, and indeed native Australians themselves, have always been half-hearted. No policy like 'Americanization' in its American usage [see White, 1983] ever operated in Australia – nor could it have done, given the widely cultivated belief in the innateness and naturalness of ethnic difference and similarity, however defined. For decades, immigrants either learned, with what was taken to be natural aptitude, to 'fit in' to the dominant mould or they did not. The latter group, harassed and often persecuted for their perceived intransigent adherence to alien ways and foreign tongues, began in the later 1960s to articulate a less fragmented opposition to the dominant so-called 'Anglo-Saxon' habitus (later 'Anglo-Celtic' – basically, English-speaking), with slogans like 'bilingual is beautiful' as their watchword.

Case 16. Making the Nation

In 1988 the Committee to Advise on Australia's Immigration Policies, chaired by Dr Stephen Fitzgerald, produced a report entitled *Immigration: A Commitment to Australia* (Commonwealth of Australia, reproduced by permission). In it, Fitzgerald traces the progression of government policies on immigration through the phases of assimilation and integration to that officially adopted since the early 1970s: multiculturalism. The Report notes that multiculturalism still has to be accepted by the very many Australians who still cling (as we might expect, given the dominant ideology) to ideals of assimilation: the more immigrants become like Us, the more acceptable They are and the more they are to be treated as equals. In this connection it is important to note, if only in passing, that the White Australia Policy, formulated in the Immigration Restriction Act of 1901 as a barrier to non-Caucasian – in practice, Asian and specifically Chinese – immigration, was only finally abandoned by the Australian government in 1973, in the face of a more organized pluralism and the arrival of boat-people from Vietnam.

Fitzgerald makes much of what the Committee calls 'community' views and perspectives on immigration, commenting on the vocabulary of migration ('DPs' or postwar Displaced Persons, 'migrants', 'New Australians' and 'ethnics') and suggesting, with some optimism, that 'Perhaps in the end, some terms will pass into the Australian vocabulary of words where context and inflection determine whether the intention is hating or loving, like bastard' [p. 22].

One of the central questions addressed by the Committee was 'What kind of Australia' was desired by the people who gave evidence to it. I cite the Report's summary at length, because it tells much about the mythologies which underpin Australian nationalist thinking on the part of both people and state:

> People were asked to identify Australian attributes that might attract immigrants, and explore how immigration contributes to the Australian way of life. [Note the assumption here of *the* Australian way of life as an identifiable reality.] We also commissioned attitude surveys on these issues.
>
> People described our quality of life in broad terms, citing freedom, equality, space, easy-going attitudes, larrikin behaviour and uncomplicated habits. Few were prepared to describe the changes wrought by immigration and fewer still were troubled by the legacy of Aboriginal dispossession.
>
> Many valued highly our peaceful history and cherished our tradition of social harmony which they saw as a positive national achievement.
>
> Throughout the consultations, overseas-born Australians knew what sort of Australia they wanted. Their interests were not limited to specific immigration policy matters. As with most Australians they expressed concern with economic development and the social well-being of the community.
>
> Australia's self-images and immigrants' images of their new home have much in common. 'Older' Australians value themselves as democratic, individualistic, loyal, egalitarian, suspicious of the powerful and the eminent, intolerant of oppression, pragmatic, fatalistic and secular. Immigrants value the society as relaxed, informal, friendly, full of opportunity, employment and education potential, free, spacious and environmentally unique.
>
> Individual letters favoured [not surprisingly] a united and prosperous Australia and were often fearful of division, racial and cultural differences and unrest. [I note here the juxtaposition of these three threats to the ideology of egalitarian individualism: division and unrest are seen to be the inevitable outcome of the existence of, and invidious attention to, 'racial and cultural differences.']
>
> Valuing Australia as 'the great leveller' [like Death?] unimpressed by differences of birth and class was also common to all generations of Australians. [pp.26–7]

Here is a portrait to warm the hearts of seekers after national harmony. As a statement of what we would like Australia to be, it is encouraging. As a description of a widespread reality, however, of the multi-stranded tensions and hostilities which lie just beneath the surface of this easy-going, tolerant and friendly image, it approaches at best wishful thinking and at worst the deceit of the simulacrum: the appearance of social harmony, but not its substance.

The economy plays a central role in the deliberations of the Committee and its witnesses. In their investigations they found that in general it was governments and 'the corporate sector' which stressed the 'need' for immigrants with specific skills. Individuals were more greatly concerned with job losses and threats to employment security: 'Clearly for many people, it makes no sense to argue that the economy needs more people when jobs are in short supply' [p.28]. Here, a crack appears in the façade of social consensus, with employers having divergent views from employees. The Master Builders Association's submission to the Committee, for example, urged the state to 'lift. . .migration intakes with a special concentration on boosting skilled and business migration' [p.28] in stark opposition to views expressed by both the trade union movement and the Department of Employment, Education and Training, both of which noted that employers have often used immigration as an excuse for failure to engage in training programmes, and oppose any increase in the size of immigration quotas.

Economic objectives are also seen to clash with social objectives, particularly when the views of immigrant communities (or, more properly, those who speak on their behalf) are compared with those of others. A central question here revolves around the value of the extended family. Leaders of business and industry claim that age and skill levels are depressed by the existence of extended family networks; social workers and church spokespeople, on the other hand, claim that the extended family is important in facilitating the settlement of newcomers. Ethnic communities stress the saving of training and education costs by the importation of skilled adults with financial resources of their own. 'A strong theme of state government submissions was the need for an emphasis on contributing to economic goals through skilled and employable immigrants and immigrant entrepreneurs' [p.29].

On the vexed question of multiculturalism per se, the Fitzgerald report had this to say:

> Of the 70 or so written submissions which expressed views specifically on multiculturalism as a policy linked to immigration, 45 were opposed to social policies which they saw as promoting community division and racial tension at the expense of 'our cultural heritage' and national security.
>
> Our consultants' research on the question suggests that:
>
> 'Compared with the 1950s there is a much greater tolerance of ethnic diversity, particularly amongst the more affluent, but this tolerance does not entail majority support for multiculturalism. The Anglo-Australian sense of the superiority of their culture, previously manifest in the policy of assimilation, is disowned by governments, but remains as a significant factor in the community'.
>
> From the [Federal Government] Office of Multicultural Affairs (OMA):
>
> 'It is fair to say that there is still a considerable degree of reluctance on the part of many Australians wholeheartedly to embrace multiculturalism. A recent small scale pilot study. . .showed that not only Anglo-Celtic Australians but also immigrants of many years standing are "very angry about multicultural policy"'.
>
> OMA notes that multiculturalism has been criticized as being divisive, and comments:
>
> 'Multiculturalism is not about institutionalization of difference, rather it is an approach which seeks to reinforce social harmony by encouraging all Australians to recognize the reality of cultural diversity in our society, promoting tolerance and equality and particularly by helping ensure effective use of all the nation's human resources.' [pp.30–1]

The advisory committee was clearly disappointed, and not a little disturbed, by the results its inquiries produced. A truly stark example arises in the strongly held views on the issue of immigrants' acquisition and use of English, with one informant stating flatly, and most tellingly, 'English unifies Australian society'. The corollary also appears: 'they use their language to keep you out' [p.31] – that is, the use of languages other than English actually divides Australian society. One other submission puts the still powerful – perhaps dominant – and implacable assimilationist view: 'Our newcomers. . .owe it to their new country to learn the language, adopt our ways' [p.33].

> Multiculturalism does not appear to have been a persuasive vehicle for analysis and community education about the beneficial social impact of immigration. In an immigration context, therefore, it does not seem to have enhanced the two-way commitment which is so essential to immigration's success.
>
> The fact that multiculturalism is so linked in the public mind with immigration and that it is also perceived negatively, as sectional and divisive, cannot be ignored in the framing of immigration policies. . ..
>
> To some the debate on multiculturalism may suggest a community still in search of an identity. That may be true, but its original intent was an outgrowth of fine ideals of justice and equality and esteem. And these ideals are an essential part of the commitment we offer to immigrants, and a far cry from the assimilationist policies of the past. . .. [p.59]

Finally, on the question of 'commitment to Australia', the Committee concludes 'Assimilation's failure was our failure to recognize human identity' [p.59] as opposed to national identity. In a sense, the Report suggests multiculturalism is also failing, as it were, from the other end. In the drive to recognize and accord parity of esteem to diverse national and ethnic identities within the framework of a unitary national policy, the policy-makers come up against the realities of the very nationalism which they seek to encourage by reference to a commitment to the ideals of justice and equality.

What is clear in the Fitzgerald Report is that notions, 'ideals', of justice and equality are open to a wide range of interpretations, and not all Australians, 'new' or 'old', are in agreement as to what these interpretations may be, or, to an even greater extent, how they might be put into practice by citizens of goodwill and of commitment to that social harmony which the Report takes to be the *raison d'être* for the establishment and prosecution of policies of multiculturalism.

When immigrants become Australian citizens, they are said to have been naturalized. The term is highly significant, especially in the light of dominant and widespread understandings of the essential similarity *in nature* of those considered to be equals. Like exotic plant species, those immigrants who can be seen to have adapted to the local environment to the extent that they are barely distinguishable from the native varieties are *made* natural. They are likely already to have been judged adaptable – suitable for naturalization – because of perceived basic similarities to the incumbent population in language, family structure, religious or political tradition, physical characteristics and so on. What concerns those who are opposed to multiculturalism, as much as those who support such policies, is that the greater the internal differentiation of the population, the greater the chance of discord. It is this arithmetic of nationalism, as B. Kapferer [1988: 190] calls it, the multiplication of difference which is seen to threaten national identity in a society which believes that each individual embodies the nation. This is why the Fitzgerald Report emphasized so greatly the necessity for immigrants to demonstrate commitment 'to Australia' and for them to learn English. It is also why the Office of Multicultural Affairs, speaking for the state, was so didactically vehement:

> Multiculturalism is *not* about institutionalization of difference, rather it is an approach which seeks to reinforce *social harmony* by encouraging all Australians to recognize the reality of cultural diversity in our society, promoting *tolerance and equality* and particularly by helping ensure effective use of all *the nation's human resources* [p.31, my emphases].

The recognition and tolerance of cultural diversity is particularly important for promoting economic success and the industrial harmony which is understood to be a necessary condition of such success. More than native-born Australians, newcomers are carefully scrutinized by a raft of bureaucrats as well as by their neighbours and workmates in an attempt to limit the range of acceptable cultural diversity to that which falls within the bounds of personal idiosyncracy and does not suggest radical difference. For radically different attitudes to work practices and labour relations, radically different evaluations of civil liberties, individual initiative and collective responsibility form the seedbeds of industrial strife and consequent social unrest.

Official policies of multiculturalism are designed to naturalize the arbitrary, to render the historically contingent and socially adventitious as taken for granted, commonsensical, 'natural'. Where the execution of such policies requires the articulation of notions of equity (as in affirmative action, positive discrimination or special assistance to the disadvantaged), the policy-makers and their administrators come up against that egalitarianism which defines equality as equivalence. There can be no suggestion in this case of 'from each according to his capacity, to each according to his needs', for in all spheres of ordinary importance every able-bodied adult Australian is already supposed to possess equivalent capacities and equivalent needs. Anything else may be and is defined as special pleading or the acquisition of special privilege at the expense of others. This harsh logic is applied, often tortuously, to special assistance for Aboriginal welfare, equal opportunity practices in employment, government grants to artists of all kinds, subsidies to private schools, broadcasting in languages other than English and hundreds of areas of everyday practice in which one group or another is singled out for 'special treatment'.

The ideology of egalitarian individualism is hegemonic in everyday life in Australia. It is the space and ground within and upon which everyday life is enacted. In recognizing and handling what they have been instrumental in creating – both the ideology itself, and the conditions of existence which bring that ideology into play – the Australian people, their elected representatives and appointed agents work in a myriad ways. I mention here three which are not in practice separable, and indeed are often in conflict with each other. The first is to adopt a punitive stance towards those who fall below some community standard as defined by researchers, commissions and committees of inquiry, powerful lobbies or a combination of these. The second is to provide conditional help with a view to allowing the formerly indigent or disadvantaged to take their place in society as equal and productive citizens. The third, related to the first two but facing the opposite direction, as it were, involves the unremitting persuasion of everyone else that special assistance is in fact deserved, will be of long-term benefit to the nation, and is after all only temporary.

The first strategy produces such practices as means testing for those who apply for special benefit, assets testing for those who seek pensions (both methods satisfying the official and populist category of 'deserving poor') and surveillance of the unemployed, sole parents or the homeless in an effort to ensure that they are truly destitute and have no means of subsistence other than those granted them by the state. The second involves the offloading of what many people, in Australia as elsewhere, see as the responsibility of the welfare state to provide for those who, *through no fault of their own* – and the qualification is all-important – cannot help themselves. Governments thus initiate and support policies of 'mainstreaming' into the public, non-specialized realm Aboriginal people, persons of non-English speaking background, the physically or mentally disabled, etc. A corollary move is privatization, as in what is euphemistically called community care (most often, family care, or care by charitable organizations) of the aged and/or infirm, the ill, the psychologically disturbed, the young unemployed and very young pre-schoolers. By these means, governments not only save money, they can be seen by those who are not in receipt of special benefits as being economical with taxpayers' funds.

The third strategy, which involves the logistics of providing minimal assistance to those in need while upholding and reinforcing the tenets of egalitarian individualism, elicits some fancy footwork on the part of the agents of the state. Popular antipathy to the idea of special treatment in the form of public subsidies, provision of special facilities, tax breaks and so forth for those already considered privileged requires the constant attention of the ideological state apparatuses. The gifted and talented, farmers, business proprietors, private schools, private hospitals and religious institutions, a vast range of special interest groups, places continuous pressure on the public purse, each in competition with all the others.

Case 17. A Natural Elite

One outstanding example of widespread popular support for the special treatment of an already privileged group is the establishment of the Australian Institute of Sport in 1981, a consequence of the Australian nation's perceived decline in athletic prowess since the 1960s. The National Athletics Stadium had been completed in 1977 and the National Indoor Sports Centre in 1980, under the aegis of the National Capital Development Commission.

Consonant with the logic of egalitarian individualism, Australians had long embraced the ideal of amateurism in sports (paralleling, perhaps, a commitment to free trade). In the period immediately following the Second World War, and indeed before it, the country's natural resources of space and climate and its egalitarian style of life which provided free access to beaches and mountains and cheap municipal facilities, such as tennis courts, swimming pools, cricket pitches, football fields and golf courses, combined with a high standard of living, abundant leisure and a deep respect for physical achievement (as evidenced by the existence of compulsory sports and gymnastics in all schools) to help produce superior athletes in quite disproportionate numbers.

This sort of public egalitarianism was only part of the story, however. As a society of recent immigrants intent upon upward social mobility, Australians found as other immigrant societies had found that success in sports was not only an avenue to higher social status but also a fundamentally egalitarian path to success. The ideal of the natural athlete cut a swathe through class and ethnic prejudice, allowing rich and poor, Anglo and non-Anglo, an equal chance to reach the heights of world championships and Olympic gold. In these efforts, the support of the family was crucial; and it is notable that many of the successes of the 1950s, prominent among them the Konrads Kids (immigrants from Hungary, swimming champions at the ages of 14 and 16), were extremely young, better able to bear the punishing training regimens insisted upon by rigorous coaches and tireless parents backed up by proud school teachers.

The success of Australian athletes fed, and fed upon, the myth of the *naturally* superior physical being. It was founded in and gave concrete expression to a mythology, even a mystique, of the ideal-typical Australian as strong, healthy, energetic and a good sport, the Australian style of life and standard of living as conducive to physical achievement, and the nation as the embodiment of these virtues. But as Europe and Asia recovered from the ravages of war, and as North Americans, the USSR and Eastern Europe began to pour money into special training facilities for international competition, Australian pre-eminence waned.

Over the objections of those who still clung to the amateur ideal [see Paddick, 1994] and the mythology of naturalism, Australians began to recognize, with the enthusiastic help of the mass media, that international athletic competition was an important prop of national status and prestige (and boycotts an important sanction against those who had offended against dominant sporting ideals), particularly for those nations who were not world leaders in economic or political affairs. Moreover, it was made clear that families and amateur coaches did not have the facilities, skills, finances or the authority to deliver the kinds of results which characterized the performance of, say, American tennis players or East German athletes. A venerable racing/gambling adage came to their rescue: 'You've got to be in it to win it', and the Institute of Sport was born.

The Institute of Sport is located, not surprisingly, in Canberra, though there are annexes in a number of other states. It is home to a selected group of athletes who show great promise or who are currently considered to be the best in their fields. Dietitians, exercise physiologists, physiotherapists, psychologists and specialist coaches are employed by the state to train and nurture these bright hopes for the future glory of the nation. It is significant, as I have already noted, that in a society which regularly confuses the term 'elite' with 'elitist' as a most pejorative description, people can and do refer to these future stars as 'elite athletes' without the slightest tremor. And this is because athletic success is not only an *expression* of egalitarianism, it is also fundamentally *productive* of egalitarianism.

In the battle for public support of private interest, much ingenious argumentation is called forth[6] in order to maintain some kind of consensus among the squabbling fractions of powerful and dominant groups, while ensuring the support, however qualified, of those who are not rich and powerful. British social policies in the 1980s are an object lesson for other national states in this respect: the appealing concept of a property-owning democracy, for example, permitted the rundown of public housing; ploys such as government schools 'opting out' of the purview of local education authorities ('going private') and National Health doctors using private hospital beds for their (public) patients allowed for increased support of conservatism and private enterprise while the scaffolding of public provision and the welfare state was steadily corroded.

Australian egalitarianism is such that the increased privatization of services regarded as traditionally provided as of right (although the tradition is not a long one) – free education and free medical care, for example – is more difficult of achievement. But a changing world economic system is made to bear heavily upon ideals, like amateurism in athletics, which increasingly come to be derided as outmoded shibboleths. Throughout the 1980s, as the gap between rich and poor widened (and the material basis of egalitarian thought in Australia was thereby undermined) the management of the economy and the market came to dominate political thinking, and Australian private enterprise worked hard to convince workers, voters and citizens that the nation's economic survival was dependent upon the adoption of new ways of seeing the world.

Schools of business management and public administration sprang up, many of them incorporated as new faculties (with privately endowed chairs and tied research funds) in the universities; indeed, private universities also began to appear and to 'upgrade' the style of all university advertising as a result. Terms like 'corporate culture' and 'management philosophy' were bandied about with increasing frequency, as were expressions like 'the bottom line' and, synonymously, 'the end of the (financial trading) day'.

In effect, Australians were being persuaded that they needed less egalitarianism and more individualism in order to continue in global economic competition. Economic downturns and recessions (but never depressions) dominated the news headlines, and governments strenuously endeavoured to persuade their constituents that the fault for economic slides lay not in their personal inability to manage, but in the global situation over which they had little or no control. Other faults were shunted off to unproductive work practices, employees with unproductive attitudes, ill-prepared school leavers and so on.

In such an atmosphere, nationalism takes on its most sinister and dangerous aspect, not only within the multicultural society itself, but also in the new world order of global economic restructuring in which all nations are embroiled. Threats to the autonomy and independence of the nation are swiftly transmuted into threats to each individual in a society which conceives of the nation as always reducible to, always already present in, each individual member. Here, individuals and communities become more self-conscious about their cultural practice, more interested in conserving it and developing it, deciding what is authentic and what is not and generating attachment to what is considered distinctively national.

As the pressure to assimilate to a new world economic and political order and a global culture increases, so does nationalist resistance to it. The challenge to myth-makers and policy-makers is one of deciding the extent to which global processes are to be welcomed or rejected: how much homogenization of cultural practice (assimilation, when it is considered at the local, that is, national level) is to be encouraged and how much heterogeneity is to be permitted? While many observers [for example, Friedman, 1990; Wallerstein, 1990; Foster, 1991] are concerned with the prospect of worldwide cultural homogeneity, Hannerz is one analyst who sees 'the world in creolization' in an optimistic light. He notes:

> Where there is strain between received meanings on the one hand, and personal experiences and interests on the other, and where diverse perspectives confront one another, cultures can perhaps never be completely worked out as stable, coherent systems; they are forever cultural 'work in progress'. [1987: 550]

This unexceptionable statement does not greatly advance the analysis of the processes of globalization of culture. Every culture in the contemporary world is a work in progress. What Hannerz ignores is the parallel economic development of the commoditization of cultures, a process in which it is in the interests of economically dominant groups (nation states and transnational corporations, for example) to extend their hegemony into the furthest reaches of everyday cultural practice in their drive to control the markets of their products [Herzfeld, 1992]. The processes of cultural creolization may be at least as convincingly understood as global multiculturalism, with all the ambivalences and ambiguities of assimilation, incorporation, conflicting loyalties and commitments which attach to that concept in national communities. Or they may be understood as one aspect of the battle to maintain collective identities as distinctive in the face of powerful forces for uniformity and homogeneity which facilitate cross-cultural and transnational control of economies and polities.[7]

The Imposition of Culture

Moves towards the globalization of culture are indicative of the efforts of transnational economic and political elites to build a transcultural hegemony. To paraphrase, or to post-modernize, Geertz' definition: *they* endeavour to tell *us* a story about *our*selves. Through an ever-tightening network of communication technologies, through the threat of military intervention, the manipulation of tariffs or economic sanctions, transnational elites reinforce the work of more easily recognizable apparatuses of cultural and ideological control: the mass media, particularly film and television, but also monopoly control of publishing; education and advertising; and tourism. As Breckenridge and Appadurai observe (cited in Foster, 1991: 248):

> The state is increasingly dominated by elites who are transnational cultural producers and consumers, forming a global class with few real

> cultural allegiances to the nation state, but who nevertheless need new ideologies of state and nation to control and shape the populations who live within their territories.

But such 'new ideologies' are difficult to create and control, opposing, as they so often do, deep-seated if frequently inchoate nationalist antipathies and unfamiliar cultural logics. The authors' rider to the above is too easy an explanation of, almost an apologia for, the power struggles attendant upon national identity formation in a changing geo-political context: 'But as these populations themselves are exposed, through media and travel to the cultural regimes of other nation-states, such ideologies of nationalism increasingly take on a global flavour' (cited above).

The independence and sovereignty of nations and their autonomy of action in the world economic system are severely limited by their debts and obligations to others more powerful than themselves. These debts and obligations are as often amorphously cultural, operating through ties of language, tradition, kinship and religion, historical partnerships and contemporary exchanges, as they are economic and political, enshrined in constitutions, pacts and treaties. In fact, as national governments are well aware, economic and political ties are immensely strengthened by the initiation and/or maintenance of cultural contacts over time. But the relation of dependency so engendered is one which grates upon the nationalist nerves of those in the position of subordinate partner or client state [Crough and Wheelwright, 1982]. Such nerves may be finely tuned by historical circumstance, economic pride and/or shame about foreign investment or foreign ownership, for example, and current internal political manoeuvring which plays upon these factors. From time to time, this anxiety about independence and identity erupts into a frenzy of nationalist affirmation and assertion which often says much about national cultural politics, even when it does little to change the global order of dominance and subordination.

Notes

1. See, for example, Alonso [1988] on Mexico; Brow [1990] on Sri Lanka; Chatterjee [1989] on India; Crain [1990] on Ecuador; Groube [1985] on Greater New Guinea; Handler [1985] on Quebec; Reynolds [1982] on Australia; and P. Wright [1985] on Britain.
2. See Alonso [1988] on the rehabilitation of Francisco Villa as Hero and the reconstitution of Villismo as a nationalist ideology by the very Mexican state against which he and others like Zapata fought and died. Villa's widow, whose home had been a personal monument to Villa's memory, died in 1982, whereupon the house was occupied by the Mexican army and transformed into the Museum of the Revolution. In the process, Villista relics came to share museum space with relics of 'their most hated enemies and assassins [1988: 43]. The Mexican state thereby 're-valued the signs of a regional and popular Villista history, bringing them into a new set of meaningful relations more in accord with the 'national interest,' with the ideological project of state-building' [ibid.]. The revolution against the state becomes equated with the nation *as* the state.
3. The following discussion draws heavily on the work of Bruce Kapferer, as indeed do many other discussions elsewhere in this book. See especially B. Kapferer, 1992. Specifically, I follow him in stating that 'I am not concerned with ideology as causation, but with the role of ideology in creating meaning and giving shape to. . .processes already in train' [1992: n.p.]. It might be noted too that this stance is in disagreement with 'the invention of tradition' thesis popularized by Hobsbawm and Ranger [1983] and White [1981].
4. 'We know. . .that certain literary procedures (other arts have equivalents) allow one to tell several stories at the same time. This is certainly the essential character of the modern work of art. It is in no way a question of different points of view on a single story understood as the same, for these points remain subject to a rule of convergence. It is, on the contrary, a matter of different and divergent narratives, as though to each point of view there corresponded an absolutely distinct landscape. There is of course a unity of the divergent series, as divergent, but it is a continually decentred chaos, itself at one with the great work. This unformed chaos, the great letter of Finnegan's Wake, is not just any chaos, it is the power of affirmation. . ..' [Deleuze, 1983: 51].
5. It should be noted, however, that with increasing economic competition and widening wage and salary differentials, often accompanied by carefully documented expense accounts (scrutinized by the taxation authorities), the division of restaurant bills in upwardly mobile business circles has lately become a more rigorously

individualist practice, freely using calculators and loudly discussing the amount of a tip, though not yet decrying – at least publicly – the meanness of those who spend less than others. But the practice of commerce has never been thought of as egalitarian in capitalist social formations.

6. In the early 1960s, much of Australia was divided on the question of state aid to non-government schools, and parents in one New South Wales town briefly withdrew their children from a Catholic school to flood the local state school. Hogan puts the state aid argument thus: 'If state aid were withdrawn, most of the private sector would collapse, and governments would simply have to take them over and fund them anyway. This was the lesson of the 1962 Goulburn school strike, the most convincing symbolic demonstration of a very pragmatic argument. Governments are going to have to pay for the education of almost all Australians whatever happens. It is preferable to support a dual system which has general community support than to socialize all education. In fact, so the argument goes, governments are today getting school education on the cheap. Catholic parish schools, for example, educate Australian children at a government expense of something like 60 per cent of the standard costs of children in state schools. ... Would it not be a very misguided economy to withdraw 60 per cent – only to finish up paying 100 per cent for an inferior product?' [1984: 41]. Leaving aside the quality of 'the product,' what is noteworthy in this argument is the assumption that schooling is entirely a question of economics.
7. The introduction of one-day international cricket matches, fast-moving and colourful, was prompted by the understanding that such contests were better suited to television than the traditional five-day Test matches and was much encouraged by media magnate Kerry Packer. Even more tellingly, the 1995 promulgation of a Super (Rugby) League by ex-Australian media mogul Rupert Murdoch, in the face of vociferous opposition from the official Australian Rugby League, supported by Packer, provided observers with a feast of localist and nationalist complaints to digest, principally the argument that a Super League of highly paid professionals (somewhat after the style of US football or basketball organisations) from all over the country would spell the demise of club or state loyalties.

CHAPTER TWELVE

A Nationalist Interlude

Case 18. Lion and Unicorn vs. Kangaroo and Emu

The last ten days of February 1992 witnessed, through the eyes of the Australian mass media, the boiling-over of a potent brew of economic argument, political point-scoring and the rekindling of ancient outrages, the temperature of which had been raised dangerously by a royal visit punctuated by lapses of protocol (or at least of traditional etiquette) and the fiftieth anniversary of a wartime bombing raid.

February is the cruellest month in Australia. It is the prime time for visits by the February Dragon [see Thiele, 1966] – the bushfire – and the time for the opening of the school year and the re-opening of Parliament after the Christmas recess. It is hot and dry, unless major flooding results from cyclones in the north. In 1992, however, natural disasters and calendrical rites receded into the background as economists warred over the most effective ways to overcome recession, politicians traded insults and monarchists battled republicans in the press.

Chronicle of Events

February 18 Beginning of twelfth royal visit to Australia. Complaints of excessive expenditure in time of economic gloom and 10 percent unemployment.

February 20 ABC-TV series *When the War Came to Australia* begins. Opening of New South Wales Parliament by Queen Elizabeth II. Two Labor MPs boycott opening. Others join them to boycott official tea party. Accused of treason by a Liberal MP.

Dame Joan Sutherland, retired diva, receives Order of Merit from Queen in private ceremony. Attacks republican sentiment.

February 24 Queen visits Canberra. Prime Minister delivers 'independence' speech. PM's wife fails to curtsey. PM touches Queen.

February 25 50th anniversary of bombing of Darwin by Japan in World War II. Prime Minister calls for Japanese apologies.

February 26 Prime Minister delivers mini-budget, called 'One Nation'.

February 27 Parliamentary budget debate: PM attacks Opposition MPs as monarchists. Refers to British betrayal of Australia in World War II – failure to secure Singapore from Japanese invasion and capture.

February 28 British press reacts.

The flavour (if not the significance or the validity) of these momentous events can perhaps best be conveyed by an unadorned selection of quotations from the Australian and British press (headlines in bold). I will return to the question of their interpretation later.

The Monarchy: Pro

Queen bestows La Stupenda's honour. 'Dame Joan [Sutherland] said how flattered she was. . .and added, a trifle grimly, that in her opinion all republicans should forthwith be sent scuttling off to Fort Denison' [*The Australian*, 21/2/92: 1. With photograph].

La Stupenda's honour [*Sydney Morning Herald*, 21/2/92: 4]. Three photographs of Queen and Duke of Edinburgh, a 'loyal royal banner' and the Queen talking 'to an eager crowd'. **Royalists reclaim the day. . .** [*SMH* 21/2/92: 1]. Photograph of Queen unveiling portrait of herself at opening of NSW parliament.

Majestic memories are made of this (six photographs, including two showing placards announcing G'DAY BETTY and WE (heart) YOU MA'AM). **La Stupenda loud for the monarchy** (small photo); **MPs thrill as Queen opens Parliament**; **Loyal mission accomplished.** 'Inside Mrs Dalmas's handbag was a camera which would capture a series of shots that she would treasure forever. . .her western suburbs home is a treasure trove of the souvenirs of royal visits to Australia over the years: Charles and Di commemorative plates, Duke of Edinburgh spoons, scrapbooks stuffed with regal clippings and an album jammed with snapshots' [*SMH* 21/2/92: 6].

Brolly good show, Your Majesty (five photos). 'The sudden downpour did not deter a big crowd. . .. The Premier. . .borrowed an umbrella from his wife to protect Her Majesty and her bright turquoise ensemble. Eventually the Queen clutched her own umbrella, produced by palace staff eager to prevent a moist monarch. Fortunately it was of the domed transparent variety, which allowed an eager crowd of 15,000 to see her' [*SMH*: 4].

The Monarchy: Con

Treason storm in a tea party [*SMH* 21/2/92: 6].

Smiles, but Paul upsets the monarchists Photo of Queen and Prime Minister. Small cartoon with leader of Opposition upbraiding PM: 'You should show a bit of respect to a billionaire who doesn't pay any tax'. 'The Prime Minister welcomed the Queen to Parliament House yesterday with a blunt speech about facing "regional realities", hailed as the first pro-republican speech by an Australian Prime Minister. . .. "Just as Great Britain some time ago sought to make her future secure in the European Community, so Australia now vigorously seeks partnerships with countries in our own region. Our outlook is necessarily independent. . .." Labor's Senator Chris Schact welcomed the speech as "reflecting the sentiments [of those who can] welcome a British monarch without resorting to sycophancy"' [*SMH* 25/2/92: 1].

An unseemly row for the Queen 'The Opposition was quite opportunistic to make such a fuss about Mr. Keating's comments. . .. The [republican] debate is now a live one and will be for years' [*SMH* 26/2/92: 12].

Queen quietens republican snarl to corgi-size volume 'Another sign of regal erosion. The corgi count was down. "I only saw five", a Palace spokesman said, recalling that on earlier visits there had been a corgi on every corner. . .. Most of the crowds, excluding the enforced presence of schoolchildren, have been made up of middle-aged and older people, mostly women. Overall, the size of the crowds has been down on previous years. . .' [*SMH* 26/2/92: 4].

Sorry, Ma'am, most Australians want a republic 'A total of 57 percent [polled] said they would prefer to see Australia become a republic, compared with 45 percent in 1988. Mr. Keating. . .in radio interviews. . .claimed that Australia's time as a "cultural derivative of Britain" was "over" and "finished"' [*SMH* 29/2/92: 1].

Most want Commonwealth, but not Queen 'Republican sentiment is stronger among Labor voters (72 percent in favour) than it is among Liberals (49 percent in favour), but support for republicanism has risen significantly among both parties. As in previous polls, women proved greater traditionalists than men' [*SMH* 29/2/92: 2].

Support for Keating republic 'The economic statement and the republican debate have given Mr. Keating a big boost in the opinion polls.' **Listen, the kids are singing our song** Photograph of 'Banner duty at Chatswood Public with Alexandra Dulson, Philip Dalley, Erika Finch, Nathan Colacino and Masumi Yamazaki, all aged 7'. 'There are 750,000 school kids in NSW – and they've all been taught the words to Advance Australia Fair. That's reassuring for the future of republicanism. [The school principal] said he encouraged his students to sing the anthem and respect the flag. "We are a 40 percent multicultural school. . .doing those things brings home to the children a sense of pride and belonging"' [*SMH* 3/3/92: 1].

Nationalism, History, the Economy and the Press

Formerly Treasurer under Prime Minister Bob Hawke, Paul Keating became Prime Minister in December 1991 after a leadership battle in the Parliamentary Labor Party. Much press reaction to his 'independence speech' and his reference to Japanese wartime atrocities was interpreted by the Australian Opposition and press as a smoke-screen to disguise the economic problems over which he presided as Federal Treasurer and for which he continued to be widely blamed.

The British press was certainly in agreement with this line of argument, though perhaps for its own populist reasons. The relationship between an erstwhile imperial power and one of its former colonies is no doubt always suffused with a certain uneasiness, even when in public the representatives of each profess admiration and respect for the other. The following reactions, culled from the Australian and British press at the time, neatly illustrate the suspicions and difficulties inherent in this relation.

Case 19. The Australian Press Reaction: 'Good Rousing Stuff'

UK press upset over royal visit incidents 'The *Daily Express*, headlining its report "Queen Sad At Insults", ran a photograph of Mr Keating under a second, smaller headline of "Australian premier stuns the royals with republican jibes". Both the *Daily Star* and *Daily Mirror* rounded on the Australian leader for putting his arm around the Queen while introducing her to officials. "Hands orf, cobber", screamed the *Star* on its front page. . .. The *Daily Mirror*: "Aussies don't give a XXXX about manhandling the Queen." They also reported the refusal of Mr Keating's wife Annita to again bow to the Queen. . .. The *Daily Star* opened its report by saying the Queen "was not amused" after "Australia's Prime Minister and his wife subjected her to a new barrage of insults"' [*SMH* 26/2/92: 4].

'A thoroughly rude blighter' 'The London tabloids are in a frenzy over Mr Keating's charge that Britain abandoned Australia during World War II [*SMH* 29/2/92: 1]. The *Sun* splashed the Prime Minister across page one as "The Lizard of Oz" and a septuagenarian MP, wheeled into the studios of the BBC, dismissed him as "a thoroughly rude blighter". . .. Defence Secretary Mr Tom King: "Pommie-bashing is a pretty well-established Australian blood-sport"' [*SMH* 29/2/92: 2].

Keating kicks history aside 'In his seemingly off-hand remarks about the monarchy and his tilt at Britain's alleged betrayal of Australia in 1942, Paul Keating is moving to place himself firmly in the tradition of the great Labor Party nationalists. . .. Mr Keating will not have forgotten what the Brits did to [NSW premier Jack] Lang in 1932 [the NSW Governor dismissed Lang for refusing to pay interest on loans from Britain]. Nor has he forgotten Britain's alleged sins of 1942. Attacking the Opposition on Thursday [Feb. 27], the Prime Minister described Britain as "the country that you people wedded yourself to, and even as it walked out on you and joined the common market, you were still looking for your MBEs and your knighthoods, and all the rest of the regalia that comes with it". Good rousing stuff, but not especially accurate' [Commentary, *SMH* 29/2/92: 2].

Keating and nationalism 'In choosing to attack [the leader of the Opposition] for a supposed lack of patriotism Mr Keating. . .has left himself open to the charge. . .that he is unable to win in the debate that matters most, on the economy, and is resorting to cheap diversionary tactics' [Leader, *SMH* 29/2/92: 20].

Save us from the class-conscious British 'I can't believe the arrogance of the British press' [Letter to the Editor, *SMH* 29/2/92: 20]. 'It is sad to see our Prime Minister trampling on the enormous goodwill that exists in the Commonwealth. If we are to promote our exports or tourism to Britain or Japan and the world, we can ill afford to offend our trading partners' [ibid.].

Is it a smokescreen or a vision splendid? 'The (not our) Prime Minister's economic package and risky vision is entitled "One Nation". Yet the very day after release of it he set about dividing the nation into two with his rhetoric about Britain and the monarchy' [Letter to the Editor, *SMH* 3/3/92: 10].

Case 20. The British Press Reaction: 'Rather Poor O Level Material'

'Australian leader's betrayal taunt.' **Keating attack on UK enrages war veterans** [photograph] 'Mr Keating yesterday: strong pursuit of independence and scorn for the opposition's "cultural cringe"' [*The Times*, 28/2/92: 1].

'Australian leader's onslaught condemned as unwise, offensive and historically inaccurate.' **Old soldiers and MPs leap to defend British reputation** 'Sir John Stokes [Conservative MP] said, "It is quite untrue to say we deserted Australia during the war. We fought in Malaya and Singapore and many British servicemen were killed. Australia was not attacked by Japan." The Foreign and Commonwealth Office noted that Mr Keating's remarks appear to have been made "in a domestic political context. . .. Our policy. . .is to work for strong and friendly relations with Australia, fully recognizing both the common interests and shared values and the different perspectives of the two countries in their different regions." Yesterday, the Palace studiously declined to enter the controversy, except to indicate that, whether or not any offence had been intended, certainly none had been taken. The veterans of the Burma railway are not so forgiving' [*The Times*, 28/2/92: 2].

The myth of abandonment. 'Colin Smith corrects the record on Britain's wartime attitude to Australia. More than 130,000 Australian, British and Indian troops were taken prisoner [at Singapore]. Of these, about 28,000 were British and 15,000 Australian. . .. Myths arising from the Gallipoli expedition in the first world war, and the fall of Singapore in the second, are essential props of pommie-bashing. The Gallipoli myth, started by Rupert Murdoch [Australian-born American citizen, proprietor of *The Times* and *The Sun* in Britain, and *The Australian*]'s journalist father, is that the flower of Australian and New Zealand manhood were squandered on a foolish gamble. The truth is that as many British and French troops fought at Gallipoli as Anzacs' [*Observer*, 1/3/92: 25].

History lesson for Mr Keating 'By the 1930s. . .Britain faced a textbook example of imperial over-stretch. The Empire lacked the military and economic might to fight a war on three fronts against Germany, Italy and Japan, but found it politically impossible to abandon any one of these commitments. . .. But from an Australian nationalist perspective the British record looks black. . .. [Churchill] kept his word [to come to Australia's aid], but it was too little too late' [*The Times*, 28/2/92: 12].

Canada plans to pull all its troops out of Europe 'In fact, Mr Keating's remarks [on British betrayal] are nearer the truth than the British denials. It is now known that in August 1940. . .the British chiefs of staff decided that. . .Singapore and Malaya were indefensible. . .. But Winston Churchill kept the news secret from the Australian government. . .' [*Guardian Weekly* 146, 10. 8/3/92: 1]. **Churchill's secret memo wrote off the Far East** Winston knew Singapore couldn't be defended – but he decided not to tell the Australians. . .. Britain went on keeping its secret, even after Japan found out. . .. The larger question of whether Churchill was right to consider Singapore – and even Australia – as dispensible continues to divide historians. . .. The Australian historian David Day. . .said Australia was placed at an unjustifiable risk because of Britain's choice to concentrate its resources in the Middle East and Europe. . .. Corelli Barnet, the Cambridge military historian: "In terms of history it's absolute and preposterous rubbish – rather poor O level material. . .. What use was Australia? [. . .] Australia was a heavy burden on us when we were fully stretched at home." Prof. O'Neill [an Australian at Oxford] says Churchill regarded Singapore as "a soft spot in the navy budget" which could easily cope with being cut. "Even this was a perfectly excusable oversight since Britain was in deep economic trouble"' [*Guardian Weekly* 146, 10. 8/3/92: 9].

Photograph of Mr Keating introducing Mrs Keating to the Queen. Caption: 'Faux pas: Paul Keating adopting a hands-on approach while escorting the Queen in Australia' [*The Times*, 28/2/92: 2].

Jumping on the anti-pom bandwagon 'Paul Keating. . .has probably done himself a power of good by tapping into the anti-[English] sentiment that is prevalent. He is shrewd enough to see that it can divert attention from Australia's economic woes. . .. While he yesterday condemned the ravages of "Thatcherite policies", he had himself learnt quite a bit from those very policies' [*The Times*, 28/2/92: 2].

Boomerang economics 'Six years ago. . .[The Australian Labor Party] tackled rampant inflation and a per capita debt bigger than Brazil's by adopting draconian measures. . .which made Thatcherism look like a minor Keynesian deviation. . .. An election looms. Paul Keating. . .has done what Britain is also in the throes of doing. Rediscovering Keynes' [commentary, *Guardian Weekly* 146, 10. 8/3/92: 1].

Spray-gunning the Poms 'At the turn of the century, the radical writers of the *Bulletin* magazine were much ruder about the monarchy and the British connection than Keating was. . .. Complaints about Australia's involvement in the Boer War on the side of the imperialists were voiced. . .long before the next generation began to feel misgivings about [Gallipoli]. . .. Without the media or rabble rousing politicians, the whole process of separation [of Australia and Britain] could be quietly left to run its course. . .. To some extent the row chiefly represents Murdoch's editors in both countries seizing on Keating's remarks in order to amuse themselves' [*The Observer*, 1/3/92: 25].

We and They: National Identities and the Global Order

The role of the mass media in the promotion of nationalist sentiment is a crucial prop to the work of state officials and ideological state apparatchiks in the building of national identity, and the concatenation of events in February 1992 gave renewed impetus to this work.

The bare 'facts' of the matter are indisputable: Queen Elizabeth II did visit New South Wales between the 18th and 24th of February; The Japanese did bomb Darwin on 25 February 1942, the first of more than sixty air raids having been launched on February 19, four days after the fall of Singapore; the Prime Minister did bring forward a mini-budget, called 'One Nation', on the night of 26th February 1992. A royal tour, an economic statement and a military anniversary are at any time occasions for wide-ranging and 'in-depth' reportage, analysis and commentary in the Australian mass media. The combination of all three, tapping into old griefs and new anxieties, provided a field-day for the press and the electronic media, as well as a prime occasion for politicians and academic commentators to advance their various causes.

The press reports cited above have gone through a more than ordinary sifting. As always, they conform to editorial policies and deadline pressures; they represent the individual views and preferences of reporters and sub-editors, the availability of materials and the co-operation of interviewees; they are culled from broadsheets, and generally conservative ones at that; and, of course, I have made my own selection from the daunting amount of materials available. But with these caveats in mind I think it is fair to say that they well illustrate the issues of national(ist) identity, and the role of the press in its formulation. What I have presented is one aspect of an abstraction, a segmentation by the British and Australian press, from the global flow of news and commentary which circulates through the offices of those transnational corporations which control access to knowledge [see Foster, 1991: 236]. These stories are constructions of the mass media, facets of global mythologies which are accepted or rejected in varying degrees by differentiated and scarcely controllable publics.

Much of the 'news value' – ephemeral by definition – of these reports rests on the appeal of the everyday and the domestic: the public personae of the famous and the 'human interest' thought to reside in the details of their most trivial activities. Mrs Dalmas is lovingly profiled to put a human face on monarchist sympathies; schoolchildren are represented as junior republicans. Questions of protocol (bowing versus curtseying; the permissibility of touching the Queen's person; the mortification of hats and/or frocks in the same colour as those of the Queen) is hotly debated, though often tongue-in-cheek. Mr Keating's background, already widely known and mythologized in Australia, is given a new airing in the British press, with some added dimensions:

> From a working class, Irish Catholic family, and the tough western suburbs of Sydney. . .Mr Keating left school at 14, and did not go to university. . .. [He] is seen as Australia's first "yuppie" prime minister. [*The Times*, 28/2/92: 2]

> On a TV programme last week, Keating allowed himself to be shown making a barbecue for his smiling young family and Dutch air-hostess wife Annita in the grounds of his official home in Canberra. Keating comes from a blue-collar background. He reached the top, displacing the leader of his party Bob Hawke with a display of ruthlessness unusual even in Australian politics; he belongs to the New South Wales Labor Right, which with its strong Irish Catholic influence might be briefly described as Australia's Tammany Hall. One of his little girls was heard to point out that this was the first time her dad had ever actually made a barbie. Still, he emerged well: not such a bad cove after all. [*The Observer*, 1/3/92: 25]

> Paul Keating's dubious accusation that Britain deserted Australia during the war may be prompted less by injured pride than by historical ignorance. According to the current headmaster of his alma mater, Keating was not a noted history scholar. . .. 'He may have studied a little history,' says Brother Adrian Watson. 'It's hard to tell'. [*The Times*, 28/2/92: 12]

Keating's working-class background, his lack of formal education, his (Irish) Catholicism, the implications of corrupt practice in the 'hard' right of the New South Wales Labor Party and his status as a 'yuppie' achiever have resonances which are not lost on a British public concerned with taxation policies, the seemingly interminable (in 1992) debacle in Northern Ireland and fears of trade-union fermentation of industrial unrest. That these resonances may be contradictory is hardly a problem for the British press; nor is the tone of these reports and the others quoted earlier (interpreted in Australian letters to the editor as patronizing, arrogant and class conscious) likely to grate upon its readers. One further example of this tone is illuminating:

> Against the Boers and in both world wars, thousands of Australians volunteered to fight for the Mother Country. Physically, the Australians

> were often magnificent specimens, proof of what decent diet and sunshine could do to the deracinated descendants of the Anglo-Celtic poor. Provided they were well trained and led, they were usually very good troops as well. [Colin Smith on 'The myth of abandonment' in *The Observer*, 1/3/92: 25]

This passage, in calling up what are mythic sources of nationalist pride for Australians – natural physical prowess and an anti-authoritarianism taken to be a hallmark of egalitarian individualism – actually has the effect of suggesting a lack of mental capacity and an inability to think or act effectively without the guidance of a superior intelligence. Similarly, Simon Hoggart, also in *The Observer* [ibid.], comments:

> The puzzling thing about Paul Keating's outburst is why he should care so much. After all, British Prime Ministers don't go round denouncing Australia. I doubt if [current British Prime Minister] John Major thinks about the place between Test matches.

The Australian Prime Minister is not the first national leader to utilize and indeed provide a spur to nationalist sentiment in order to further both long- and short-term political aims. The turning of attention to the threat or perfidy (whether real or imagined makes no difference) of an Other outside and beyond the national Self has the important effect, for the purposes of weaving a national consensus, of demarcating boundaries within which 'sameness overrides difference' [see Handler, 1988].

But in a global economic system in which cultural goods and services are mass-produced and mass-marketed by non-national entities – trans-, inter- or multi-national corporations, the ownership and management of which resides in a global capitalist class – the emanation of nationalist fervour can be dismissed, as it was in the case described above, as a storm in a historical (more properly, perhaps, a historiographical) teacup.

This is not to suggest, however, that such local issues have no relevance for the health of capitalist enterprise and the smooth functioning of its global markets, for indeed they do. The maintenance of amiable international relations – in which tariff barriers and trade restrictions can be used as political weapons (economic sanctions) and in which the costs of accelerated economic competition between trading blocs (the European Community, the fledgling bilateral agreements in North America) are unacceptably high in terms of pollution, land degradation and mass starvation – depends upon the maintenance of international economic optimism, and vice versa. And in middle-range, developed economies like that of Australia, the pressure to offend no one regularly produces lapses in economic judgement and planning which have effects entirely opposite to those intended. Thus faith in British assurances of support left Australian agricultural policy in tatters after Britain's abrupt entry into the European Economic Community in 1972, while 'rural Australia [which] had taken seriously America's tub-thumping on free trade. . .was shocked to discover the Bush administration could, under America's Export Enhancement Programme, out-subsidize the EC on grains'. [*The Economist*, 1992: 14]

The incidents which I have outlined here address long-standing and widespread questions of national pride and honour, preferred forms of governance, war and peace and international relations played out on a global stage. They are indeed global questions, touching upon the everyday lives of millions who are caught up in the torrents and eddies of global flows. While they form part of a universal problematic, however, they are also peculiarly inflected through local histories and cultures. In Australia, a federation of states and territories each claiming internal sovereignty, the big questions of relations among national states are transposed as questions of multiculturalism, of the limits of welfarism, of the disbursement of tax monies by 'big' governments and faceless bureaucrats and debates about allegiance to family, locality, region, state and nation. In all these, the national state appeals to the egalitarianism, mutual aid and sense of justice characteristic of community, while at the same time its apparatuses strive to individuate that community. Fragmentation works against the collectivist impulse, and communal feeling is pitted against the atomization of the social world.

The incidents of February 1992 illustrate some of the dangers of playing nationalist games in an international league. Despite, and at the same time because of, the efforts of the mass media and the pronouncements of politicians of both the right and left, economic consensus in a national state characterized by ever-widening gaps between the haves and the have-nots is as difficult of attainment as political consensus. The political production of a local economic statement entitled 'One Nation' – always in competitive relation with other nations – must then be viewed as global whistling in the dark, a wistful tune falling on deaf ears at home and abroad.

Epilogue: Such is Life

The discursive practices of those imagined communities we call nations are nothing other than the life work of millions who strive to fashion for themselves and their neighbours a world fit for all humanity in its diversity and unity. The structures of social action within which this work takes place are the hard-won outcomes of histories and cultures, in turn the products of human social interaction – sometimes harmonious, sometimes discordant. The trick, as always, is to minimize the discord while we struggle for the harmony. I have argued that nation states are not the best means of achieving such a consummation, that rather it is the people themselves who most nearly approach, fleetingly and chaotically, the dream of human community.

Yet as Australians approach the centenary of the federation of British colonies which formed the independent Commonwealth of Australia in 1901, their debates about nationhood and identity and thereby *national identity* take on renewed significance and urgency, crystallizing around the notion of republicanism. Opinion polls in 1995 suggested that most Australians favour the idea of their nation becoming a republic, and in this the majority of their elected representatives are at last in tune with them, even if some of those representatives have only lately come to accepting the inevitability of a republican form of the state, and even if they have done so by reading the will of the people in terms of electoral advantage.

In June 1995, the Prime Minister offered the Australian people a carefully minimalist vision of an Australian republic, the basis of which was the conviction that an Australian Head of State must be an Australian citizen, not the hereditary sovereign of another State with no allegiance to anything Australian beyond a professed affection for the people of the Commonwealth. It was also proposed that the President of the new dispensation should not be a politician (this elicited sighs of relief all round) but rather an eminent person who embodied the best of what were taken to be Australian characteristics and who had demonstrated these in the service of his or her country. So far, so good. But then came a parting of the ways: the President of the Commonwealth would, preferably, be chosen by a two-thirds majority of both Houses of Parliament, in other words, by politicians. But the same opinion polls indicated that the people, whose mistrust of party politics runs strong and deep, want a direct, popular election. Many believed that the Prime Minister was trying to put one over on them, a suspicion assiduously fostered by members of the Opposition. Despite the Prime Minister's fairly credible claim that an election would politicize the office of President, the Leader of the Opposition seized on the possibility of a 'People's Convention' to decide the issue – politicizing by another, populist route.

So the debate continues. It is one in which egalitarian individualists are ranged against the holders of national office, both elected and appointed. Their utopianism wars with their pragmatism, and the ruling groups of the national state seek about to find their own advantage. Over all hovers the endless quest for a defined national identity, the search for a totality of characteristics by which we might discover 'true' Australianness.

This work was partly conceived of as participating in that quest, with the knowledge that no definitive answers would ever be possible, and recognising that it is the quest for even a transitory understanding of human being that itself constitutes one of the most enduring and universal human endeavours. Thus I have tried to loosen up, deconstruct and rearrange various aspects of Australian cultural practice which might illuminate some paths to understanding the multiple and changing identities of contemporary Australians. In this journey, I have taken a generally (though by no means exclusively) post-structuralist approach to the questions thrown up by human social relations in this part of the world. These questions, of relations between large and recognizable collectivities grounded in gender, class, racial and ethnic difference, have been observed and puzzled over by means of exploring a range of people, places, activities and events which are the intersubjective creations and negotiations of Australians themselves.

That cultures are always and everywhere in the process of

becoming, that they can never be finished products, is the reason for their elusiveness. Pinning them down, categorizing and pronouncing upon their essential characters, is a fruitless task for the social scientist, for it is their very sociality and mutability which is what makes them so intriguing, and so human. Since Australians have become more easily articulate about our quest for a national identity, we have produced an extraordinary amount of work, in art, film, literature, music and dance, in learned theses and bureaucratic reports, all interrogating ourselves and our everyday lives. That the search is continuous is inscribed in the titles of many of the popular scholarly works of the last few decades: *Inventing Australia* [White, 1981]; *Constructing a Culture* [Burgman and Lee, 1988]; *Making a Life* [Burgman and Lee (eds.), 1988]; *Reinventing Australia* [Mackay, 1993]; and *Creating a Nation* [Grimshaw et al., 1994]. The use of the present continuous tense is testimony to the writers' understanding that cultures are always 'work in progress'. Creating, constructing, making, inventing and reinventing a way of life is a central concern of these works. But so also, on the part of these and other writers, is the vague belief that the whole attempt might be something of a hoax. The suspicion that what has been 'invented' might therefore be untrue hovers over titles like the following: *National Fictions* [Turner, 1986]; *Myths of Oz* [Fiske et al., 1987]; and *Mistaken Identities* [Castles et al., 1988], perhaps inspired by earlier and highly influential British works like Anderson's *Imagined Communities* [1983] or Hobsbawm and Ranger's edited volume *The Invention of Tradition* [1983]. The theme of invention and construction is not uncommon in the United States literature on nationhood, nationality and nationalism either [see Foster, 1991]. No doubt we are right to be worried that someone somewhere might be 'inventing' or concocting mythical worlds for us, artificial worlds which we might misrecognize as real, in which we have no voice and over which we can have no control. But it would be perilous to believe that ordinary citizens are so much the pawns of Fate in the process of living cultures, whether of their own or anyone else's construction. Cultures are not invented, though they may be diverted down paths which their progenitors did not or could not foresee. The elements of cultures are always drawn from the practice of everyday life in particular times and places, including the practice of thinking about and reflecting upon the meaning of mundane existence.

And it is these practices which are reflected in the ways people think about themselves as members of collectivities. This is why individual and group identities are always being de- and re-mythologized, reworked, revalued and reoriented to the task of making sense of human lives spent, in Thomas Carroll's words, in 'efforting' to support themselves and those they love in what is always an obdurate social world.

In this, they are heroic. Ordinary Australian men and women who will never be elected to high office, who will never be feted as Australian of the Year, nor chosen (by whatever means) to be President of an Australian republic, cast about themselves for ways in which to form passionate human bonds. In their secular Australian ways, those who stumblingly seek the means of grace and the hope of glory are always aware, however dimly, that they cannot achieve their high humane ideals of community without the company of others like *and unlike* themselves. It is the endeavour to make sense of the rhizomic chaos in which we live that powers the journey towards all the conversations and jokes together, the intersubjective idealisms that are the building blocks of community and the expression of our humanity. In this, Australians, like everyone else, are always on the road, engaged together in ceaseless movement, explorations and wanderings, forever waltzing their Matildas.

Bibliography

Abercrombie, Nicholas, S. Hill and B. Turner [1980] *The Dominant Ideology Thesis*, London: Allen and Unwin.

Aitkin, Don [1988] '"Countrymindedness": the spread of an idea', in S.L. Goldberg and F.B. Smith (eds), *Australian Cultural History*, Cambridge: Cambridge University Press.

Alonso, Ana Maria [1988] 'The Effects of Truth: Re-presentations of the Past and the Imagining of Community', *Journal of Historical Sociology* 1, 1: 33–57.

Althusser, Louis [1971] *Lenin and Philosophy and Other Essays*, London: New Left Books.

Anderson, Benedict [1983] *Imagined Communities*, London: Verso.

Apps, B.F.G. [1943] *Children's Playgrounds*, Department of Health, Canberra: Government Printer.

Ashbolt, Allan [1966] 'Godzone: (3) Myth and Reality', *Meanjin Quarterly* 25, 4: 373–88.

Australian Stockman's Hall of Fame (ASHOF) [1988] *Glossary of Outback Terms*, Longreach: ASHOF.

— [1990] *Outback*, Kensington, N.S.W.: Bay Books.

Bachelard, Gaston [1969] *The poetics of space* (transl. Maria Jolas), Boston: Beacon.

Bakunin, Mikhail [1966] 'Marx, the Bismarck of Socialism', in L. Krimerman and L. Perry (eds), *Patterns of Anarchy*, Garden City: Anchor Books.

Baudrillard, Jean [1988] 'Simulacra and Simulations', in M. Poster (ed.), *Jean Baudrillard: Selected Writings*, Cambridge: Polity Press.

Becker, Howard [1970] *Sociological Work*, Chicago: Aldine.

Bell, Daniel [1960] *The End of Ideology*, Glencoe, Ill.: Free Press.

Berger, Peter [1966] *Invitation to Sociology*, Harmondsworth: Penguin Books.

Berneri, Marie Louise [1950] *Journey Through Utopia*, London: Freedom Press.

Bernstein, Basil [1959] 'A Public Language: Some Sociological Implications of a Linguistic Form', *British Journal of Sociology*, 11: 271–6.

— [1971] 'On the Classification and Framing of Educational Knowledge', in M.F.D. Young (ed.), *Knowledge and Control*, London: Collier Macmillan.

Blainey, Geoffrey [1966] *The Tyranny of Distance*, Melbourne: Sun Books.

— [1975] *The Triumph of the Nomads*, Melbourne: Macmillan.

Blau, Peter [1964] *Exchange and Power in Social Life*, New York: Wiley.

Bloom, Allan [1987] *The Closing of the American Mind*, New York: Simon and Schuster.

Bodnar, John [1992] *Remaking America: Public Memory, Commemoration and Patriotism in the 20th Century*, Princeton: Princeton University Press.

Bourdieu, Pierre [1973] 'Cultural Reproduction and Social Reproduction', in R. Brown (ed.), *Knowledge, Education and Cultural Change*, London: Tavistock.

— [1977] *Outline of a Theory of Practice*, Cambridge: Cambridge University Press.

— [1984] *Distinction: A Social Critique of the Judgement of Taste* (transl. R. Nice), London: Routledge and Kegan Paul.

— [1990] *In Other Words*, Stanford: Stanford University Press.

— [1993] *The Field of Cultural Production*, Cambridge: Polity Press.

— and Passeron, Jean-Claude [1977] *Reproduction in Education, Society and Culture*, Beverley Hills: Sage Publications.

Boyd, Robin 1980 [1960] *The Australian Ugliness* (revised edition), Ringwood, Vic.: Penguin Books.

— [1978] *Australia's Home* (second edition), Ringwood, Vic.: Penguin Books.

Brow, James [1990] 'The Incorporation of a Marginal Community within the Sinhalese Nation', *Anthropological Quarterly* 63, 1: 7–17.

Bulbeck, Chilla [1991] 'Australian History Set in Concrete? The Influence of the New Histories on Australian Memorial Construction', *Journal of Australian Studies* 28: 3–16.

Burgmann, Verity and Jenny Lee [1988] *Constructing a Culture*, Fitzroy: McPhee Gribble.

Burgmann, Verity and Jenny Lee (eds) [1988] *Making a Life*, Fitzroy: McPhee Gribble.

Carmichael, Laurie (chair) [1992] *The Australian Vocational Certificate Training System*, Canberra: AGPS.

Castles, Stephen, Mary Kalantzis, Bill Cope, and Michael Morrissey [1988] *Mistaken Identity: Multiculturalism and the Demise of Nationalism in Australia*, Sydney: Pluto.

Chatterjee, Partha [1989] 'Colonialism, Nationalism and Colonized Women', *American Ethnologist* 16, 4: 622–33.

Clark, C.M.H. [1962] *A Short history of Australia*, Cambridge: Cambridge University Press.

— [1962–1987] *A History of Australia* (4 vols.), Melbourne: Melbourne University Press.

Clastres, Pierre [1977] *Society against the State*, Oxford: Blackwell.

Clifford, James [1988] *The Predicament of Culture*, Cambridge, Mass.: Harvard University Press.

Coleman, James S. [1976] 'Learning through games', in J. Bruner, A. Jolly and K. Sylva (eds), *Play – Its Role in Development and Evolution*, New York: Basic Books.

Commonwealth of Australia [1980] *Educating for Leisure*, Canberra: AGPS.

— [1987] *In the National Interest* (Schools Commission), Canberra: AGPS.

—, Fitzgerald, Stephen (chair) [1988] *Immigration: A Commitment to Australia. Report of the Commission to Advise on Australia's Immigration Policies*, Canberra: AGPS.

— Joint House Department (J.H.D.) [1989] *Australia's Parliament House: The Meeting Place of our Nation*, Canberra: AGPS.

— Johnston, Elliott (Commissioner) [1991] *Royal Commission into Aboriginal Deaths in Custody: National Report. Overview and Recommendations*, Canberra: AGPS.

— [1993] *The National Report on Australia's Higher Education Sector*, Canberra: AGPS.

— [1994] *Diversity and Performance of Australian Universities*, Canberra: AGPS.

Connell, R.W. and T.H. Irving [1980] *Class Structure in Australian History*, Melbourne: Longman Cheshire.

Connell W.F., R.E. Stroobant, K.E. Sinclair, R.W. Connell and K.W. Rogers [1975] *12 to 20: Studies of City Youth*, Sydney: Hicks Smith.

Corrigan, Peter [1985] No title, pp. 19–29, in C. Johnson (ed.), *The City in Conflict*, Sydney: Law Book Co.

Corrigan, Philip and Derek Sayer [1988] 'Editorial', *Journal of Historical Sociology* 1,1: 1–5.

Cottam, Susan [1988] *Winton to Longreach*, Bowen Hills, QLD: Boolarong.

Cowan, L. Gray, James O'Connell and David Scanlon [1965] *Education and Nation-Building in Africa*, New York: Praeger.

Crain, Mary [1990] 'The Social Construction of National Identity in Highland Ecuador', *Anthropological Quarterly* 63, 1: 43–59.

Crough, Greg and T. Wheelwright [1982] *Australia: A Client State*, Harmondsworth: Penguin Books.

Culler, Jonathan [1975] *Structuralist Poetics*, London: Routledge and Kegan Paul.

Dark, Eleanor [1941; 1963] *The Timeless Land*, Sydney: Collins.

David, Miriam [1980] *The State, the Family and Education*, London: Routledge and Kegan Paul.

Debord, Guy [1970] *Society of the Spectacle*, Detroit: Black and Red.

De Certeau, Michel [1984] *The Practice of Everyday Life* (transl. S Rendall), Berkeley: University of California Press.

Deleuze, Gilles [1983] 'Plato and the Simulacrum', *October* 27: 45–56.
— [1986] *Cinema I: The Movement Image*, Minneapolis: University of Minnesota Press.
— [1991] 'What is philosophy?', *Critical Inquiry* 17, 3: 471–8.
— and Felix Guattari [1987] *A Thousand Plateaus*, Minneapolis: University of Minnesota Press.
Derrida, Jacques [1987] '*Geschlecht* II: Heidegger's Hand', in J. Sallis (ed.), *Deconstruction and Philosophy: The Texts of Jacques Derrida*, Chicago: The University of Chicago Press.
Dominguez, Virginia [1986] 'The Marketing of Heritage', *American Ethnologist* 13, 3: 546–55.
Donzelot, Jacques [1980] *The Policing of Families*, London: Hutchinson.
Douglas, Mary [1966] *Purity and Danger*, London: Routledge and Kegan Paul.
Dovey, Kim [1994] 'Dreams on Display: Suburban Ideology in the Model Home', in S. Ferber, C. Healy and C. McAuliffe (eds), *Beasts of Suburbia*, Melbourne: Melbourne University Press.
Dumont, Louis [1977] *From Mandeville to Marx*, Chicago: The University of Chicago Press.
Dutton, Geoffrey [1981] *The Australian Heroes*, Sydney: Angus and Robertson.
Eagleton, Terry [1990] *The Ideology of the Aesthetic*, Cambridge: Blackwell.
Eliot, T.S. [1959] *Four Quartets*, London: Faber and Faber.
Fergie, Deane [1995] 'Whose Privilege? Whose Sacred Sites? Determined Positions in the Hindmarsh Island Bridge Debate', *Current Affairs Bulletin* (in press).
Finn, Brian (chair) [1991] *Review of Young People's Post-Compulsory Education*, Canberra: Australian Education Council.
Fiske, John, Bob Hodge and Graeme Turner [1987] *Myths of Oz*, Sydney: Allen and Unwin.
Fitzgerald, Alan [1983] 'The history of Canberra', in A. Fitzgerald (ed.), *Canberra and the New Parliament House*, Dee Why: Lansdowne Press.
Foster, Robert J. [1991] 'Making National Cultures in the Global Ecumene', *Annual Review of Anthropology* 20: 235–60.
Frank, Andre Gunder [1969] *Capitalism and Underdevelopment in Latin America*, New York: Monthly Review Press.
Friedman, Jonathan [1990] 'Being in the World: Globalization and Localization', *Theory, Culture and Society* 7: 311–28.
Garfinkel, Harold [1967] *Studies in Ethnomethodology*, Englewood Cliffs: Prentice Hall.
Geertz, Clifford [1973] *The Interpretation of Cultures*, New York: Basic Books.
Gilbert, Alan [1988] 'The Roots of Australian Anti-suburbanism', in S.L.

Goldberg and F.B. Smith (eds), *Australian Cultural History*, Cambridge: Cambridge University Press.

Gillis, John R. (ed.) [1994] *Commemorations: The Politics of National Identity*, Princeton: Princeton University Press.

Gouldner, Alvin [1979] *The Future of Intellectuals and the Rise of the New Class*, London: Macmillan.

Gramsci, Antonio [1971] *Selections from the Prison Notebooks* (ed. and transl. Q. Hoare and G. Nowell Smith), London: Lawrence and Wishart.

Grathoff, Richard [1970] *The Structure of Social Inconsistencies*, The Hague: Nijhoff.

Greenblatt, Stephen [1991] *Marvelous Possessions: The Wonder of the New World*, Chicago: The University of Chicago Press.

Grimshaw, Patricia, Marilyn Lake, Ann McGrath and Marian Quartly [1994] *Creating a Nation*, Fitzroy: McPhee Gribble.

Groube, Les [1985] 'The Ownership of Diversity', in I. McBryde (ed.), *Who owns the past?*, Melbourne: Oxford University Press.

Hamilton-Smith, Elery and Robert Robertson [1977] 'Recreation and Government in Australia', in D. Mercer (ed.), *Leisure and Recreation in Australia*, Malvern: Sorrett.

Handler, Richard [1985] 'On Having a Culture: Nationalism and the Preservation of Quebec's *Patrimoine*', in G.W. Stocking Jr. (ed.), *Objects and Others: Essays on Museums and Material Culture*, Madison: University of Wisconsin Press.

— [1988] *Nationalism and the Politics of Culture in Quebec*, Madison: University of Wisconsin Press.

Hannerz, Ulf [1987] 'The World in Creolisation', *Africa* 57, 4: 546–59.

Hasluck, Paul [1977] *Mucking About: An Autobiography*, Melbourne: Melbourne University Press.

Heney, Helen [1943] 'Caroline Chisholm: Pioneer Social Worker', *Royal Australian Historical Society Journal* 29, 1: 21–34.

Herbert, Xavier [1975] *Poor Fellow My Country*, Sydney: Collins.

Herzfeld, Michael [1986] 'Of Definitions and Boundaries: The Status of Culture and the Culture of the State', in P. Chock and J. Wyman (eds), *Discourse and the Social Life of Meaning*, Washington: Smithsonian Institution Press.

— [1992] *The Social Production of Indifference*, Oxford: Berg.

Hewison, Robert [1987] *The Heritage Industry*, London: Methuen.

Hobbes, Thomas [(1651) 1962] *Leviathan*, London: Collier, Macmillan.

Hobsbawm, Eric [1969] *Bandits*, London: Weidenfeld and Nicholson.

— and Terence Ranger (eds) [1983] *The Invention of Tradition*, Cambridge: Cambridge University Press.

Hodge, Bob and Vijay Mishra [1993] *Dark Side of the Dream: Australian Literature and the Post-Colonial Mind*, Sydney: Allen and Unwin.

Hogan, M. [1984] *Public versus Private Schools*, Harmondsworth: Penguin Books.
Hoggart, R. [1958] *The Uses of Literacy*, Harmondsworth: Penguin Books.
Holston, J. [1989] *The Modernist City: An Anthropological Critique of Brasilia*, Chicago: The University of Chicago Press.
Horin, Adele, D. Jopson, D. Hickie and P. McCarthy [1985] 'Living the Australian Dream', in Rob Pullan (ed.), *The Way We Are*, Sydney: Unwin.
Horkheimer, Max and Theodor Adorno [1972] *Dialectic of Enlightenment* (transl. J. Cumming), New York: Seabury.
Horne, Donald [1964] *The Lucky Country: Australia in the Sixties*, Ringwood, Vic.: Penguin Books.
— [1984] *The Great Museum: The Re-presentation of History*, London: Pluto.
— [1986] *The Public Culture*, London: Pluto.
Hoskins, Ian [1994] 'Constructing Time and Space in the Garden Suburb', in S. Ferber, C. Healy and C. McAuliffe (eds), *Beasts of Suburbia*, Melbourne: Melbourne University Press.
Hughes, Everett C. [1958] *Men and their Work*, Glencoe: Free Press.
Hughes, Robert [1987] *The Fatal Shore*, London: Collins Harvill.
— [1994] *Culture of Complaint*, London: Harvill.
Hume, David [1911] *A Treatise of Human Nature*, London: Everyman.
Indyk, Ivor [1988] 'The Semiotics of the New Parliament House', in H. Beck (ed.), *Parliament House Canberra: A Building for a Nation*, Sydney: Collins.
Irvine, Nancy [1987] *Mary Reibey – Molly Incognita*, North Sydney: Library of Australian History.
Jameson, Frederic [1984] 'Postmodernism, or the Cultural Logic of Late Capitalism', *New Left Review* 146: 53–92.
Johnson, Pauline [1984] *Marxist Aesthetics: The Foundations within Everyday Life for an Emancipated Consciousness*, London: Routledge and Kegan Paul.
Juneja, Renu [1988] 'The Trinidad Carnival: Ritual, Performance, Spectacle and Symbol', *Journal of Popular Culture* 21, 4: 87–100.
Kammen, Michael [1991] *Mystic Chords of Memory*, New York: Knopf.
Kapferer, Bruce [1988] *Legends of People, Myths of State*, Washington: Smithsonian Institution Press.
— [1992] Unpublished manuscript.
— and Judith Kapferer [1993] 'Monumentalizing Identity: The Discursive Practices of Hegemony in Australia', *Stanford Literature Review* 10, 1–2: 67–84.
Kapferer, Judith [1978] 'Social Control and the Extracurriculum', *Australian Journal of Education* 22, 3: 262–76.
— [forthcoming] 'Heritage Tourism and Identity Instruction: Whose Heritage? Whose Benefit?'

Kerr, Colin and Margaret Kerr [1983] *Royal Show*, Adelaide: Stock Journal Publishers.

Kiddle, Margaret [1990] *Caroline Chisholm* (4th edition), Melbourne: Melbourne University Press.

Klapp, Orrin E. [1962] *Heroes, Villains and Fools: The Changing American Character*, Englewood Cliffs: Prentice Hall.

Konrad, G. and I. Szelenyi [1979] *The Intellectuals on the Road to Class Power*, New York: Harcourt Brace Jovanovich

Lang, J.T. [1970] *The Turbulent Years*, Sydney: Alpha Books.

Larson, Magali S. [1994] 'Architectural Competitions as Discursive Events', *Theory and Society* 23: 469–504.

Lasch, Christopher [1977] *Haven in a Heartless World*, New York: Basic Books.

Lass, Andrew [1988] 'Romantic Documents and Political Monuments: The Meaning-Fulfillment of History in Nineteenth-Century Czech Nationalism', *American Ethnologist* 15, 3: 456–71.

Lefort, Claude [1986] *The Political Forms of Modern Society*, Cambridge: Polity Press.

Lippman, Walter [(1922) 1965] *Public Opinion*, New York: Free Press.

Lowenthal, David [1985] *The Past is a Foreign Country*, Cambridge: Cambridge University Press.

Lyotard, Jean-François [1984] *The Postmodern Condition: A Report on Knowledge*, Manchester: Manchester University Press.

McBryde, Isabel (ed.) [1982] *Who Owns the Past?*, Melbourne: Oxford University Press.

— (ed.) [1985] *Who Owns the Past?*, Melbourne: Oxford University Press.

McGregor, Craig [1968] *Profile of Australia*, Ringwood: Penguin Books.

Macintyre, Stuart [1985] *Winners and Losers*, Sydney: Allen and Unwin.

Mackaness, Joan S. and George Mackaness (eds) [1934] *The Wide Brown Land*, Sydney: Angus and Robertson.

Mackay, Hugh [1993] *Reinventing Australia*, Sydney: Angus and Robertson.

McQueen, Humphrey [1970] *A New Britannia*, Ringwood, Vic.: Penguin Books.

— [1988] *Suburbs of the Sacred*, Ringwood: Penguin Books.

McQuilton, J.F. [1979] *The Kelly Outbreak*, Melbourne: Melbourne University Press.

Manne, Anne [1995] 'Children in the New World Order', *Quadrant* 39, 6: 29–39.

Mannheim, Karl [1968] *Ideology and Utopia*, London: Routledge and Kegan Paul.

Mattelart, Armand [1979] *Multinational Corporations and the Control of Culture*, Brighton: Harvester Press.

— [1983] *Transnationals and the Third World*, South Hadley: Bergin and Garvey.

Matza, Donald [1967] *Delinquency and Drift*, New York: Wiley.
Mead, George H. [1934] *Mind, Self and Society*, Chicago: The University of Chicago Press.
Michaels, Eric [1988] 'Bad Aboriginal Art', *Art and Text* 28: 59–73.
Milner, Andrew [1991] *Contemporary Cultural Theory*, Sydney: Allen and Unwin.
Moerman, Michael [1968] *Agricultural Change and Peasant Choice in a Thai Village*, Berkeley: University of California Press.
Morgan, Sally [1987] *My Place*, Fremantle: Freemantle Arts Centre Press.
Morris, Meaghan [1988] 'Panorama: The Live, the Dead and the Living', in P. Foss (ed.), *Island in the Stream: Myths of Place in Australian Culture*, Leichardt: Pluto.
— [1990] 'Banality in Cultural Studies', in P. Mellencamp (ed.), *The Logics of Television*, Bloomington: Indiana University Press.
Mosse, George [1975] *The Nationalization of the Masses*, New York: Howard Fertig.
Murray, Les [1991] *Collected Poems*, Manchester: Carcanet.
Nietzsche, Friedrich [1983] *Untimely Meditations* (transl. R.J. Hollingdale), Cambridge: Cambridge University Press.
Nimon, Maureen [1987] *Children's Reading in South Australia 1851–1900*, Flinders University: Unpublished Ph.D. thesis.
Paddick, Robert [1994] 'Amateurism: An Idea of the Past or a Necessity for the Future?', *Olympika* 3: 1–15.
Parker, Stanley [1971] *The Future of Work and Leisure*, New York: Praeger.
Partington, Geoffrey [1995] 'Determining Sacred Sites: The Case of the Hindmarsh Island Bridge', *Current Affairs Bulletin* 71, 5: 4–11.
Quarry, Neville [1983] 'Three Capital Cities', in A. Fitzgerald (ed.), *Canberra and the New Parliament House*, Dee Why: Lansdowne Press.
Quinney, Richard [1980] *Class, State and Crime*, New York: Longman (second edition).
Reiger, Kerreen [1985] *The Disenchantment of the Home: Modernizing the Australian Family 1880–1940*, Melbourne: Oxford University Press.
Reynolds, Henry [1972] 'Violence, the Aboriginals and the Australian Historian', *Meanjin Quarterly* 31, 4: 471–7.
— [1982] *The Other Side of the Frontier*, Ringwood, Vic.: Penguin Books.
Robinson, Portia [1988] *The Women of Botany Bay*, Sydney: Macquarie Library.
Rolfe, Patricia [1979] *The Journalistic Javelin: An Illustrated History of The Bulletin 1880–1980*, Sydney: Wildcat Press.
Rolls, Eric [1981] *A Million Wild Acres*, Melbourne: Nelson.
Rorty, R. [1979] *Philosophy and the Mirror of Nature*, Princeton: Princeton University Press.

Rowse, Tim [1978] 'Heaven and a Hills Hoist: Australian Critics on Suburbia', *Meanjin Quarterly* 37, 1: 3–13.
Rydell, Robert [1984] *All the World's a Fair*, Chicago: The University of Chicago Press.
Sahlins, Marshall [1976] *Culture and Practical Reason*, Chicago: The University of Chicago Press.
— [1985] *Islands of History*, Chicago: The University of Chicago Press.
Sartre, Jean-Paul [1970] *Anti-Semite and Jew* (transl. George Bocker), New York: Schocken.
Schutz, Alfred [1962] *Collected Papers, Vol. I: The Problem of Social Reality*, The Hague: Nijhoff.
Shaw, A.G.L. [1966] *The Story of Australia*, London: Faber and Faber.
Short, John R. [1991] *Imagined Country: Environment, Culture and Society*, London: Routledge.
Slaughter, S. and L. Leslie [1995] 'Entrepreneurial Science and Intellectual Property in Australian Universities', in J. Smyth (ed.), *Academic Work: The Changing Labour Process in Higher Education*, Buckingham: SRME and Open University Press.
Stephen, Sir L. and Sir S. Lee (eds) [1967–8] *Dictionary of National Biography*, Vol. VII. Oxford: Oxford University Press.
Stephenson, M.A. and S. Ratnapala (eds) [1993] *Mabo: A Judicial Revolution*, St Lucia: University of Queensland Press.
Stocking, G.W. Jr. (ed.) [1985] *Objects and Others: Essays on Museums and Material Culture*, Madison: University of Wisconsin Press.
Stretton, Hugh [1970] *Ideas for Australian Cities*, North Adelaide: privately published.
Summers, Anne [1975] *Damned Whores and God's Police*, Ringwood: Penguin Books.
Symes, Colin and Bob Lingard [1988] 'From the Ethnographic to the Aesthetic', in P. Foss (ed.), *Island in the Stream: Myths of Place in Australian Culture*, Leichhardt: Pluto.
Szelenyi, Ivan and Bill Martin [1988] 'The Three Waves of New Class Theories', *Theory and Society* 17, 5: 645–67.
Thiele, Colin [1966] *February Dragon*, London: Angus and Robertson.
Thomas, W.I. [1928] *The Child in America*, New York: Knopf.
Trigger, David S. [1993] Review of Hodge and Mishra 1993, *The Australian*, 20th January 1993.
Turner, Graeme [1986] *National Fictions*, Sydney: Allen and Unwin.
Uzzell, David (ed.) [1989] *Heritage Interpretation*, London: Belhaven.
Veblen, Thorstein [(1899) 1970] *The Theory of the Leisure Class*, London: Unwin.
Vergo, Peter (ed.) [1989] *The New Museology*, London: Reaktion.
Wallerstein, Immanuel [1990] 'Culture as the Ideological Battleground of the Modern World-System', *Theory, Culture and Society* 7: 31–55.

Ward, Russel (chair) [1986] *The Greats: Heroes, Larrikins, Leaders, Visionaries: The Fifty Men and Women Who Shaped Australia*, Sydney: Angus and Robertson.

Watson, Sophie [1989] 'Social Spatial Connections' and 'Family Fortunes', pp. 7–13, and 73–5, in D. Modjeska (ed.), *Inner Cities*, Ringwood: Penguin Books.

White, Richard [1981] *Inventing Australia*, Sydney: Allen and Unwin.

— [1983] 'A Backwater Awash: The Australian Experience of Americanization', *Theory, Culture and Society* 1, 3: 108–22.

Wilkes, G.A. [1981] *The Stockyard and the Croquet Lawn*, Melbourne: Edward Arnold.

Williams, Raymond [1965] 'Base and Superstructure in Marxist Cultural Theory', *New Left Review* 32: 3–16.

— [1971] 'Literature and Sociology: In Memory of Lucien Goldman', *New Left Review* 67: 3–18.

— [1975] *The Country and the City*, St Albans: Paladin.

Wolff, Kurt, Barrington Moore Jun. and Herbert Marcuse [1969] *A Critique of Pure Tolerance*, London: Cape.

Woolf, Virginia [1929] *A Room of One's Own*, London: Hogarth.

Wright, Judith [1959] *The Generations of Men*, Melbourne: Oxford University Press.

— [1971] *Collected Poems 1942–1970*, Sydney: Angus and Robertson.

Wright, Patrick [1985] *On Living in an Old Country: the National Past in Contemporary Britain*, London: Verso.

Index